The Essence of
Total Quality Management

The Essence of
Total Quality Management

Second Edition

John Bank

An imprint of **Pearson Education**

Harlow, England · London · New York · Reading, Massachusetts · San Francisco · Toronto · Don Mills, Ontario · Sydney
Tokyo · Singapore · Hong Kong · Seoul · Taipei · Cape Town · Madrid · Mexico City · Amsterdam · Munich · Paris · Milan

Pearson Education Limited
Edinburgh Gate
Harlow
Essex CM20 2JE
England

and Associated Companies throughout the world

Visit us on the World Wide Web at:
www.pearsoneduc.com

First published Prentice Hall Europe 1992
Second edition published 2000

© Prentice Hall Europe 1992
This edition © Pearson Education Limited 2000

The right of John Bank to be identified as author of
this work has been asserted by him in accordance with
the Copyright, Designs and Patents Act 1988.

ISBN 0 135 73114 3

British Library Cataloguing in Publication Data
A CIP catalogue record for this book can be obtained from the British Library.

10 9 8 7 6 5 4 3
04 03 02 01 00

Typeset by 35 in 10/13pt Sabon
Printed and bound in Great Britain by T J International

This thing here, which looks like a wooden club, is actually several pieces of particular wood cunningly put together in a certain way so that the whole thing is sprung, like a dance floor. It's for hitting cricket balls with. If you get it right, the cricket ball will travel two hundred yards in four seconds, and all you've done is give it a knock like knocking the top off a bottle of stout, and it makes a noise like a trout taking a fly. . . . What we're trying to do is to write cricket bats, so that when we throw up an idea, and give it a little knock, it might . . . travel. . . .

Tom Stoppard, *The Real Thing**

* Tom Stoppard, *The Real Thing* (London: Faber & Faber, 1988, p. 52).

For

Susan and Daniel,
Jade and Alex,
Rebecca and Nicholas

and in memory of
Sue H. Bank

Contents

Preface to the second edition

The Atlanta Olympics was a shambles before the explosion in Centennial Park. Competitors, coaches, spectators, support staff, vendors and the media complained about the collapse of virtually everything from the transport system to the computer set-up, from inadequate provisions for the predictable, debilitating hot and humid climate to security lapses. Quality planning and provisions to meet customer requirements seemed to have been left out of the equation and this will tarnish the 1996 Olympics and a great city's reputation far more than a mindless act of violence.

People's expectations and demands for total quality are increasing all the time. Their impatience with systems that are poorly planned, services that fall ludicrously short of expectations and managers who fail to manage well is increasingly vocal. Cunard learned this costly lesson in the farcical QE2's transatlantic crossing at Christmas 1994 and the cruising company's future in the hands of its new Norwegian owners is still in jeopardy (*see* p. 16).

Since the publication of this book's first edition six years ago, Total Quality Management (TQM) has grown, not diminished. Total quality management continues to be a historically unique opportunity to improve organizational effectiveness while revealing how organizations actually work in practice.

TQM now permeates all areas of society from business and industry to commerce and education, health and welfare, public life and professional organizations. Unlike management fads of the past, total quality management has staying power as a unifying business philosophy in the run-up to the new millennium. Most TQM programmes remain true to the ideas of the founders of the quality movement. The quality concepts and words have not been devalued or debased despite their widespread popularity. The quality words still have a ring of reality about them, a potent sense of purpose that can capture the imagination of managers and employees alike and truly motivate them to excel.

The quality message has the potency Aldous Huxley attributes to words in his *Brave New World* when he writes 'Words can be like X-rays, if you use them properly – they'll go through anything. You read and you're pierced.'

The relaunch of America's space shuttle programme in October 1988 required over 400 design changes and replacement of critical components in the shuttle fleet costing $2.4 billion. In the nearly three years it took to recover from the spectacular in-flight break-up of *Challenger*, NASA was completely reorganized. Yet 13 years after the *Challenger* accident cost-cutting and financial pressures in NASA, similar to those at the time of the accident, are setting off alarm signals.

Events leading up to 'the major malfunction' of *Challenger* provide the raw material of a classic case study on how *not* to manage a complex technological project where lessons are timeless. The prodigious cost of poor quality engineering and poor processes in the space shuttle programme – including the loss of seven lives – still argue for the need of total quality management in NASA even as it moves irrevocably towards total privatization by a consortium of aerospace companies.

Poor quality processes in its Bhopal pesticide plant cost the Union Carbide Corporation £420 million in compensation claims in March 1989. More than 3,400 people have died since a cloud of deadly methyl isocyanate gas leaked out of a storage tank at the Bhopal plant and floated over a city of 672,000 population in the early hours of 3 December 1984. It was the worst industrial accident in history with over 200,000 people hurt and 15,000–20,000 suffering lasting injuries. The pesticide factory simply did not have the quality safety processes that exist in a similar pesticide plant in Germany (owned by Bayer) and one in America (Union Carbide's own) which include towers that rain down foam to neutralize escaping gases. The three men with garden hoses at Bhopal – two of whom wisely ran away – were a ludicrous substitute for a fail-safe system.

The space shuttle fireball or the tragedy at Bhopal are not accidents that result from human error. They are part of seriously flawed business processes where quality is ignored. They are part of the unacceptably high cost of poor quality which companies and their customers are increasingly refusing to pay.

Who is accountable for disregarding quality procedures? There was public outrage in Britain over the sinking of the British ferry *Herald of Free Enterprise* after it sailed from Zeebrugge on 6 March 1987 with open bow doors. Anger over the loss of 193 lives was reflected by a court case in which former employees of P & O European Ferries were charged with manslaughter at the Old Bailey in October 1990. As a result of the case, although those charged were acquitted, corporate manslaughter is legally admissible in an English court. Another roll-on roll-off ferry, the *Estonia*, with bow door problems foundered off the coast of Sweden in 1994 with the loss of 852 lives highlighting the intrinsically unsafe design of the ferries. The fire on Occidental's Piper Alpha oil platform in the North Sea which claimed 167 lives on 6 July 1988 showed a similar disregard for life when submitted to the white-hot scrutiny of public inquiry and legal action. Earlier there was the tragedy of the drug thalidomide. Today there is the scandal of mistakes and sloppy practices across the entire cervical smear testing system which are putting women's lives at risk, according to a 1998 National Audit Office report. These events again reveal an alarming lack of proper quality procedures. But it should not take a national disaster to alert managers to bad practices and procedures. Engineers or shopfloor workers who discover flawed design should have been encouraged to 'blow the whistle' by their company's own commitment to continuous improvement and to quality processes rather than wait to play dramatic parts as witnesses in an inquiry.

An insistence on total quality as the fundamental business principle in organizations everywhere has the force of an unstoppable idea whose time has come. Managers are grappling with total quality now to ensure a future for themselves and their companies. Anyone who ignores quality today does so as great jeopardy to his or her business.

In the run-up to the new millennium, managers have to focus on the right priorities. They should lead their companies with clear vision to fulfil their missions, unleashing the creative powers of all employees in diverse teams to meet competitive challenges from a global market-place. Coping with change and uncertainty, managers need an overall framework within which to work that will provide practical norms while capturing the imagination of managers and workers alike. Managers needs to create a corporate culture where quality products and services, business processes and people are central. In short, managers need a working understanding of total quality management (TQM).

Rooted in the research and teachings of American quality pioneers W. Edwards Deming and Joseph M. Juran, the home-grown management synthesis of Kaoru Ishikawa and many others, the TQM message empowered Japanese managers and gave them the quality vehicle with which they established global trade supremacy.

The quality gurus told Japanese managers and politicians what they were gradually discovering for themselves, that the only way they could survive as an island nation with virtually no natural resources was to make quality products and service the national imperative. And this they did, producing steel, ships, motorbikes, cars, medical equipment, transistor radios, stereo components, television sets, video recorders, cameras, camcorders, calculators, computers, photocopiers and other office machinery, musical instruments, hand tools, machine tools, radial tyres, electric motors, food processors, microwave ovens, sports equipment, heavy machinery, computer games, industrial robots, electron microscopes and microcircuits – where the Japanese measure defects in 'parts per million' (six sigma) rather than the traditional Western percentages. In all these sectors the Japanese sell their products on quality as well as price. They perfected the idea of continuous improvement and competitive benchmarking. And the West is still reeling from the results. In 1985 the US foreign trade deficit reached a record $148.5 billion of which $49.7 billion – a third – applied to trade with Japan.

During the last decade, however, the quality thrust came back to America and Europe bringing great benefits in its wake. The benefits of TQM programmes include greater competitive advantage and massive financial savings to do with the cost of quality' (the total business cost in achieving quality) which is exhibited in the costs of prevention, appraisal, internal failure, external failure, exceeding customer requirements and lost opportunities.

Although first taken advantage of in the industrial sector, total quality management has been found to be just as effective in the service industry – in banking, insurance, hotels and restaurants, travel and holidays, health and the administration of public affairs. In fact, whenever an organization has a sequence of activities directed towards a defined end result it has business processes which can be analysed and improved by TQM techniques.

In addition to marketing advantages and financial savings, TQM programmes increase customer satisfaction producing a tidal wave of goodwill, customer retention and additional business. They encourage the production of new products and services. They help develop a more effective management focused on the right priorities. By empowering people, these TQM programmes improve company morale and encourage genuine improvement in decision-making. They help turn companies into learning organizations. They ultimately enhance a company's image and, in so far as is possible in an uncertain world, attempt to assure a company's viability.

UK companies have been following the lead of Japanese and American firms taking on TQM programmes to capture these benefits. Getting it right first time, zero defects, prevention, the internal customer, competitive benchmarking, 'cost of quality', synergy in teamwork, self-management, self-inspection – these are key words and phrases in the move towards total quality. Behind the words and concepts are techniques and actions. Instead of focusing on products and services in isolation, they are looked at in their integral connection with business processes and the people who do the work. New systems are created. New orientations such as relationship marketing are undertaken.

The focal point of it all is the customer. In fact, quality is defined as fully satisfying agreed customer requirements at the lowest internal price. The rewards are great for those companies who meet customer requirements because they win repeat business.

This book presents the essence of total quality starting in Chapter 1 with a focus on the customer. Chapter 2 analyses total quality management core concepts, which are: profiting from quality, right first time, zero defects, a rejection of acceptable quality levels (AQLs), cost of quality, competitive benchmarking, involving everyone, synergy in teamwork, ownership, self-management, reward and recognition, managers as role models, leadership and the quality delivery process. What major writers have said about total quality management in the past is the subject of Chapter 3. We look at the work of the Americans: Deming, Juran and Crosby, and at the Japanese 'Father of Quality Circles' Professor Karou Ishikawa and the British expert John S. Oakland.

Cutting the cost of quality is the subject of Chapter 4 in which each of the traditional costs of quality – prevention, appraisal, internal failure, external failure, exceeding requirements and lost opportunities – is analysed and illustrated by relevant examples, including a more detailed look at the *Challenger* accident. On average firms waste 20–30 per cent of their revenue or turnover on 'cost of quality' issues. Halving the cost of quality (over two years or so) could double their profits.

Case studies in Chapter 5 show TQM programmes at British Airways, IBM, Xerox, the Paul Revere Insurance Group, the Royal Mail and The Body Shop – famous for its effective customer care. These programmes illustrate the key concepts of TQM in real business situations. Here we also look at the challenge of changing company culture to the more positive total quality management culture.

The major tools and techniques of total quality management are summarized in Chapter 6. Chapter 7 opens up the critical discussion of how to determine the success or failure of total quality initiatives. It also examines quality award criteria. Finally a selective and annotated guide to further reading containing a dozen of the best books in the field is included in Chapter 8.

The potential readership of this book includes MBA students who need to pick up ideas swiftly and run with them, and practising managers, some of whom seek out business schools to delve into new management practices before returning to the hurly-burly game of survival. The book is intended for all those managers who know instinctively that quality must mean something more than just the basics outlined in BS 5750 or ISO 9000. That in no way is to belittle the importance of these two standards – the former for Britain, the latter for Europe and the world. Customers are constantly asking their suppliers for confirmation of their accreditation to BS 5750 and ISO 9000 and the requests have fuelled much quality activity. Further, the Department of Trade and Industry (DTI) through its Quality Initiative had certified a large team of consultants nationwide and will fund up to half the consultancy cost for small companies (under 500 employees) who launch quality programmes which often lead to BS 5750 or ISO 9000 accreditation. Impact on global trade can be immense as when the US Navy announced that it could not deal with a supplier unless they had ISO 9000 certification. The standards are the floor of the quality building, not the edifice of total quality, or to use Bonington's terminology, BS 5750 is the base camp while total quality is the ascent up Everest.

Armad Feigerbaum, the head of quality at General Electric in the United States and who coined the term 'total quality management', had also stated that 'quality is a way of managing not a technical activity'.

Management is one of the most challenging, exhilarating and risky activities in the real world. People's livelihoods and their families' well-being, personal fortunes and communities' social health, and the wealth of the nation state, all depend on the skill and prowess of managers who create their own luck and read the changes new technology and global marketing are pushing rapidly forward. They latch onto total quality management with its unique combination of systems, techniques and employee involvement to gain the management equivalent of Olympic gold – glittering competitive edge.

Total quality management is an approach to business which looks critically at the products and services a company produces in relation to the processes it takes to recreate them and the people who do the work to make certain that outputs fully satisfy agreed customer requirements. Internal customers – anyone who receives the work of another within the company – are as important as the external customer or end user of the goods or services because they create a chain of quality which reaches out to the consumer. The approach is called 'total' because it encompasses everything the company does – all its processes and all of its employees at every level in the company all the time. It is a restless approach since it aims at continuous improvement, the elimination of waste and costs, and the strengthening of loyal relationships with suppliers and customers. Although statistical quality control techniques, such as statistical process control (SPC), are used, the approach is more concerned with management than with specific techniques. The purpose of this book is to demystify the topic and provide managers with a concise, clear guide to total quality management.

The new edition updates and expands certain chapters, particularly Chapter 1, 'Focus on the Customer', Chapter 4, 'Cutting the Cost of Quality', and Chapter 5, 'Case Studies of Total Quality Management'. A new case study on The Body Shop, the international cosmetic retail chain, has been added to illustrate effective customer care. A completely new Chapter 7, 'Evaluating TQM' opens up the critical discussion of how to determine the success or failure of total quality initiatives. It also examines quality award criteria. The annotated bibliography in the final chapter is also altered to reflect some new titles. Throughout the book I have tried to give illustrations of TQM in small businesses as well as in the global corporations.

Writing a book on TQM fills an author with anxiety for he/she must, as Shakespeare exhorts in *A Midsummer Night's Dream*, 'Take pains to be perfect'.

John Bank
London, 1999

Acknowledgements

Looking after this book has been a bit like tending a bonsai tree. It grew slowly and steadily to its gnarled, stumpy height and needed pruning, nurturing and continual care for nearly a year. None of that would have happened without the 'green fingers' of my secretary, Joan Edwards. 'Inspire me!' I would say to her and she would respond with another improved draft of a chapter on her computer. So my 'thank you's' start with her rather than end with her for caring for both editions of the book.

Louise Edwards and staff of the Management Information Resource Centre and Doreen Dunbar and Simon Bevan of the staff of the Cranfield University Library were very helpful in providing books and articles I needed for research and in running swift computer checks on certain facts (proving time and again their case for a paperless office).

I am grateful to the many colleagues who have shared their ideas with me as we have worked together on quality consultancy assignments. They include Alison Dawson, Mike Robson, Duncan Case, Carolyn Ritchie, David Cropper, Trevor Griffiths, Jim Underwood, Les Rix, Peter Angus, Eric Knight, Mike Brown, Bob Cardow, David Borthwick, Dick Fletcher, Jim Thomas, Patrick Dolan, Geoff Spriegel, Mike Regan, Mike Miller, Michael Frye, Trevor Smith, Jackie Holman, Mike Thompson, Richard L. Shacklady, Chris Binmore, Tim Belcher, Steve Appleyard, Jim Kennedy, Peter Conway, Ron Mayo, Oliver McLaren, Dai Thomas, Nic Birtles, Shamim Khan, Jimmy Kane, Steve Carver, Nicholas C. Walsh, Bob Philip, Chuck Townsend and Peter W. Schlesiona, both of IBM (USA), Liam Strong, Farid Muna of MEIRC, Abdul-Redha Ishaq, Titus Earle, Graeme Lynam, Robin Young, Manuel Marcet, Michelle Berkowitz at Restoration Hardware, Columbus, Ohio, for superb customer service and, most importantly, John D. Huckett, CEO of Crandelta International, with whom I have developed TQM programmes and training materials. Messages from the joint effort with John Huckett surface throughout the entire book and are too entwined with my own thoughts to identify, Sir Chris Bonington has contributed greatly to my understanding of leadership over the years and deserves a vigorous thank you, and a special thank you to Mr Zhong-Liang Xu (MPhil) for his hard work on the index to the first edition.

I have been fortunate to have Julia Helmsley, MBA, Senior Editor at Prentice Hall, as a skilful and patient publisher – for both editions of the book – and owe her a round of applause for her superb efforts.

Acknowledgements

Over nearly two decades at the Cranfield School of Management and before that at the London Business School I have discussed ideas about quality and employee involvement with thousands of MBA, MSc and other management students. I believe in the Latin axiom 'We learn by teaching', and owe much to my students in the business schools and in boardrooms, offices and factories, for making the learning a two-way process. Their ideas are reflected here.

My wife Susan Vinnicombe has her own career as a management academic and consultant and her own books to write. She has been supportive of my effort to make the publisher's deadline and very helpful with ideas when I got stuck. She has also played the 'devil's advocate' when the attributions I made to TQM became too overarching and arrogant for her liking and cast a critical eye over the text. Anyone like us living as a dual career couple does a non-stop juggling act with work and conferences, research and writing, children and their education, sports and leisure. It's a demanding double act. The book became another fluorescent ball in the air and Susan skilfully added it to the others flying in a small orbits overhead at our house in Highgate or at the university. Her brother Mike and his wife Bev Vinnicombe, proprietors of the Star Inn in Perigueux in the Dordogne, shared their rural house with us in August 1991 when I pulled the first edition of the book together.

By design the book is a derivative one, attempting to sum up the entire field of total quality management, research, thinking and practice. Most of the ideas, then, are those of other writers, some of whom are legends in the quality business. In that sense, the words of Sir Isaac Newton are appropriate. We see further 'by standing on the shoulders of giants'.*

John Bank
London, 1999

* Letter to Robert Hooke, 5 February 1675/6.

We are grateful to the following for permission to reproduce copyright material:

Fig 1.1 reprinted with permission from *The Independent Magazine*, 3 August 1991; Fig 2.6 from IFALPA; Fig 2.9 from Research International; Fig 2.17 from BS 7750: 1992 (British Standards); Fig 3.4 and Fig 3.5 from *Total Quality Management*, Oxford: Butterworth Heinemann (J.S. Oakland, 1994); Fig 4.1 from *Time Magazine*, 10 October 1988; Fig 4.4 reprinted with permission from *The Far Side Gallery 4*, London: Warner Books (Gary Larson, 1993); Fig 5.4 from Xerox Training Material; Figs 5.6 and 5.7 adapted from 'Total Quality Benchmarking', USA Study Tour, 1–5 October 1990; Tables 5.4 and 5.5 adapted from a Royal Mail Internal Publication; Fig 6.2 and Fig 6.4 adapted from Eli Lilly and Company, Florida Power and Light Company, 1989; Fig 6.7 from 'A New Ambiguous Figure', *American Journal of Psychology*, (Edwin G. Boring, July 1930). Originally drawn by cartoonist W.E. Hill published in *Puck*, 6 November 1915. As printed in *Games Trainers Play*, McGraw-Hill Book Co. (John W. Newstrom and Edward E. Scanneil, 1980); Fig 6.15 adapted 'How to Implement a Competitive Quality Program', *Quality in America*, Homewood, Ill.: Business One, Irwin (V. Daniel Hurst, 1992); Fig 6.16 adapted from *Total Quality Management: A Cross Cultural Perspective*, John Wiley & Sons (Rao, Carr, et al., 1996); Fig 7.1 adapted from *The Corporate Guide to the Malcolm Baldrige National Quality Award*, 2 edn, Milwaukee, Wis.: SAQC Quality Press (Marion Mills Steeples, 1993); Fig 7.3 from 'Business Process Redesign – Hype or Hope?', *Management Focus*, Cranfield School of Management, no 2, (Gerard Burke, Autumn 1993); Fig 7.4 from 'The Balanced Scorecard Links Performance Measures', Harvard Business Review (Robert S. Kaplan and David P. Norton, Jan–Feb 1992).

Epigraph on p. v and quotation on p. 31 from *The Real Thing*, London: Faber & Faber (Tom Stoppard, 1988); Epigraph on p. 31 from *Trouble Shooter*, London: BBC Books (John Harvey-Jones (with Andrea Massey), 1990).

Whilst every effort has been made to trace the owners of copyright material, in a few cases this has proved impossible and we take this opportunity to offer our apologies to any copyright holders whose rights we may have unwittingly infringed.

Chapter 1

Focus on the customer

Get thee glass eyes, and, like a scurvy politician, seem to see the things thou dost
not.   Shakespeare, *King Lear*, Act IV, Scene 5.

'We want to turn this sham Citizen's Charter into a real people's Charter,' deputy
leader John Prescott said. Instead of cutting red tape and redressing wrongs, it
has become 'vague, inaccessible and impractical.' A Blair government would make
its 'People's Charter' accessible to people and would set meaningful targets.

Later Tory vice-chairman Charles Hendry attacked Labour's plans for the
Citizen's Charter, claiming they ignored 'the transformation in the quality of public services' achieved over the past five years. 'From health to housing, power to
post, tough targets have been set and achieved.' Mr Hendry said.[1]

The customer as king

When Ally Svenson moved to London from Seattle, Washington, with her
husband Scott in 1990, she anticipated some culture shock as a customer, but
she did not expect to be denied her favourite daily cup of coffee. She was
employed by the US publishing company Comag as head of the import sales
department with a mission to introduce American magazines to European
readers. She despaired of ever finding a choice of coffees to drink in London
cafes where insipid cappucinos were their most creative offerings.

Five years later in April 1995, she opened her first coffee cafe called the Seattle
Coffee Company in Covent Garden. This first coffee shop catered to tourists and
exploited the cafe's link with Seattle, the coffee capital of the world. But the
next two coffee shops – one in the Canary Wharf business sector of the Docklands
and the other inside a Cambridge book store – were aimed at British customers.
By April 1998, there were 56 Seattle coffee shops (including one in Heathrow
Airport and one shop on the High Street in North London's Muswell Hill),
and plans to double that number by the end of the year were announced.

Ally Svenson's husband had left his job as chief executive of the largest
public health care company in Britain to manage the finances of the Seattle
Coffee Company, which has a turnover of £21 million. His wife at age 31 is
managing director.

The entire business is built on Ally Svenson's belief that coffee drinkers are customers who should be given greater choice. For her coffee is 'an affordable luxury'.[2]

Total quality management is focused on the requirements of the customer. On the personal front people only go back to restaurants that fully satisfy them and they shop regularly at stores that meet their needs. They fly on airlines that provide friendly, efficient service. Industrial customers, likewise, have a set of expectations and requirements that must be met for the supplier to win repeat business. An industrial customer has the same range of emotions as a personal customer to being disappointed, cheated or short-changed. The industrial customer's response to poor service is similar – withdrawal of business and buying elsewhere.

A popular poster for display in shops, offices and factories drives this message home. It reads as follows:

Customers are:
- The most important people in any business.
- Not dependent on us. We are dependent on them.
- Not an interruption of our work. They are the purpose of it.
- Doing us a favour when they come in. We're not doing them a favour by serving them.
- A part of our business, not outsiders.
- Not just a statistic. They are flesh and blood human beings with feelings and emotions, like ourselves.
- People come to us with their needs and wants. It's our job to fill them.
- Deserving of the most courteous and attentive treatment we can give them.
- The lifeblood of this and every other business. Without them we would have to close our doors.
  (Don't ever forget it!)

There are problems about defining quality as fully meeting agreed customer requirements when the awareness of customer service in British culture is so low. People are simply not conditioned to expect a high level of customer care in their private dealings and hence do not have models that transfer easily to the business or work context.

To *serve* the customer in Britain is not the expected thing. The motto of British Airways (BA) is 'we fly, to serve', but only in the last decade has BA begun to deliver consistently on the service side. Sales personnel in shops often cluster together talking among themselves totally ignoring the customer. For example, should a female customer approach them with a query about an item of clothing she would like to purchase, she is made to feel as if she were intruding. 'Excuse me', she says, 'do you have this dress in a size 10?', to which a likely reply is 'if it's not on the rack, we haven't got it'. Rarely will the sales assistant actually attend to the customer's requirements by checking computer printouts of stock or looking at display windows, or talking about when the item might arrive on a reorder or whether another branch has it in stock.

It may be that serving the customer in this country gets confused with servitude and class barriers come up quickly. It may be that pay and other rewards are so poor in the retail trade that people are not motivated to look after customers. Perhaps they are just not trained or managed skilfully to do so. It could be that by allocating 'low status' to service jobs those employees are 'programmed' for delivering poor service. Part of it must be down to the customers themselves, who are not assertive about what they want.

However, the tide is beginning to change in favour of the customer. The Conservative government's Citizen's Charter, first announced in July 1991, seeks to set standards, ensure greater competition and accountability and provide redress for customers who are victims of poor service. The Citizen's Charter makes consumer rights the 'central theme of public life' for the 1990s. The goals of total quality management, at least, have surfaced in government.

The proposed new protections for ordinary people extend throughout the National Health Service, education and transport to the privatized gas, water, electricity and telecommunications utilities. The government White Paper promised legislation to bring the powers of the utility regulators 'up to the level of the strongest, including making sure that the regulators have adequate powers to require the award of compensation in response to legitimate customer complaints'.

That means a clearer commitment to quality of service, fixed appointment times and 'more considerate mechanisms for dealing with customer complaints'. There will be a charter standard for public service quality which will entitle those who can prove they meet the high standards to use a new 'Chartermark'. This Chartermark would denote publication of standards of service that the customer can reasonably expect, and of performance against those standards. It would also certify 'evidence that the views of those who use the service have been taken into account'. And, show that clear information about the range of services on offer had been given by staff who would be 'normally prepared to identify themselves by name' to help rid the public of the faceless bureaucracy – public servants where appropriate would wear name badges.

To qualify for the Whitehall Chartermark of excellence public services and utilities would need to erect 'well-signposted avenues for complaint if the customer is not satisfied, with some independent review whenever possible'. The final requirement, of course, would be 'independent validation of performance against standards and a clear commitment to improve value for money'.[3]

The Prime Minister in announcing the charter insisted that bodies in all areas of public service would be required to publish 'explicit standards of performance and the results they actually achieve – targets will be set for improvement year by year'. Examples of how this would benefit consumers include the following:

- The waiting time before taking the driving test would be reduced.
- There would be more proposals accepted for motorway service areas from private developers.
- Road contractors would be penalized for coning off sections of a motorway when work is not being done.
- A network of lay adjudicators would be established to 'help the citizen to get swift resolution of those small but irritating complaints which cause so much frustration'.

Summing up his proposals Prime Minister John Major said:

> It is a programme for a decade. The charter programme will find better ways of converting the money that can be afforded into even better services. I want the people of this country to have services in which they as citizens can be confident, and which public servants themselves can take pride.[4]

Although the Citizen's Charter was launched in July 1991, with an eye to the general election that summer, it did catch the mood of the nation in so far as quality services is concerned. As a leader in a daily newspaper put it so well:

> Many of Mr Major's frustrations are refreshingly mundane. He complained of motorway lanes unnecessarily coned-off for long periods. He talked of the delays caused by hospital administrators who book dozens of out-patients for the same time because it is more convenient for the consultants to have a queue of patients waiting. He spoke of people waiting at home all day because telephone engineers and those who service gas, electricity and water supplies often refuse to give and keep fixed appointments.
>
> Some commentators might be inclined to smirk at what they would see as the lack of sophistication demonstrated by the Prime Minister. They would be wrong. Mr Major's workaday preoccupations are shared by millions of people. They are quietly furious at the incompetence and casual arrogance that has come to characterise producer-dominated public services and the privatised utilities. They do not want their services battered or humiliated. They want them improved. There are votes aplenty to be won here.[5]

In the run up to the last general election in 1997, both political parties took positions on the Citizen's Charter. While the government lauded the Charter as a bold beginning, the Labour opposition attacked it as a bungled attempt far inferior to what a Labour government would put in place to protect the people when they came to power.

Ann Taylor, a front-bench Labour MP and a spokesperson for the Citizen's Charter, argued that this flagship Tory policy was a Labour idea initially. A Labour leader Herbert Morrison coined the phrase 'Citizen's Charter' in 1921. Labour councils used the idea in the 1970s and Neil Kinnock drafted the phrase in two policy documents in the late 1980s. 'We are looking for something that is bolder and more meaningful – the basic concept of ensuring quality and providing redress has got to be re-established,' said Ann Taylor.

Public reaction to the Citizen's Charter has been mixed. The 'Charterline', a telephone helpline, was abandoned as a pilot scheme in the East Midlands because it prompted only 25 calls per day on average at a cost of £68 each. Too often the Charter standards are mocked by poor public performance as when an elderly lady waited 81 minutes for a London ambulance when the Patient's Charter states that 95 per cent of people who live in urban areas should be able to get an ambulance in 14 minutes. Yet in one way even this failure is paradoxically a sign of the Charter's success for without the Patient's Charter there would be no publicized targets for the ambulance service and therefore no measure of success or failure. As it was, the failure was apparent, picked up by the media and the London Ambulance Service immediately set up an inquiry to see what had gone wrong.

The Patient's Charter gave rise to a 56.7 per cent increase in written complaints to the NHS in one year bringing the number to nearly 60,000. The Charter requires that a patient be seen within half an hour or be given the reasons for the delay.

The £2.7 million spent on the Parent's Charter, head teachers pointed out, could have been better used to have operated a medium-sized comprehensive school for 18 months. Unfortunately most adults regard standards to have fallen in the NHS, railways, roads, policy and council housing according to a government survey which itself cost £75,000 to undertake. A full third of those interviewed had not even heard of the Citizen's Charter.[6]

Another opinion poll run by the TUC concluded that two out of three people regarded the Charter idea as a public relations exercise and that only 2 per cent had used one of the over 40 charters set up to improve public services.

TUC General Secretary John Monks said: 'Our poll shows that the Citizen's Charter is an expensive irrelevance which plays no part in delivering quality in our public services. It goes unseen, unread and unused by a vast majority of British citizens.'

One of the proponents of the Citizen's Charter, Roderick Nye, Director of the Social Market Foundation, complained that the Charter was too one-sided placing an onus on the public service to be more responsive, whereas the public itself needed to be reminded to use services more responsibly.

The Consumers' Association magazine *Which?* concluded a detailed test of five of 40 charters with a list of failings that included information not being on display or easy to find, neglect in providing details of how to claim compensation or a refund and punctuality targets unacceptable to commuters at British Rail stations. Benefits Agency offices were found negligent in displaying local service standards. Hospitals were careless about waiting time standards in casualty departments or having copies of the Patient's Charter on hand.

A third of 35 main post offices failed to display their customer charter and only six main branches displayed local service standards.

'There have been some successes,' said Paul Kitchen, the Consumers' Association spokesperson, 'but some of the charters fall well short of the commitment to overall improvement promised. Charters need to be more than paper promises.' The Institute of Public Policy Research echoed those ideas when its spokesperson Ian Bynoe said: 'We must learn from the Charter's mistakes but build on its potential, giving the public clear rights and greater influence in the planning and running of their services.'

Customer complaints in rail travel are finally being heard. In May 1998, rail companies were fined £4m for running trains late or with too few carriages. According to an Office of Passenger Rail Franchising bulletin, punctuality worsened on 35 routes over the previous 12 months and improved on only 77 routes during the same time span. John O'Brien, the franchising director, warned the train operators that most needed to dramatically improve their punctuality and reliability figures, which were 'unsatisfactory'. He said: 'Passengers have a right to expect performance to improve year to year.'[7]

These sentiments are captured in the cartoon shown in Figure 1.1.

Fig. 1.1 The Citizen's Charter

Source: The Independent Magazine, 3 August 1991.

Consumer power

Part of the thrust for total quality management comes from consumer demands that grow stronger and better organized. *Consumer Reports* was founded in the United States 62 years ago as a publication of the Consumers Union (CU) which was started by trade unions in the 1930s. The organization has published CU's ratings for thousands of products and services – from cars to life insurance, from drain cleaners to refrigeration – without ever losing a libel suit. The circulation for its monthly magazine is over 4 million. These subscribers, their friends, relatives and others, refuse to buy anything until they consult the magazine. A Consumer Report summed up customer complaints about US airlines based on a poll of 140,000 passengers as follows:

> Passengers are flying in more crowded planes and sitting in more cramped spaces. They are waiting in more congested airports, for more delayed flights and visiting cities they have no desire to go to, simply to change planes.
>
> In short the product they are buying today is a shadow of the product they could have bought 13 years ago, since the airlines industry was deregulated. . . .
>
> The US government sets space standards for airlines transporting cats and dogs. No such rules apply to human cargo. Thirty per cent of readers listed 'very crowded' as a problem with their flight and almost half our respondents called the seat comfort less than good.[8]

The main areas of complaint were: seat comfort, 49 per cent; in-flight catering, 37 per cent; ventilation and cabin temperature, 21 per cent; in-flight service, 13 per cent; check-in, 10 per cent.

Nearly a decade later the customer view of the US airline industry is still low. Airlines in the United States – in the hope of heading off plans by Congress to introduce two passengers' bill of rights – are pulling together a package of voluntary measures.

These measures include:

- telling customers what the lowest fare is to a destination even if it is offered by another airline;
- better explanations of flight delays;
- a pledge to answer written complaints within 60 days;
- the prompt provision of ticket refunds; and
- better hospitality to passengers during runway delays.

Britain came much later to the consumer protection business. The Consumers' Association (CA) was started by Michael Young, now Lord Young of Dartington, in March 1957. Seven months later the first issue of *Which?* was published. From its beginnings in a converted garage in the East End of London to its modern office block on Marylebone Road, CA has grown into an influential organization with an income of more than £38 million a year and a membership of one million.

The Association for Consumer Research (ACR) is a registered charity which undertakes research and comparative testing of goods and services. Its trading subsidiary, Consumers' Association Limited, publishes these findings (in *Which?* magazine and its other publications), represents the consumer interest and campaigns for improvements in goods and services.

Every month *Which?* gives independent verdicts based on testing and research, much of which is undertaken at ACR's test laboratories in Harpenden, Hertfordshire. It also publishes the *Drug and Therapeutics Bulletin* (fortnightly) which provides impartial and expert information for doctors about the clinical use of drugs. Separate periodicals deal with wine and gardening and holidays and health issues.

The mobile phone customer and competitive advantage

Britain had more than 17 million mobile phone users by the spring of 1999 and the market was expected to grow from 28 per cent of Britons having cellular phones to 35 per cent within the year.

Yet research by the Consumers' Association[9] shows that one in three users of mobile phones is unhappy with the product. The survey found that customers are obliged to sign lengthy contracts with unreliable networks for phones that often cut off in mid call. The report said that nearly three-quarters of mobile phone users had experienced problems with their phones. About four out of ten users were so dissatisfied that they would return their mobile phones, change tariff or move network if they could do so without paying a financial penalty.

More than a third of the 2,891 respondents to the survey said they were unhappy with at least one core aspect of the mobile phone service. They complained of being cut off for no apparent reason, failing to connect to their network and having to take their mobile phone in for repairs.

There are four competing networks for the mobile phone market. Cellnet and Vodafone were the rival pioneers in the business. Mercury's One-2-One network was launched in September 1993 followed by Orange, whose tag line 'The future is bright, the future is Orange' could be predictive as the survey showed Orange customers to be least dissatisfied with the network. Customers of Mercury One-2-One and Vodafone registered the highest level of dissatisfaction.

Customer care the American way

Most British tourists visiting America are impressed with the friendly and efficient service they get in restaurants, from the unasked-for glass of iced water and the first-name introduction of the waitress as in 'I'm Cheryl and I'm your wait-ress' to the extra cup of coffee. The level of customer expectation is high. The willingness to serve the customer seems there. There are stunning examples like Disney and McDonald's and with such a broad middle class there are few class barriers to serving. But even in America there has been a noticeable slippage in service to the customer. And people are unhappy about it. A cover story in *Time Magazine* asked what had happened to service. It began with a parody of poor service:

> For Harry Hapless, it was a rough day in the service economy. His car, a Fiasco 400, started sputtering on the highway, so Harry pulled into a gas station for help. 'Sorry, no mechanics, only gas!' shouted the attendant. 'How can you call this a service station?' yelled Harry. He went to the bank to get some emergency cash for a tow truck, only to find the automatic teller machine out of order again. 'Real nice service!' he muttered. Then Harry decided to use a credit card to buy a tool kit at the Cheapo discount store, but he couldn't find anyone to wait on him. 'Service! Anyone, please! Help me!' was his cry.
>
> It had been a trying day indeed, Harry thought as he rode a bus home, but at least he could look forward to a trip to Florida the following week with his wife Harriet. That is, until Flyway Air called: 'Sorry, Mr Hapless. Due to our merger with Byway Air, your Florida flight has been cancelled.' Harry got so angry he was going to call the Federal Aviation Administration immediately. But just then his phone went dead – no doubt because the Bell System had been split up, he imagined. Well, that was the last straw. A few minutes later a wild-eyed Harry burst into the newsroom of his local newspaper. 'I've got a story for you!' he cried. 'There is no more service in America!'
>
> More and more consumers are beginning to feel almost as frustrated as Harry Hapless. Personal service has become a maddeningly rare commodity in the American marketplace. Flight attendants, sales clerks and bank tellers all seem to have become too scarce and too busy to give consumers much attention. Many other service workers are underpaid, untrained and unmotivated for their jobs, to the chagrin of customers who look to them for help. The concept of personal service is a difficult quantity to measure precisely, to be sure; the U.S. Government keeps no Courtesy Index or Helpfulness Indicator among its economic statistics. But customers know service when they miss it, and now they want it back.[10]

The root cause of the fall-off of service is economics. The great inflation of the 1970s, set off by the oil crisis, caused businesses to cut service to keep prices from rocketing. This was followed by deregulation, which increased com-petition and caused more cutbacks. Labour shortages in many areas, then, left fewer people available for the service sector. Computers and self-service replaced service personnel as further cost-cutting took place. Company account-ants grew happier at the expense of consumers, who may have enjoyed self-service to keep prices down but now want old-fashioned quality service.

The demand for customer service comes at a time in the United States when manufacturing has declined in importance relative to the service sector: 85 per cent of the 12.6 million new jobs created in the United States between 1982 and 1987 were in the service sector. As America's economy becomes more dependent on the service sector, the real danger exists that service organizations will make the same strategic mistake over quality that manufacturing did.[11] Japanese banks are already a threat. *Time Magazine* said: 'The potential of service business losing touch is chilling because it was the U.S. that practically invented the concept of good service on a mass-market scale . . . The country's huge appetite for reliable service gave rise to such pioneers as AT&T, IBM, American Express.'[12]

The service sector, if it cares to read recent history, has enough case studies to learn from. In the late 1970s quality circles blossomed on the American scene – by the mid-1980s 90 per cent of the *Fortune* 500 companies had quality circle programmes. But for most companies, it was just a fad that soon faded when it became clear that they could not conjure the quick fix that most firms were looking for.[13] Too often quality circle programmes became something the top told the middle to do to the bottom of the organization. They lacked solid company-wide support. Today companies realize that total quality means a sweeping renewal of a firm's entire culture, a complete change in a company's philosophy, and an unswerving commitment to continuous improvement.

Apart from aerospace and agriculture where the United States competes mightily, there are few markets where the United States holds its own in international trade. Poor quality in products and services became the number one brake on the nation's productivity and competitiveness in global markets. The car makers discovered this in the early 1980s when they realized that Americans were not buying Japanese cars just because they were cheaper, but because of their superior quality. US car makers are now closing the gap. Semiconductor manufacturers lost the market to the Japanese for computer memory chips in the late 1970s and have yet to win it back, although they have improved their quality.

It is not surprising that GM, Ford and Chrysler were among the first US companies to take on TQM in a massive way returning to a clear customer focus and the time when 'made in the USA' was a badge of quality.

The search for longevity

GM, Ford and Chrysler are looking for longevity. Arie de Geus won the Financial Times / Booz-Allen & Hamilton Global Business Book Award for the 'most insightful management book' in 1997 with a small masterpiece called *The Living Company* in which the author offers his practical ideas for how a company as a living being might plan, learn, manage and govern itself. His starting point was the alarming data that showed that the average life expectancy of a multinational company – Fortune 500 or its equivalent – is between 40 and 50 years, a lot less than the average human life of 74 years or more.[14]

This experience-based work of a practitioner from Shell found corroboration from a more rigorous, academic source. In their book *Built to Last*[15] Stanford University Professors James C. Collins and Jerry I. Parras, describe visionary companies as 'premier institutions – the crown jewels – in their industries, widely admired by their peers and having a long track record of making a significant impact on the world around them.' Both books make the same point that the visionary companies with staying power put a low priority on maximizing shareholder wealth or profits. Both books assert that the admired, long lived companies are sensitive to their environment and have a strong sense of identity. They identify Hewlett-Packard as such a visionary company, a real organization, an institution, and the words of co-founder William R. Hewlett echo their definition of a visionary company.

'As I look back on my life's work, I'm probably most proud of having helped to create a company that by virtue of its values, practices, and success has had a tremendous impact on the way companies are managed around the world. And I'm particularly proud that I'm leaving behind an ongoing organization that can live on as a role model long after I'm gone'

Collins and Parras, 1995, page 1

Small businesses count

The customer-focus required by TQM, of course, is as vital for small businesses as it is for the global players. A small, London-based sandwich company with a French name 'Pret à Manger' is proof that a customer-focus and quality service pays.

'I went back to the service counter and told the girl there that I felt the bread was slightly stale. The girl immediately went to get the manager, who without even looking at the sandwich, apologised and offered me a replacement with a free drink and a complementary sandwich and a drink for my friend who was with me. I have probably told this story five or six times now.'[16]

These words from a Pret à Manger customer sum up the bias to action a customer experienced in one of the company's sandwich shops.

The chain of sandwich shops was founded on TQM principles in 1986 by two entrepreneurs, Julian Metcalfe and Sinclair Beecham. It grew in a decade from a single shop in Victoria, London, to 80 shops with an average turnover of £18,500 per week per shop. The shops are mostly at prime locations in London but also include Birmingham, Cambridge and Croydon. In human terms, Pret à Manger serves over a million customers each week. Plans for 2000 will expand the chain of sandwich shops to 200 outlets throughout England, maintaining the same tight focus on satisfying the customer.

Pret à Manger entered the highly crowded and competitive market with a clear, well-defined and relentlessly communicating the mission statement: 'The mission is to create hand-made, natural food, avoiding additives and preservatives common to so much of the "prepared" and "fast" food on the market today.'

This statement is placed in the middle of the company's red five-point star logo. It is found on all packaging, window displays and all Pret consumables. 'Passionate about food!' is its simple tag line. The company trades on a consistent quality of production and quality of service to the customer. It follows Deming's 14 points with particular attention to point 4 (*see* p. 90) for developing, loyal, high-quality suppliers of its raw materials.

Pret à Manger chooses its 11 major suppliers on three criteria:

1 quality of goods;
2 quality of service;
3 price.

Pret à Manger managers realize their dependency on their suppliers because they, themselves, do not manufacture their food. They simply take the raw materials and assemble them into sandwiches and other lunch dishes. To motivate their regular suppliers they even give a 'supplier of the month' award to recognize the supplier's role in their continuing success. They demand that their suppliers meet their high-quality standards for main ingredients.

All Mediterranean and walnut bread and sun dried tomato loaf are baked without preservatives, chemicals or yeast enhancers. Hams are prepared by hand, roasted in a traditional oven and basted with honey and cloves. Chicken is restricted to only fresh chicken breast – no leg or brown meat is permitted. Lamb is from an organic farm. Pasta is hand-made using fresh not dried pasta. Eggs are all free range from a farm where no artificial colourants or hormones are added to the chicken food. Salmon is from Scotland and is poached in the shops daily and tuna is carefully selected. Mayonnaise is made with fresh herbs. A professional coffee buyer chooses only the finest Arabica beans for their cappuccinos.

Having suppliers committed to quality goods and service is a starting point at all 80 outlets. At a Pret à Manger shop in central London, staff were reminded to check their suppliers' ingredients for quality and size with two charts stuck to the refrigerator. On the bottom of the vegetable suppliers' charts was the name of a loyal fruit and vegetable supplier who 'knows how important it is to get us at Pret the right stuff' – if he doesn't, staff are told to give him a hard time: 'Send the stuff back, don't pay for it and demand a replacement immediately.'

Production then begins with top quality goods from faithful suppliers. Pret demands from them:

- *Perfect ingredients.* All ingredients must be of the highest quality to create amazing food. Clerks are reminded to never accept poor quality ingredients in shops, but to weigh, wash and ensure they are fresh.
- *Picture perfect.* People eat with their eyes. Customers expect the same quality food and drinks each time they visit. To ensure this staff carefully follow the recipe for each and every single thing. They prepare and follow the cooking times for hot foods.
- *Passionate about perfection.* To ensure perfection in their food, staff pay attention to detail. They spread sauces on the sandwiches completely to the edges. They ensure fillings are full and showing, not allowing bread crusts to touch, and they ice pastries correctly. They are exhorted to take pride in what they are making – someone's lunch.
- *Perfect packaging.* Staff are instructed not to top and wrap more than five sandwiches at a time to keep sandwiches fresh. After they build the required number of sandwiches they are instructed to return all items to the fridge immediately after use and to send all finished food straight to the shop.

The production process includes 'Pace' – great service means offering the best range possible of the best products possible to as many customers as possible. The staff are responsible for their own production targets which are achieved by a prompt start, good preparation and methodical working practices, cleaning as they go and having a sense of urgency and teamwork.

Everything at Pret à Manger is aimed at exceeding customer expectations. The commitment to this level of service, then, includes the cleanliness of the shop itself and the staff uniforms.

Customers are delighted with a wide choice and attractive displays of food. They are served coffee and food within 60 seconds of requesting it. Queues are kept to a maximum of three people and regular customers are greeted and recognized and valued. Everyone is left in no doubt about the value of their repeat business.

Systems to train new staff and structures to empower employees, of course, are in place to be able to deliver a quality service to the customer. Feedback from customers is sought through suggestion boxes. All recycled carrier bags carry an invitation from the founder and managing director, Julian Metcalfe to get in touch about anything to do with Pret à Manger at his office phone number.

The company uses the 'mystery shopper' idea, sending its own staff into Pret shops posing as customers to check on the quality of service. In addition operations managers carry out a detailed Quality, Service, Cleanliness and Development audit each quarter.

Every fortnight the MD invites staff members to a quality meeting (for which they are paid to attend) to brainstorm ways of improving their business. The openness of the top management to continuous improvement is matched by a reward package that includes bonuses and perks and recognition awards from gift vouchers to free holidays (£35,000 worth of vouchers were given to staff in 1995). Keeping the staff well-trained, highly motivated and interested in improving the business means that customer satisfaction comes naturally, not by accident but by design.

Julian Metcalfe explains:

> I try to create a culture where people aren't afraid to fail, and, if they do fail, don't worry but have another go . . . We don't have any customer service training. It's a question of listening to people and treating them with respect. Staff come in with low self-esteem, but if you give them hope, training, good working conditions and good managers, they get on.[17]

The Richer way

Julian Richer is an entrepreneur in the mould of Julian Metcalf. He is obsessed with people and quality service. He started his own group of businesses, now worth over £50 million, with one small shop called 'Richer Sounds'. He is now the biggest and most profitable hi-fi retailer in the UK with the highest sales per square foot of any retailer in the world, a claim recorded in the *Guinness Book of Records* six years running. He is a believer in 'Kaizen', the Japanese word for continuous improvement, and uses a traditional employee suggestion scheme as the way of ensuring the ongoing progress. 'It is the engine of self-improvement in the business,' he writes. 'Ideas come from the staff and they power the company forward.'[18]

Disregarding the customer

The tragic case of Gerald Ratner, a British jewellery entrepreneur, provides a global warning not to joke about one's customers. Gerald Ratner had been in his family's high street retail jewellery business since he left school at 16. He started serving customers in the shops, which on later reflection, he said he found harder work than being chairman of the company.

In 1983, while he was still in his thirties, Gerald Ratner persuaded his father, Leslie, who founded the business in 1947, to retire at the age of 62 and give him control. He then introduced a new marketing approach to sell high-volume cheap jewellery to capture the lucrative youth market. He moved the average spend in jewellery shops from over £300 to just £20, referring to Ratners as the 'McDonald's of jewellery'. By a policy of aggressive acquisition he took over H. Samuels (in 1986), an existing middle-market chain of high street jewellery shops much larger than Ratners. He crowned his acquisition strategy later by buying the upmarket jewellery chain Zales. During his heady rise to the position of the world's leading jewellers in 1991 with 2,400 shops worldwide and a profit of £112 million, Gerald Ratner enjoyed good press. Positive articles about the shy, attractive millionaire regularly appeared in the British press and he was an established household name and a popular personality.

Gerald Ratner spoke to the Institute of Directors conference at the Royal Albert Hall in London on 23 April 1991. To lighten his 24-minute talk he injected some humour, telling the audience of 6,000 that they could get through the recession by selling junk as he did in his shops. He claimed that his cut-price jewellery shops gave people what they wanted, cheap fun. 'We even sell a pair of earrings for under a pound – gold earrings as well,' he said, 'and some people say it's cheaper than a prawn sandwich from Marks & Spencer. But I have to say the sandwich will last longer than the earrings.'

He said his shops had sold a quarter of a million imitation open books with curled up corners and antique dust, which were in 'the worst possible taste'. He added: 'We also do this nice sherry decanter – it's cut glass and it comes complete with six glasses and a silver-plated tray that your butler could bring you in and serve your drinks on and it really costs £4.94.' Ratner continued: 'People say to me "how can you sell this for such a low price?" I say because it's total crap.' (Earlier the young woman who ran the teleprompter at the Royal Albert Hall that night was the only one who had queried his use of the words 'total crap', asking if it was a misprint.)

Apparently Ratner was oblivious of how the general public that purchased his products would respond to his cynical words once they were amplified in the popular press. He did not anticipate how deeply he had offended his customers who bought his jewellery and other products as gifts for friends and relatives.

'Our Ratner shops will never win any awards for design', he continued. 'They're not in the best possible taste, I admit that. In fact, some say they can't even see the jewellery for all the banners and posters smothering the shop windows. So it's interesting that these shops that everyone has a good laugh about take more money per square foot than any other retailer in Europe. Why? Because we give the customer what they want,' he boasted.

On immediately finishing the talk Gerald Ratner felt relieved and pleased with himself. It went down well with his audience. He delivered the speech correctly with energy and style and got the laughs he wanted. He was totally unprepared for the pillorying in the press that followed over his remarks and the disquieting contempt for the customer that they conveyed.

The Sun, a popular tabloid paper with a circulation of 4.2 million and a readership of over 10 million, led the charge with a banner headline playing on the family name and changing it to '*Rot*ners'. The so-called 'quality press' also reported the speech with critical commentary. In the Ratner shops across Britain chaos broke out as customers, offended by Gerald Ratner's words, returned items they had purchased. Ratner shops became the butt of an epidemic of jokes.

Gerald Ratner apologized to his shareholders for his comments at the annual general meeting, but by mid-September of that year he had to explain why his company had showed a pre-tax loss of £17.5 million for the first half of 1991, compared with a £7.3 million profit for the same period in the previous year.

In his own defence Ratner said: 'My approach has been to be honest with our customers and to make jewellery affordable for the man in the street. How else could we have sold £5 billion of jewellery in seven years [the period of time he had been the head of the family business]. We couldn't have done that by tricking people.' But the damage was irreversible and eventually cost him his job.

Much later, when he was in a new position selling stores in new shopping developments to companies, Gerald Ratner had time to reflect on the scale of his mistake. He talked about it in a BBC film, a short documentary entitled *Ratner Lord of the Rings*.[19]

At the time of writing Gerald Ratner is out of the jewellery business, running his own gymnasium near Henley-in-Thames. When he was forced to resign in November 1992 from Ratners, Gerald Ratner did not get a big pay off. 'I got a year's salary', he said in an interview in 1998,[20] 'which had just been reduced from £600,000 to £375,000, which was taxed, so I didn't walk away with a large cheque.'

Cunard's QE2 Christmas cracker

Another spectacular miscalculation of customer anger, when a company failed to manage the heightened customer expectations its own advertising and success had created, took place in the Christmas season of 1994. Cunard was determined to conduct a major refit of its superliner *Queen Elizabeth II* in 24 days spanning November–December in time to make a lucrative Christmas crossing from Southampton to New York City – the first leg of a world cruise proceeding to the Caribbean from where the QE2 was to continue around the world.

The German contractor, Blohm & Voss, in Hamburg, finished the work on time avoiding serious penalty clauses of $300,000 per day. The British contractors, however, did not finish their plumbing work and remodelling on schedule. To complicate matters, Cunard managers, against advice from their parent company Trafalgar House, wanted to salvage as many of the transatlantic/Caribbean cruise fares as they could and start the world cruise on schedule. They decided to sail as scheduled on 17 December. In a damage limitation exercise, at first Cunard informed 300 passengers about their refit problem and told them *not* to turn up. But the company had to cancel a *further 190* passengers on the spot in face-to-face confrontations. The total number of disappointed passengers rose to 500, nearly half of the intended passenger list of 1,100.

From the passenger's point of view having one's voyage cancelled on the pier was inexplicable and offensive. David Steene, a solicitor from Hertford-shire, England, paid the Cunard Line £19,000 (nearly $30,000) to take his wife Diane and their three children to America for Christmas on the *Queen Elizabeth II* superliner. When the family showed up at the QE2's Southampton dock on Saturday, 17 December 1994, they were told that they were among the 190 passengers who would *not* be able to go on the transatlantic cruise.

They were offered a full refund and a free replacement cruise the following year with a £250 spending credit. But the angry solicitor Steene responded to the treatment he and his fellow passengers received by organizing a legal action group to sue Cunard. 'Cunard must have known the boat would not be ready and they should have told us last week instead of just a few hours before the ship left,' Steene argued.

Not surprisingly other passengers like Steene, who were cancelled at the QE2 terminal a few hours before they had expected to sail off to America on the luxury Christmas cruise, took it badly. Chaos broke out – tempers flared and a few fist fights started up, creating mass confusion which delayed the departure of the ship. No one could find a chart of the cabins which had been completed, so the assignment of passengers to their cabins (which normally was precise) became guesswork. The QE2 left Southampton over six hours late and in a state of serious disorder with plumbers and other workmen on board. They were using the ship's nursery as sleeping quarters.

The £30 million ($45m) refit comprised the fitting of new bathrooms in the 936 passenger cabins (materials and fittings of about 350 items per cabin) and included the refurbishment of public areas such as the shops and the Lido deck, the latter to be refitted with a purpose-built alternative buffet dining area with its own adjoining preparation kitchen.

Disgruntled passenger David Steene and members of his passenger action group took their protest to Cunard's then headquarters in Pall Mall, Central London. Cunard's unwise response was to lock their doors. For three hours Steene and his action group posed for photos and gave interviews to the press, while Cunard management and employees peeked out from windows and the locked doors. By the time they decided to let the angry passengers into the headquarters, the media damage had been done and Cunard had unwittingly added another chapter to a case study on how not to handle a public relations situation.[21]

Meanwhile on board the QE2 the disaster increased as many passengers among the chosen 600 grew increasingly disturbed at the disorder on the luxury liner and the unfinished state of their passenger cabins.

Peter Ludlow, a 48-year-old diamond-setter and one of the passengers, was on his third luxury cruise that year with Cunard. Accompanied by his fiancée, Merrilyn Wesley, he was horrified at the state of the ship. The corridor outside their cabin was littered with debris including a floor-sweeper, a life-jacket, a roll of carpet. In several other corridors in their part of the ship the ceilings were not secured and wires were dangling from open panels.

At 2.30 am Ludlow couldn't sleep. It was a Sunday morning and he and his fiancée were so worried about the safety issues they decided to report their concerns to the purser, but the deck to the purser's office was impassable. He called out the ship's safety officer and asked him to officially record his complaints. The embarrassed officer agreed with their complaints and logged them. In doing so the safety officer exposed Cunard to legal action.

Peter Ludlow and Merrilyn Wesley described their reactions to the situation, saying they felt like bit-part players in a television sitcom. After catching a few hours sleep they were awoken by drilling from workmen in the cabin above them which began at 9 am and continued unabatedly.

Ludlow said his £7,400 (over $10,000) trip to New York and on to the Caribbean 'was supposed to be a dream holiday but it had turned into a nightmare. I don't think we will be travelling with Cunard again.'

Other passengers complained about sharp and jagged edges left by unfinished work and the fear they had of tearing their expensive ballgowns and clothing. Some had to swill out their lavatories with water from ice buckets and sleep on mattresses on the floor. It was a far cry from Cunard's 'luxury trip of a lifetime' advertised in travel brochures and video tapes. One passenger compared it to living in an unfinished Spanish hotel, but with a difference – he was 700 miles west of Ireland in the Atlantic ocean.

Public areas were often no better than the rooms. The Yacht Club bar was full of welding equipment, the Lido deck was closed and an outside swimming pool was being used for rubbish like a builder's skip. The theatre was closed for the first two days of the voyage; new panels were falling off walls, and toilets and lights in some cabins did not work. Water leaks in the cabins were so common the staff developed their own code for dealing with these emergencies: 'Niagara, Niagara, Niagara!'

Peter Ludlow went on to organize passengers into an action group. They relayed their complaints to the press over satellite phones and faxes. They threatened a sit-in on the QE2 when it reached New York. Passengers who were to disembark in New York City threatened to remain on the ship, blocking the entry of the New York passengers joining the cruise to the Caribbean. Cunard responded by cancelling the 158 passengers scheduled to join the cruise in New York.

Ludlow's action group demanded that Cunard directors come aboard the ship to sort out their complaints and to offer meaningful compensation. He summed up the company's attitude as 'cavalier'.

They won their demand and John Olsen, Cunard's chairman, agreed to board the liner as it reached New York to deal with their grievances. They wanted a formal apology and a clear compensation package. They rejected Cunard's earlier offer that each passenger write separately to Cunard after the cruise requesting compensation.

Two days before Christmas the QE2 sailed in to New York and was declared unfit to sail by the US Coast Guard inspectors headed by Commander Michael Karr. The ship was declared a fire hazard and a safety risk. Britain's flagship was disgraced. The planned six-hour turnround for the ship to sail to the Caribbean was scrubbed. Cunard was ordered to put things right. Banner headlines announcing the QE2 unfit to sail in Great Britain and elsewhere and news flashes throughout the world made the international embarrassment complete.

A Coast Guard spokesman said: 'This may be a shocking day for British shipping, but it is a great day for the passengers who would have been on board. Their safety is not going to be compromised.' The inspectors filled six handwritten sheets with safety problems that had to be fixed before they would allow the QE2 to sail.

John Olsen, who had come out to the ship on a pilot boat as it approached Manhattan, spoke to the passengers and promised them compensation. After the great ship docked at Pier 9 on New York's West Side, company chairman Olsen and other Cunard managers conducted tours for the press. A Japanese TV crew boarded the ship and was preoccupied with plumbing failures in the passenger cabins.

Olsen showed the reporters parts of the refurbished ship and they admitted in their reports that much of the refitting did look splendid. 'The bars and restaurants gleamed with their new carpeting and neo-Deco finishings,' wrote David Usborne in *The Independent* (24 December 1994). But the work was still unfinished. There were missing panelling, wires dangling from the ceiling and stories of erupting toilets. The condition of parts of the ship still contradicted the glossy brochure written and published to boast of a perfect refit long before the disastrous chain of events touched off by the late British plumbers and their mates. Teams of British workers flew home for Christmas, leaving their American counterparts to finish the job. The American workers cleared up the fire hazards and safety violations first and continued the finishing work on the ship as it sailed to the Florida coast and on to the Caribbean.

Cunard then faced multi-million pound class action suits by at least 50 passengers – an American system in which plaintiffs can team up. Trafalgar House offered to pay £7.5 million ($11.5 million) in compensation to passengers whose transatlantic Christmas voyage was wrecked by the refitting work. That estimate was added to the original refit bill of £30 million ($45 million) which did not include the massive overruns en route to New York City and the safety work in the harbour.

The QE2 was launched on the Clyde in 1967 – the same year as Concorde made its test flight. But while the supersonic aircraft only scrapes a living because the immense capital cost of the project was paid for by British and French taxpayers, the QE2 makes a fine profit in its own right. That profit depends on repeat passengers which are its lifeblood. According to Captain Robin Woodall, a legendary QE2 captain (who is now retired), one-third of all passengers are repeats.

The consequences of the Christmas saga were far reaching. Within six months of the disaster, Cunard chairman, John Olsen, who took responsibility for the Christmas voyage, had resigned from his £506,000 a year position. Cunard losses for 1995 were set at £16.4 million, shares fell to an all-time low of just 17p and the entire management team was changed. Cunard itself, with its flagship the QE2, was sold in March 1996 along with Trafalgar House to the Norwegian group Kvaerner.

Relationship marketing puts customers centre stage

The origins of the idea of relationship marketing can be traced back to the writings of American marketing experts. Theodore Levitt of the Harvard Business School in a seminal article in the *Harvard Business Review* argued that:

> Economic conditions, business strategies, customer wishes, competitive conditions, and much more can determine what sensibly defines the product. One thing is certain. There is no such thing as a commodity or, at least from a competitive point of view, there need not be.[22]

The traditional marketing model based on the 'Four Ps' (product, price, place and promotion) was reappraised in the early 1980s and found wanting, except where the exchange was a brief, single transaction in a mass consumer market. It seemed inadequate in industrial or service contexts where relationships with customers were long term and of critical important. If fell short for global marketing where trade barriers and politics could deny entry. Studies undertaken in Northern Europe concentrated on the customer's perspective of marketing. Researchers Hakan Hakansson in the industrial area and Evert Gummesson and others of the so-called Nordic School in the service sector proposed a new marketing paradigm which they called 'interactive marketing' or 'interactive relationships'. About the same time a number of American writers including Barbara B. Jackson, Lawrence Crosby and Nancy Stephens were also looking at the role of relationships in the industrial marketing and services sectors. They created the label 'relationship marketing'.[23]

V.A. Zeithaml, A. Parsuraman and L.L. Berry made their contribution to the concept of relationship marketing from their extensive research on delivering quality service in the United States. They found that service quality is deeply subjective, but that, while the precise determinants of quality were undefined, there is a universal acceptance that quality is very important. In fact, perceived quality is largely determined by the gap between customers' expectations of service and perceptions of the actual experience. The three consultants developed an instrument called 'SERVQUAL' to measure the ten determinants which impacted on a customer's perception of services. These ten determinants were later distilled to five core dimensions:

- *Tangibles* – physical facilities, equipment, and appearance of personnel.
- *Reliability* – ability to perform the promised service dependably and accurately.
- *Responsiveness* – willingness to help customers and provide prompt service.
- *Assurance* – knowledge and courtesy of employees and their ability to inspire trust and confidence.
- *Empathy* – caring, individualized attention the firm provides its customers.

Relationship marketing, then, involves managing an entire network of relationships between customer and supplier and other supporting and interlocking relationships both inside and outside the organization. It involves the creation and strengthening of trust. The Nordic School emphasizes the pivotal role of promises in a relationship and mutual assurances of commitment. Theodore Levitt, likewise, in stressing the need for promise-keeping and commitment likens sustaining quality long-term relationships to maintaining the quality of a marriage. When promises are not kept between businesses and their customers, trust suffers and the entire quality of the relationship deteriorates, eventually ending it and eliminating future prospects. In summary, then, the most important issue in marketing today is to establish, maintain and enhance long-term customer relationships at a profit, so that the objectives of all the parties involved are met.

Jonathan R. Copulsky and Michael J. Wolf, two US-based marketing consultants, describe the process in a product-led manner, saying:

> Relationship marketing combines elements of general advertising, sales promotion, public relations and direct marketing to create more effective and more efficient ways of reaching customers. It centres on developing a continuous relationship with customers across a family of related products.[24]

Customer retention and loyalty is core to the concept. Regis McKenna, an international marketing consultant, argues that 'We must build lasting relationships with our customers so that they do not move from product to product and supplier to supplier as the technology and options present themselves.'[25] Study after study demonstrates that by increasing service quality and consequently customer satisfaction a higher percentage of customers are retained.

Sandra Vandermerwe's celebrated book *From Tin Soldiers to Russian Dolls: Creating Added Value through Services*[26] pulls together the author's several years of research and takes as its starting point the premise that every high-value enterprise is in the business of providing services. By interviewing hundreds of executives and academic colleagues globally – 130 interviews done specifically for the book in 35 companies in Europe, North America and Japan – the author shows how managers are thinking and behaving to actualize contemporary service concepts. She used the metaphor of tin soldiers into Russian dolls.

The tin soldiers stood for the rigid one-dimensional models and frameworks of the past. These were ideal for producing tin soldiers. But what is needed today are Russian dolls. Surprisingly the Russian doll – the matrushka – arrived in Russia from Japan at the end of the nineteenth century. A woodcarver in the town of Zagorsky near Moscow carved the doll after a Japanese character, Daruma, who had lost the use of his legs due to his constant practice of meditation. The woodcarver made the dolls in a series, each one smaller than the previous one to fit smoothly inside it. The dolls, he explained, symbolized a continuing regeneration.

Sandra Vandermerwe asked:

> But how, writers in both manufacturing and services had been asking, were managers going to eradicate the seeming gap between producers and consumers? . . . A new orthodoxy began to surface late in the 1980's which had a different kind of nuance, based on relationships more 'connective'. Connective because it meant doing things not only *for*, but also *with* customers. Partnering between a firm and its customers . . . entered the general management vocabulary. What it intended to convey was an end to the distancing between corporations and their customers. It implied collaboration.[27]

General Motors' Saturn division provided a powerful illustration of this type of collaboration between company and customer in June 1994. At the Saturn car plant in Spring Hill, Tennessee, the company played host to nearly 30,000 Saturn owners and family members with a 'homecoming hoedown' that offered free food and drink, country music and dancing, tents and tours of the car plant. The camaraderie of Saturn owners was designed to eliminate any cognitive dissonance about the first purchase of a Saturn and set the customer up for the next purchase. According to Saturn research 60 per cent of current customers intend to buy another Saturn.

'How has Saturn created this almost cult-like devotion to a sturdy, well-designed, but hardly spectacular subcompact?' Tom Peters asked and then answered:

By embracing the customer as a friend – an *intelligent* friend – from the moment the customer first steps into the showroom. With salaried sales people, low-pressure tactics, superb listening skills, no-hassle pricing . . . free car-care clinics, and 'family' barbecues, Saturn dealers have created a welcoming atmosphere that has become the envy of the industry.[28]

It also put Saturn into profitability for the first time in 1993 with bright prospects for the car's future.

Perhaps one of the most spectacular case studies of relationship marketing was BT's Global Challenge, a 30,000-mile yacht race round the world the 'wrong way'. On 29 September 1996, 14 identical yachts with 14 randomly chosen teams left Southampton to participate in the world's toughest yacht race, sailing against prevailing winds and currents.

The crew volunteers had extensive training by Sir Chay Blyth's Challenge Business, but most had little experience. They faced an environment of extreme danger – violent weather, equipment failure, complex tactical decisions, fatigue and demanding daily workloads.[29]

For BT, the sponsors, the race provided a massive exercise in relationship marketing which they mounted during all the preliminary organizing for the race and at each port of call from Southampton to Rio de Janeiro, Wellington, New Zealand, Sydney, Australia, Cape Town, South Africa, Boston, Massachusetts back to Southampton. As a global player in the telecommunications industry BT used the world-wide race as an unparalleled opportunity to meet business leaders, politicians and their customers and potential customers at each port of call, holding press conferences and parties for the crew and the public.

Customer requirements

What does the customer require? The customer will have five questions, consciously or unconsciously. These are the five dimensions of quality. The traditional view of quality is simply 'conformance to specification'. However, this is only part of total quality. Quality involves all of the five dimensions for the customer to be satisfied. The measurement of quality will reflect each of these elements – specification, conformance, reliability, cost (value) and delivery.

The five questions are as follows:

1 What can I expect when I buy your product? – the *specification* for the product or service. For example, most vacuum cleaners for the car simply are not designed to do the heavy work of vacuum cleaning the debris found in cars. Run as they are by small batteries they have a specification more suited to sucking up crumbs from a toaster than the bits of gravel, dirt and foreign matter that invade cars.

2 Is it what I expected? – the *conformance* to the specification. For example, a horse trailer should conform to the technical specification in the literature and manuals. A car that claims economic fuel consumption driven at 55 mph should deliver on its promise. A hotel that advertises 'old world' luxury and service should provide the proper level of opulence and excellent service.

3 Does it continue to do what I expected? – the *reliability* (or conformance through time). For example, products should not fall apart – a person does not purchase a radio for a few weeks' use. It should last for years. Laws governing guarantees support commonsense demands for reliability. The Labour Party's Citizen's Charter includes consumer protection provisions about guarantees.

4 How much do I have to pay? – the *value* for money aspect. For example, people who visit Disney World in Orlando, Florida, do not complain about the price of admission because the spectacle is splendid, the customer care is dazzling and the day itself, 8.30 am to midnight, could hardly be longer.

5 When can I have it? – *delivery* (quickly and on time). For example, once the delivery data is agreed, it should be adhered to. Some customers often want products as soon as possible. Others require them just-in-time. Speed of delivery is usually a factor. If one's competitor can make an earlier delivery date he or she has an advantage. This is not always the case – as when a person joins an eight or nine year queue by ordering a Morgan car. Even here by exporting only 200 Morgans per year and keeping the same number for domestic sale, the company denies itself many sales opportunities. But normally there should be a definite delivery day which is met promptly.

What, then, is quality itself? How does one define it? Quality is:

fully satisfying agreed customer requirements at the lowest internal cost.

Each of these words in the definition are important and meaningful.

People who splash out £40 to £100 for an evening meal for two expect the restaurant to be *fully satisfying*. The setting and service must be correct. The food has to be excellent and properly prepared. Any aspect of the dinner that goes wrong – cold soup, or an over-cooked roast beef, or the wrong wine, or a surly waiter, or a noisy room, or loud or inappropriate music – can diminish the satisfaction and even spoil the evening.

Ken Cusack, a global manager at ICL, whose firm has had a spurt of phenomenal growth in the computer maintenance business, refuses to let anyone in his firm talk about 'satisfying' the customer: 'We aim to positively *delight* the customer not just satisfy him.' In doing so he is in line with Deming's latest thinking: 'It will not suffice to have customers that are merely satisfied,' Deming wrote. 'An unhappy customer will switch. Unfortunately a satisfied customer may also switch, on the theory that he could not lose much, and might gain. Profit in business comes from repeat customers, customers that boast about your products and service, and that bring friends with them.'[30] Often experts, including Deming, talk about satisfying customers' needs now and in the future. The idea is to stay ahead of the customer, to anticipate his or her needs in the next few years so that when he or she articulates the need you have already planned for it and are ready (ahead of the competition) to meet it.

Ken Cusack tells the story of his arriving at an Oxford hotel to find a fresh bowl of ice in the room to his great delight. He had arrived at the hotel at 8.00 pm and was curious as to how the bowl of ice was there as the hotel did not know his arrival time. On asking he was told that the bowl was placed in the room at 3.00 pm and changed every 30 minutes until he arrived.

In what may be an aprocryphal story, the Hilton Hotel chain was celebrating a major anniversary. The celebration was a newsworthy event and well covered by the media. Conrad Hilton, the founder, was asked to say a few words and he, speaking to a blaze of television cameras, said that he would just like to remind the guests of Hilton Hotels that when they use the shower they should make sure the shower curtain is inside the bath tub. Later when some brave senior members of his staff said to him that he should have used the media opportunity to say something more meaningful to the public, he defended himself saying that the hotel business is all about attending to detail. Conrad Hilton did put a lot of emphasis on attending to detail in meeting customer requirements as his book *Be My Guest* shows. He would look at daily reports from all the hotels including international properties.

Requirements should be *agreed*. The waiter's ready question 'how do you like your steak?' is a simple example of agreeing a customer requirement. It is a serious question for most people not a throwaway line. A person who orders a rare steak or medium rare steak is not very pleased to have a well-cooked or burnt steak and vice versa. A steak not properly prepared should be returned to the chef.

The emphasis for *customer requirements* must be on what the customer requires not on what the company wants to foist on the customer. As seen above, customer requirements include specification, conformance, reliability, value for money and on-time delivery. The insurance industry is awakening (lately) to the concept of meeting genuine customer requirement – as opposed to inventing new products almost in isolation from the customer and pushing them on to the market.

Finally, concerning *at the lowest internal cost*, part of a quality delivery process must be concerned with cost control. Having money to throw at a product to improve its quality is a rare phenomenon and is becoming rarer.

IBM's 'quality focus on the business process' programme aims at improving all processes with a natural cost-cutting element.

The internal customer

To meet the customers' requirements means to listen to the customer and to respond to what he or she wants and to what is agreed. But customers are not only external to the company – the people outside who are the end users of a firm's products and services. There is also the *internal customer*, the person within the company who receives the work of another and then adds his or her contribution to the product or service before passing it on to someone else. In manufacturing the internal customer is the next person down the line who builds the product. For example, at Bally Shoes in Norwich a pair of shoes will pass through a hundred pairs of hands from start to finished product – the chain of internal customers stretches round the factory. In software engineering as the 'man years' grow the computer program passes from one internal customer to another until a 'bug free' program is offered to the external customer. In a restaurant, the chef has the waiters and waitresses as internal customers and the chef must meet their requirements if they are all to please the guests.

If the internal customers' requirements are agreed and met, a chain of quality is made that reaches out to the external customer. To get people to identify the internal customers for the main outputs of the work group is to make a start at a total quality process. To touch off a dialogue between the internal 'supplier' and the internal customer that leads them to agree customer requirements is the beginning of creating a total quality culture. 'You'll never achieve quality externally until you have quality internally,' Ken Cusack tells his managers. 'It's the way you trust each other internally which will eventually lead to how the engineer, when he carries that tool bag on site, treats the customer.'

Moments of truth

Scandinavian Airlines System (SAS) provides a clear illustration of focusing on the customer. In 1981 Jan Carlzon became president of SAS and began to analyse why his company was about to lose $20 million. By looking at customer requirements and meeting them head on Carlzon turned the loss-making threat into a $54 million profit in one year. His unique frame of analysis was called 'the moments of truth'.

A simple analysis of his airline told him that the asset base was strong with many jets, hotels, restaurants and travel agencies. The management team was experienced and worked well together, but they were still losing money. He went back to basics to determine a customer focus. An airline, after all, simply takes a passenger from point A to point B – an airline seat is a commodity product. He multiplied the number of passengers – 10 million per year – times five 'moments of truth' each and arrived at 50 million 'moments of truth'. The task of management was to look after 50 million 'moments of truth' – face-to-face encounters between the customers and front-line supervision in which the customer decided whether he or she was being treated well or badly.

As Carlzon puts it:

> Last year, each of our 10 million customers came in contact with approximately five SAS employees and this contact lasted an average of 15 seconds each time. Thus, SAS is 'created' in the minds of our customers 50 million times a year, 15 seconds at a time. These 50 million 'moments of truth' are the moments that ultimately determine whether SAS will succeed or fail as a company. They are moments when we must prove to our customers that SAS is their best alternative.[31]

In the process of dealing with moments of truth Carlzon found that he had to *empower* front-line people and front-line supervision. Why should the decision to issue luncheon vouchers to delayed passengers be made five levels up the managerial hierarchy instead of on the spot by people dealing with the frustrated passengers?

Carlzon was not the only manager to learn the benefits of empowering people. In an extensive study of peak performers in management Charles Garfield found that the idea of empowerment was essential to their notion of team building:

> . . . peak performers discover time and again that releasing the power in others, whether in co-workers or customers, benefits them in the long run. In developing, rewarding, and recognizing those around them, they are simply allowing the human assets with which they work to appreciate in value. The more they empower, the more they can achieve, and the more successful the whole enterprise becomes.[32]

One of the messages of *The Managed Heart*[33] is that for a company to get staff to treat customers well, the company must treat the staff well. For Christmas 1982 Carlzon sent every SAS employee a personal letter and a gold watch with its second hand in the shape of a tiny aeroplane, a second 'little red book' on the customer-driven strategy and an invitation to a party celebrating their success. Eighteen months after launching the new SAS, the employees were given new uniforms. As the employees spent all their time at work in uniforms, the best quality was provided and were designed by Calvin Klein.

At the same time a new corporate image was created by Landor Associates which encompassed aircraft livery and interiors, reservation offices, tickets – everything was given a new look. The presentation of the new image took place in Copenhagen, Oslo and Stockholm with successful press conferences. *The Financial Times* said:

> In place of the technical production orientated attitude which used to underpin almost all company actions has come almost evangelistic dedication to putting customer service above all else. It is this totally marketing geared approach which the stylishness of the new SAS livery and logo in gleaming white with diagonal red, yellow and blue strip is intended somehow to reflect.[34]

The results were stunning. In 1982 SAS showed a profit of $80 million, while the airlines business as a whole suffered $2 billion losses. Over the following years SAS continued to increase profit and market share. In 1983 Fortune named SAS the best airline for business travellers in the world and the following year SAS was voted *Air Transport World*'s 'Airline of the year'.

Customer care at Ascot

Fourteen months after installing a customer care programme, Ascot racecourse began enjoying the dividends. Crowd figures for 1995 showed an increase of more than 15 per cent compared to an average national rise of less than one per cent for Britain's 59 racecourses.

Ascot's racecourse director, Douglas Erskine-Crum, who began running Ascot in October 1994, attributed the success to customer care.

> We have put considerable emphasis in the last 12 months on developing customer relations, improving facilities and making the racecourse accessible and friendly. We have also worked hard to maintain a programme of the highest quality across our 24 race-days.

He indicated that new plans for continuous improvement in the future were designed to provide Ascot's racegoers with the

> best possible entertainment, enjoyment, comfort and value for money. Racing has to compete for its market with a growing number of other sports and rival entertainments, so strong marketing and promotion, as well as improved customer-care, have to be a key part of any strategy.[35]

Notes

1 David Cracknell, 'Labour Plans Hi-Tech Shake-Up of Citizen's Charter', *Daily Telegraph*, 30 July 1996.
2 Glenda Cooper, 'All the Perks of a Coffee Renaissance', *The Independent*, 1 April 1998, p. 3.
3 Extracts from Citizen's Charter, Cmd. 1599, July 1991.
4 Statement to the House of Commons, Hansard, 22 July 1991.
5 *The Independent*, 23 July 1991.

6 'Citizen's Charter, an "irrelevance"', *The Financial Times*, 17 October 1994.

7 Louise Jury, '£4m Fine for Rail Firms that Run Late', *The Independent*, 12 May 1998.

8 *Consumer Reports*, July 1991.

9 Robin Young, 'One in Three "Unhappy" with Mobile Telephones', *The Times*, 8 February 1996.

10 *Time Magazine*, 2 February 1987.

11 James Quinn and Christopher Gagnon, 'Will Services Follow Manufacturing into Decline?', *Harvard Business Review*, Nov.–Dec. 1986.

12 *Time Magazine*, op. cit.

13 Of all the 'quality circles' started in the United States in 1982, 75 per cent had been discontinued by 1986, according to Richard Tanner-Pascale, *Managing on the Edge* (Harmondsworth: Penguin, 1990). In the United Kingdom, according to David Hutchins (the British consultant largely responsible for introducing the concept into the United Kingdom), 90 per cent of all quality circle programmes have failed. See D. Hutchins, *In Pursuit of Quality* (London: Pitman, 1990), p. iv. *See also*: Edward E. Lawler III and Susan A. Mohrman, 'Quality Circles – After the Fad', *Harvard Business Review*, Jan.–Feb. 1985; Edward E. Lawler III and Susan A. Mohrman, 'Quality Circles – After the Honeymoon', *Organizational Dynamics*, Spring 1987.

14 Arie de Geus, 'The Living Company, growth, learning and longevity in business' (London: Nicholas Brearley, 1997), p. 7.

15 James C. Collins and Jerry I. Parras, *Built to Last: Successful Habits of Visionary Companies* (London: Century Press, Random House, 1995), p. 1.

16 Robert J. Cave, 'Total Quality Customer Care Elective: Pret à Manger', unpublished Cranfield School of Management MBA student paper, July 1996.

17 *Entrepreneurs: The New Generation*, talk delivered to the Royal Society for the Encouragement of the Arts, Manufacturing and Commerce (RSA), 27 November 1996 (privately printed).

18 Julian Richer, *The Richer Way* (London: Emap Business Communications, 1996), p. 21.

19 *Ratner Lord of the Rings*, BBC Education, Executive Producer Jonathan Drori, Producer Nick Mirsky.

20 John Walsh, 'Lord of the Ring Returneth', *Independent Saturday Magazine*, 15 February 1998, pp. 17–18.

21 *See* BBC for Business, *Cruise Wars: Carry on QE2*, Business Case.

22 Theodore Levitt, 'Marketing Success Through the Differentiation of Anything', *Harvard Business Review*, Jan.–Feb. 1980.

23 *See* B.B. Jackson, 'Build Customer Relationships that Last', *Harvard Business Review*, Nov.–Dec. 1985, pp. 120–8; Lawrence Crosby and Nancy Stephens, 'Effects of Relationship Marketing on Satisfaction, Retention and Prices in the Life Insurance Industry', *Journal of Marketing Research*, vol. XXIV, November 1987, pp. 404–11.

24 Jonathan R. Copulsky and Michael J. Wolf, 'Relationship Marketing: Positioning for the Future', *Journal of Business strategy*, July/August 1990, pp. 16–20.

25 Regis McKenna, *Relationship Marketing* (London: Century Business, 1992), p. vii.

26 Sandra Vandermerwe, *From Tin Soldiers to Russian Dolls: Creating Added Value through Services* (Oxford: Butterworth-Heinemann, 1993).

27 Ibid., p. 53.

28 Tom Peters, *The Pursuit of WOW! Every Person's Guide to Topsy-Turvy Times* (London: Macmillan, 1995), p. 189.

29 H. Walters, P. Mackie, R. Mackie and A. Bacon, *Global Challenge Leadership Lessons from 'The World's Toughest Yacht Race'* (Sussex: The Book Guild, 1997).

30 W. Edwards Deming, *Out of the Crises* (Cambridge: Cambridge University Press, 1986).

31 Jan Carlzon, *Moments of Truth* (Cambridge, Mass.: Ballinger, 1987), p. 3.

32 Charles Garfield, *Peak Performers: The New Heroes in Business* (London: Hutchinson Business, 1986), p. 182.

33 A.R. Hochschild, *The Managed Heart* (Berkeley, Calif.: California University Press, 1983).

34 *The Financial Times*, details unknown.

35 Richard Evans, 'Ascot Rewarded with Increased Crowds', *The Times*, 8 February 1996.

Chapter 2

....

Core concepts of total quality management

In Tom Stoppard's play, *The Real Thing*, Henry, a professional playwright, picks up a script written by Brodie, an amateur. He says:

> Now, what we've got here is a lump of wood of roughly the same shape trying to be a cricket bat, and if you hit a ball with it, the ball will travel about ten feet and you will drop the bat and dance about shouting 'ouch!' with your hands stuck into your armpits. [Indicating the cricket bat.] This isn't better because someone says it's better, or because there's a conspiracy by the MCC to keep cudgels out of Lord's. It's better because it's better.[1]

Sir John Harvey-Jones wrote in the *Trouble Shooter*:

> There is a 1950s glamour about the Morgan car. The appeal is dripping with nostalgia. It conjures up images of wholesome Grace Kelly lookalikes with Hermes' scarves, and clean-shaven young men in tweed sports jackets off for a spin in the country.
>
> Marketing people use nostalgia quite cynically to sell everything from jam to soap to luggage. The product may be the same as a supermarket brand sold at half the price, but with the help of some pretty packaging we are quite prepared to be conned into believing that we are keeping alive some ancient craft . . .
>
> The Morgan car is not the product of the fertile mind of some marketing man – it is the real thing.[2]

Quality for profit

There is a great deal of profit to be made by quality improvements in products and services, business processes and people. Internal analysts at IBM, for example, put the cost of non-conformance or failure to meet quality standards in its products and services at a minimum 11 per cent[3] of revenue or $5.6 billion in 1986.[4] (They suggested that companies of similar size had comparable cost.) To this figure can be added the costs of having poor business processes. Launched in May 1985, IBM's 'Quality Focus on the Business Process' was targeted to save a conservative $2 billion, world-wide, in improving processes alone. The two estimates taken together, understated as they are, represented $7.6 billion worth of potential savings.

Saving on the cost of people is still another potential area for adding to the profit margins. Labour turnover in the UK restaurant industry runs at about 60 per cent each year. In one company alone – a division of one of the largest UK restaurant companies – the labour turnover for hourly-paid staff was 295 per cent per annum. The amount of money spent in recruiting software engineers in high-tech companies runs into hundreds of thousands of pounds. The scope for savings here is staggering. The conclusion that quality improvement in products and services, business processes and people is profitable is inescapable. 'Expressed in business terms, quality – or the lack of it – is the single greatest factor in achieving market success for any company,' said Peter W. Moir, a former Senior Writers Editor, Advertising and Publications, IBM, 'and must therefore be a matter of prime importance for executive management.'[5]

Most major companies have launched full-scale quality programmes. A few of them are the following:

- Leadership Through Quality (Xerox);
- Quality the ICL Way (ICL);
- Quality Service Programme (NatWest);
- Total Quality Culture (Texas Instruments);
- Total Quality Excellence (Ford);
- Quality Focus on the Business Process (IBM);
- Quality Enhancement Strategy (National Semiconductors).

In these companies and thousands of others additional profit is achieved through quality improvement. Rather than rely exclusively on the route of increasing sales to gain profit, which of course increases operating costs, quality improvement becomes a short cut to improved profits (*see* Figure 2.1). The actual quality improvement also increases sales by generating customer demand which has its own momentum in the market (*see* Figure 2.2).

Dell Computers has been singled out as the most profitable investment of the decade. By May of 1998, its share value had risen by 29,600 per cent. *Fortune Magazine* ranked Dell no. 7 among the Fortune 500 in return on shareholder equity – ahead of Coca-Cola, Intel and Microsoft. It is the only Fortune 500 company that has increased its sales and earnings by more than 40 per cent a year in 1995–8. The magazine called Dell 'a runaway money train'.[6] Its formula for success is based on going directly to customers to meet their needs, eliminating the middleman and selling over the Internet.

A small case study from First Union's capital markets group reveals how Dell meets customer requirements in the fiercely competitive computer business

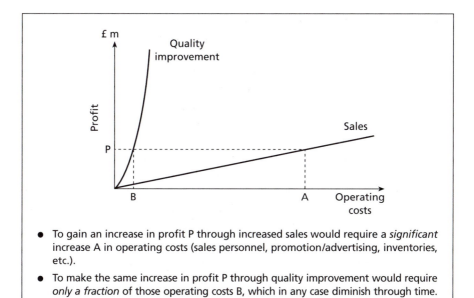

Fig. 2.1 Quality pays for itself in cost reduction

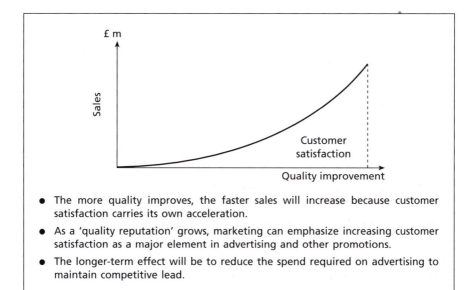

Fig. 2.2 Quality pays for itself in sales growth

where price-cutting is a daily occurrence and where the product a company makes – essentially boxes similar to those of its competitors – is out of date within months.

Peter Mojica, the IT Manager of First Union's capital markets group in Charlotte, North Carolina, was a customer with very demanding requirements. His part of the business made 20 per cent of the group's profits and his traders had to be high performers with the best equipment for their jobs. As Peter Mojica put it, 'For us, having the right technology is do or die. We needed to have 50 PCs available at any given time for delivery within 24 hours. But our resellers were never able to provide us with that.'[7]

When he arrived to take charge two years ago Mojica's unit depended on 2,500 PCs and 75 Windows NT servers together with a mix of different generations of Compaq and DEC computers. The mix caused him stocking problems, difficulties with the installation of software and networking challenges. The installation of new machines was a big event as Nojica describes it:

> UPS would deliver the PC and a purchasing guy would open the box, pull out the machine, tag it, power it up, and program its electronic address. Then he would put the PC back in the box and store it in a holding station. Later another guy would take the PC out of the box again, load in our software, and stick it back in the box. Then it would go to someone's desk to be installed. If we were doing this in an office outside of Charlotte, we'd have to send a guy there for two days. Can you believe how much money we were throwing out the window?

Mojica called Dell. 'They were priced below the other guys, and Dell could tag and address the machines and load our software in its factory,' he says. 'That alone saves us $500,000 a year.' Mojica has now cleaned out the Compaqs and DECs and replaced them with Dell PCs. Next comes a rollout of Dell machines in the Asian offices that First Union picked up in its recent acquisition of CoreStates. Like the US machines, the Asian PCs will come fully loaded according to Mojica's specs, only these machines will be made in Dell's plant in Malaysia.

Dell's business is built on such stories. In 1997 Dell had $12.3 billion in sales and $233 million of inventory. Gateway 2000, who also sell directly, by comparison had about half the sales ($6.3 billion) and a similar inventory ($249 million). Dell is working to exploit even more just-in-time (JIT) systems to lower inventory costs. In 1997, 31 per cent ($3.8 billion) of Dell's sales came from the international market. Dell's sales are growing by 50 per cent annually in Europe.

Michael Dell, the CEO of Dell Computers, explains that his success and prodigious growth is the sum of many little things done right. He segments the business into discrete parts to focus his plans of action for continuous improvement in his working.

Right first time

The failed mission of Apollo 13 – NASA's fifth journey to the moon in April 1970 – was caused by a series of defects that converged to create a cataclysmic event. Fifty-five hours into the flight a mysterious explosion rocked the spaceship causing its oxygen (and power) to drain away.

> It was in late spring that the Cortright Commission released its findings, contritely acknowledging that none of these technical problems should have happened in the first place, but implying that the problems were *merely* technical – that NASA had at least avoided the spectre of three dead astronauts perpetually orbiting the Earth in an equally dead spacecraft . . . By that time, the men whose lives had been most directly affected by the fused thermostat and the low-pegged thermometer and the blasted tank and the steaming sublimator were out of the country altogether, busy with the five-nation tour the Agency had planned for them as one of the final chores associated with their mission.[8]

At the heart of TQM is the conviction that it is possible to achieve defect-free work most of the time. This assertion is phrased in various ways as right first time, working smarter or zero defects. The idea is to strive for perfection in the work, the way an archer aims for the bull's eye on a target, or the single-minded way Torville and Dean strove for ice skating supremacy in the international competitions that made them world champions. The row of 5.9 or 6 point scores from the judges became the norm for the two dazzling ice skaters. One may not always achieve the target, but the 'mindset' to strive for perfect work is important. 'It's better [in this sense], to aim at perfection and miss than it is to aim at imperfection and hit it,' said Thomas J. Watson, the founder of IBM (*see* Figure 2.3).

Right first time or zero defects is the result of an emphasis on prevention, the diligent use of measurement and process controls and the data-driven elimination of waste and error. It serves as a goal for continuous improvement. Prevention is the aim of all quality assurance. Through planned and systematic action such as documentation of work processes or cost of quality audits, quality assurance prevents quality problems.

Quality management is all about prevention. As Philip B. Crosby said:

> The purpose of it [quality management] is to set up a system and a management discipline that prevents defects from happening in the company's performance cycle. To accomplish this you have to act now on situations which may cause problems some time from now. Act now for reward later.[9]

The idea of prevention is a difficult one to find practical support for. Yet it is pivotal to a TQM programme. Why should anyone spend time sorting out complicated quality problems when they could have been prevented in the first place? Yet while most people subscribe to the desirability of prevention, it remains

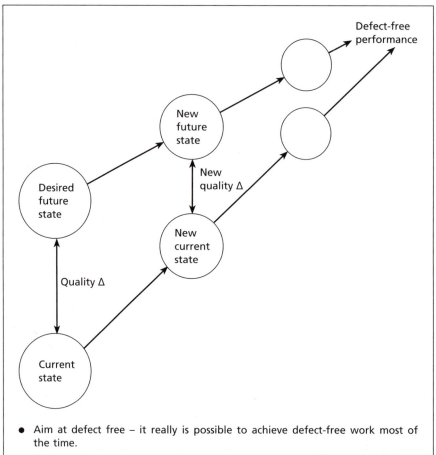

- Aim at defect free – it really is possible to achieve defect-free work most of the time.
- A 'prevention' culture must be created – most poor quality can be avoided through good design, structured processes and trained people.
- Total business quality approach is essential – all business functions must be involved in quality improvement.
- Quality is free – it pays for itself.

Fig. 2.3 Reaching for the desired state

for most illusionary, impractical or simply unattainable. That to err is human becomes a universal 'let-out clause' for poor performance. Right first time or zero defects are simply performance standards that fly in the face of conventional work practices that seem to have an anticipation of failure built into them.

For many managers and employees, then, the TQM preoccupation with prevention involves a 360 degree shift from their normal attitude to work performance. It means breaking from the dual standard that they often set up – one standard for their own personal lives where they expect quality service and good products up to standard and one for their work life where they expect safety nets to catch mistakes and put right shoddy work.

Acceptable quality levels

Out of the dual performance standard arises a willingness to put up with acceptable quality levels (AQLs) at work. The concept is best illustrated by a real case. An IBM firm in Windsor, Ontario, ordered a shipment of components from a Japanese firm, specifying the AQL as three defective components for every 10,000 parts. In a covering letter from the Japanese supplier to the IBM firm (which was reprinted in the *Toronto Sun*) that accompanied the order the Japanese company explained how difficult it was to produce the defective parts and said: 'We Japanese have hard time understanding North American business practices. But the 3 defective parts per 10,000 have been included and are wrapped separately. Hope this pleases.'

Acceptable quality levels which have arisen in industry since the end of the Second World War offer a diametrically opposed mind-set to total quality. Instead of getting it right first time, focusing on zero defects, the company encourages defects by setting AQLs (*see* Figure 2.4). In reality as quality improves, defects are reduced and costs decline (*see* Figure 2.5).

If one sets an acceptable quality level of 99 per cent the results are: at least 200,000 wrong drug prescriptions each year; more than 30,000 newborn babies accidentally dropped by doctors/nurses each year; unsafe drinking water almost four days each year; no electricity, water, heat for about 15 minutes each day; no telephone service or television transmission for nearly 15 minutes each day; newspapers not delivered four times each year; at least one misspelled word on every page of a book. The US government spent approximately $785 billion on goods and services in 1984. A 99 per cent AQL would have meant that 1 per cent of those goods and services were waste or scrap – a staggering $7.8 billion worth.

Edward J. Kane, director of quality for IBM, gave an example of a quality focus on the business process:

> The billing process consists of 14 major crossfunctional activities which are logically related but physically dispersed among 255 marketing branches and 25 regional offices, a similar number of field service locations, and several headquarters operations and manufacturing sites. The work is crossfunctional and nonsequential within any function. It is tied together by a complex information system.
>
> Overall, 96% of the invoices are accurate, but because of the high cost of adjusting those that are incorrect, 54% of the total resource was devoted to cost of quality. Some of that cost is for prevention and appraisal (98.5% of the invoices delivered to the customer are correct), but most of all the errors can be attributed to failure of some kind. This is testimony to the need to prevent errors rather than to fix them after the fact.[10]

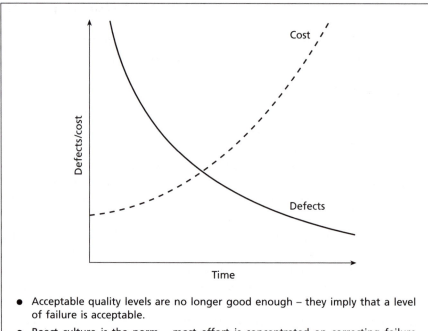

- Acceptable quality levels are no longer good enough – they imply that a level of failure is acceptable.
- React culture is the norm – most effort is concentrated on correcting failure ('putting out the fires').
- Achieving quality is expensive – defects are reduced over time only by increasing cost through extensive inspection, checking and progress chasing.

Fig. 2.4 'Traditional' quality

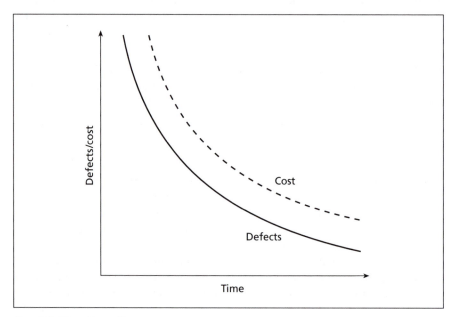

Fig. 2.5 'Total' quality

Of course the cost of not putting prevention in place can be staggeringly great. In the autumn of 1996 new allegations were made that the European Community tried to cover up the danger to public health posed by mad cow disease up to six years earlier according to *The Financial Times*:[11]

> Leaked letters reveal that the top civil servant responsible for farm policy in Brussels sought to limit discussions about BSE, bovine spongiform encephalopathy or mad cow disease, in committees charged with managing public health and animal welfare.

The letters, written in 1993 and published in the French newspaper *Libération* three years later gave fresh impetus to a European Parliament inquiry into earlier charges of a Brussels cover-up.

A leaked internal Commission memorandum claimed that the European Union's standing veterinary committee concluded in 1990 that it was 'necessary to minimise the BSE affair by using disinformation'.

The medical world has known the importance of prevention for decades and yet it still must remind itself and others of pre-emptive measures. Take TB, for example. In 1995 a record number of people – 3 million – were killed worldwide from tuberculosis, a disease which most Westerners feel had been vanquished. However, unless governments and the pharmaceutical industry increase their spending on prevention and research, the World Health Organization warns that TB will kill over 30 million more people in the coming decade.

In the business world prevention often remains a hard idea to sell despite its centrality to total quality management. There is often not much kudos in designing systems for prevention or expensive fail-safe mechanisms which do not immediately reflect on bottom-line profitability.

The need for preventative actions is no more urgently felt than in the airline industry. A growing number of serious incidents have led to efforts to improve ramp safety procedures.

The Civil Aviation Publication (CAP) No. 642 *Airside Safety Management* has been produced as a stage-one process towards legislation in the area. While this initiative attempts to improve safety on the ground, dangers in the air continue to escalate. Nowhere is the danger more palpable than over African skies. The International Federation of Airline Pilots' Associations (IFALPA), representing over a hundred thousand pilots in ninety countries, broke with tradition in 1996 to issue a public warning about air safety over the African–Indian Ocean region (*see* Figure 2.6).

The Federation claims that at least 75 per cent of the region's air traffic systems are unable to handle safely the new rises in air traffic volume. Routes to the post-apartheid South Africa have increased by an alarming 300 per cent on the north–south route as the number of airlines serving South Africa has more than quadrupled to over 80. The Federation said there were 57 'incidents'

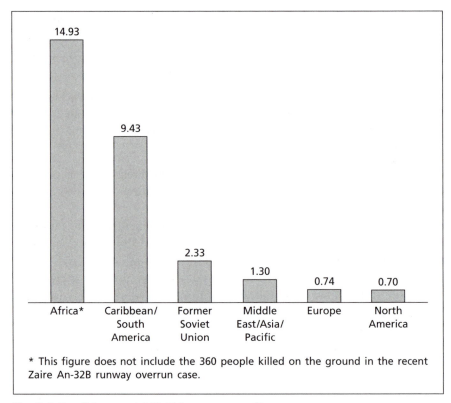

* This figure does not include the 360 people killed on the ground in the recent Zaire An-32B runway overrun case.

Fig. 2.6 Fatalities per 1,000,000 passengers flown
Source: IFALPA

in the 15 months up to November 1996 which included near misses that could have resulted in mid-air collisions like the one in India in November 1996 that killed 351 people.

IFALPA is demanding improvements in ground equipment to enable traffic controllers (too few in numbers anyway) to communicate better with pilots in the air and controllers in adjacent regions. In much of Africa, IFALPA pointed out, open long-range high frequency bands are used instead of the newer very high frequency (VHF) bands for radio communications links.

Cost of quality

The cost of quality is a shorthand formula for all the business costs incurred in achieving a quality product or service. These include prevention costs, appraisal costs, internal failure costs, external failure costs, the cost of exceeding customer requirements and finally the cost of lost opportunities. Taken together these costs can drain a company of 20–30 per cent of its revenue or turnover

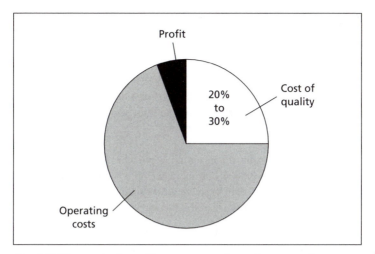

Fig. 2.7 The cost of quality as proportion of revenue/turnover

(*see* Figure 2.7). Key areas of waste in a company include material, capital and time, of which time is perhaps the biggest cost. Cutting the cost of quality is so central a concept to TQM that Chapter 3 deals with it exclusively.

The question here arises about terminology. Should these costs not be called the 'cost of *poor* quality', or the cost of non-conformance. Although, on the face of it, there is a valid argument for referring to the 'cost of poor quality', there are stronger arguments for using 'cost of quality' as a catch-all category. Logically quality costs include 'prevention' which is not a cost of poor quality. On the contrary prevention costs are incurred in getting it right first time and in setting up a total quality programme. Most importantly, in much of the quality literature of the last 50 years, the category cost of quality is referred to with the specific meaning given here – as the total cost in achieving quality, including prevention, appraisal, internal and external failure, exceeding requirements and lost opportunity.

Benchmarking

'While others use starch to thicken their tomato ketchup, Heinz just uses tomatoes' – as a total quality management company, under the leadership of Tony O'Reilly, Heinz decided to wrap this message around the neck of a ketchup bottle in an advertisement which is part of a series to show its commitment to produce quality food. O'Reilly used competitive benchmarking to achieve Heinz's mission:

> We have taken our company from being a rather stodgy, mid-performing, rather unromantic pickle and ketchup company, into a multi-dimensional, international

Table 2.1 Competitive benchmarking

Aim: 'To be better than the best competitor'

Means: By benchmarking the following:

- Products: products and services delivered to external and internal customers.
- Processes: business processes in all departments/functions.
- People: organization, business culture and calibre of people.

---

corporation . . . both in terms of conceptual approaches to the food industry and nutrition in general. . . . So if you ask me what my vision is for the future, it is to maintain the dominance that we have established over the past 10 years as one of the leading food innovators in the world.[12]

Comparing one company's performance with that of another is a reflex of TQM. Competitive benchmarking is a continuous management process that helps firms assess their competition and themselves and to use that knowledge in designing a practical plan to achieve superiority in the market-place. To strive to be better than the best competitor is the target. The measurement takes place along the three components of a total quality programme – products and services, business processes and procedures, and people (*see* Table 2.1).

The idea is to benchmark performance, not only with one's direct competitors, but with other firms as well to discover best practice and bring that practice back to one's own company. It may be that 3M's practice of bootlegging, whereby the firm promotes employees unofficially using 15 per cent of their time, as well as company resources, to develop their own pet projects, is something that other companies will want to copy. (The sticky yellow notes called Post-it notes, one of 3M's most successful global products, came from Arthur Fry and Ben Silver, two 3M employees bootlegging.) Adopting such a programme of bootlegging and adapting it to one's own firm would be a clear example of competitive benchmarking. Effective appraisal systems or team briefings used in rival firms, can be brought back into the company and improved. Likewise an airline adopting a similar empowerment of front-line people to deal with customer service as in SAS's moments of truth would be an act of competitive benchmarking. Defects in cars that surface after delivery to the customer can be benchmarked, as well as warranty costs.

When done correctly competitive benchmarking produces the hard facts needed to plan and execute effective business strategies that fully satisfy agreed customer requirements.

The competitive benchmarking process has the following five steps:

1 Decide what is going to be benchmarked. These may include products and services, customers, business processes in all departments and the organization, business culture and the calibre and training of employees.

2 Select the competitors who are the best in terms of products and services, business processes and people, aspects that one's firm wants to measure. (Usually firms will be looking at their direct competitors. But they may go outside these companies to compare themselves with an outstanding leader in some aspect of business which is famous for certain practices.)

3 Decide on the most appropriate measurements which will be used to define the performance levels in the competitor's business and in one's own company and develop a strategy for collecting the data needed to make meaningful and valid comparisons.

4 Determine one's competitors' strengths and assess those strengths against one's own company's track record or performance. Ask questions such as:

(a) Is the competitor better? If so, how much better?

(b) If they are better, why are they better?

(c) What can we learn from them? How can we apply what we have learned to our business?

5 Develop an action plan. Use the analysed data to set company goals to gain or maintain superiority and to include these goals in the formal planning process. Gaining senior management's acceptance of the results of the competitive benchmarking is crucial to getting commitment to the action plans. A staged problem-solving process is often used to achieve the action plans.

Accordingly competitive benchmarking can be defined as the continuous systematic process for evaluating companies recognized as industry leaders to develop business and working processes that incorporate best practice and establish global performance measures.

Benchmarking is a vital component of any total quality programme. The practice was first used in Japan. 'Dantotsu', the Japanese word for benchmarking, in fact means 'striving for the best of the best'. In the West, the Xerox Corporation was the first company in 1979 to make widespread use of the technique. Xerox was devastated to learn that Canon's selling price of a photocopier was identical to Xerox's production costs for a comparable machine. By 1981 Xerox was using benchmarking throughout its organization. Other companies began to use the method as an integral part of their company-wide quality programmes. The technique has become so popular, today it has developed a life of its own apart from TQM programmes. Benchmarking clubs and support organizations have sprung up across the world. (*See* Appendix A at the end of the book for global benchmarking organizations.)

Seven solid reasons for using the technique are to:

1 Define customer requirements.
2 Establish effective goals and objectives.
3 Develop true measures of productivity.
4 Become more competitive.

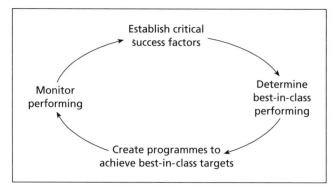

Fig. 2.8 The benchmarking cycle

5 Determine industry best practice.
6 Foster proactive change.
7 Encourage collaboration, information sharing and relationship building with other companies on a regional, national or global basis for mutual benefits.

There are three types of benchmarking. *Internal benchmarking* takes place within one's own organization, comparing similar processes within the company's subsidiaries or branches. The US health products giant Johnson & Johnson used internal benchmarking to compare 25 separate finance functions in the month-end closing of books. The goal was to cut the time down from an average of three weeks to two days.[13]

External benchmarking can be competitive which compares work practices within the same industry, either with direct competitors or with companies operating within the same industry but in a different market. The aim is to isolate outstanding performance.

Benchmarking can also be about *best practice*. Regardless of the industry, the nature of the business, the type of product or kind of work, this type of benchmarking seeks excellence. Taking a cross-industry approach this type of benchmarking is looking for leading-edge practices and processes – the kind that lead to quantum leaps in performance. A good example of this type of benchmarking occurred when Bradford Community Trust in search of better ways of transporting its patients with special needs benchmarked Britannia Airways to see how the airline transported people.

A simple approach to benchmarking called the benchmarking cycle shows four separate sequential activities (*see* Figure 2.8). The cycle starts with discussions and debates which establish the critical success factors in the business. Once these are decided on, it is essential to determine best-in-class performance among competitors. Data collection should eliminate high performance in terms of products and service, business processes and procedures and people. The

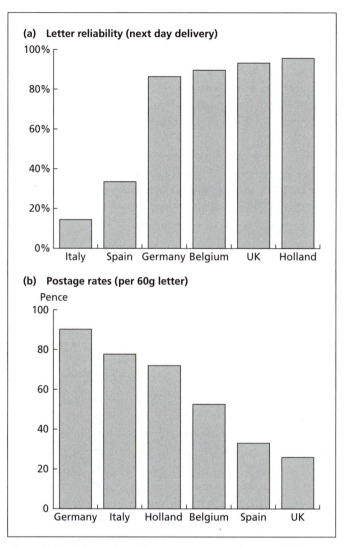

Fig. 2.9 Postal services: European comparisons 1995
Source: Research International

task, then, is to create programmes and projects to achieve best-in-class targets – to be better than the best competitor. Having put real measurements in place, performance is monitored, progress measured, the entire cycle is repeated and improvement spirals upwards.

In its own exercise in competitive benchmarking, the Royal Mail claims to have the second best post service in Europe. A survey of the postal service in six European countries puts Britain second from the top of the performance league table (*see* Figure 2.9). 'The rest of Europe does not even come close to us when it comes to letter reliability,' Sir Bryan Nicholson, Post Office chairman, said.

Letters were posted in the United Kingdom, Germany, France, The Netherlands, Italy and Spain and the time measured to handle the mail from post-box to doormat. The United Kingdom in terms of value for money came top. Royal Mail's then postal rate of 25 pence for a 60 gram first-class letter is significantly lower than any other European postal service (*see* Figure 2.9(b)).

Benchmarking against other firms' best practices with their people is a salutary experience. For example, Federal Express, which moved into the United Kingdom only in 1985, already holds the number two position in the British parcel business behind Parcel Force Limited. Federal Express's philosophy is about the link between people–service–profits. 'Take care of the people; they in turn will deliver the impeccable service demanded by our customers who will reward us with the profitability necessary to assure our future' is how the philosophy is formally put. The company was founded in 1973 by Frederick W. Smith, a Yale MBA. He wrote a paper at Yale University suggesting an overnight delivery service based on the hub and spoke system. He got a 'C' grade on the paper, but he stayed with the idea and turned it into a TQM company. He is now the chief executive officer of a $14 billion company employing 145,000 people world-wide.

The people focus of the philosophy works through the organization in practical ways such as a 'no layoffs' policy. When its business venture 'Zapmail' failed, all 1,300 employees were redeployed to other parts of Federal Express.

British Airways (BA) makes use of competitive benchmarking in its attempt to deliver the highest quality service to its customers. According to Liam Strong, when he was Director of Marketing and Operations benchmarking was used especially where he knew the comparisons would become a spur to action. He cited Japanese engineers who took only 40 minutes to turn a jumbo jet around when BA needed three hours to do the same task.

Whether the competitive benchmarking results are used internally within the company or published in advertising campaigns, great care must be taken to ensure accuracy and meaningful comparisons. British Rail opened an advertising campaign in which it claimed to run more high speed trains than any other European country. The benchmark British Rail chose to advertise was trains travelling at more than 100 miles per hour. Although its claim is valid at 100 miles per hour, above 110 miles per hour British Rail drops down in the league, and as the benchmark goes higher British Rail eventually is out of the competition. When the benchmark is raised to 125 miles per hour – the speed that gave British Rail's InterCity premium trains their brand name – Germany has more trains at that speed than Britain. Above that speed, British Rail falls off the table.

This boastful, misleading and expensive advertising campaign had the opposite effect from that which the transport company intended. The claim was not amusing to passengers on British Rail trains crawling through Sunday engineering works. The television commercial showed a train wrapped in black silk flying past landscape and the voice-over said: 'The French TGV train, the Japanese Bullet. All over the world faster trains are being unveiled. But the fact is, here in Britain with the launch of the new InterCity 225 we have more trains going at over 100 miles per hour than any country in Europe.'

The advertisement left British Rail open to criticism in the press. *The Sunday Times*, for example, in a page-one critical response commented:

> What the commercial does not say is that by more ambitious measures, British Rail fails to compete: above 136 miles per hour, Japan runs 407 trains a day, France 142 and Germany 40. Britain has none.
>
> Even the 225 electric train which the commercial was commissioned to celebrate will not help. It is named the 225 because it is capable of 225 kilometres an hour (141 miles per hour). But you will not find any travelling at the speed until signalling is upgraded.[14]

Meanwhile, high-speed trains that top 300 kilometres per hour are being used by French, German, Swiss, Italian, Swedish and Canadian companies. They now link major cities on 12,000 kilometres of track and offer increased services that include hot meals and drinks served at seats, TVs and telephones and fax machines for business passengers, family sleeping areas and special playground rail cars for children travellers. The stations they stop at are being designed for comfort and are located in the centres of destination cities, unlike their rivals the airports which are found in far-flung outskirts and suburbs.

In whatever area of modern life – services or product development – only companies that keep an alert eye on the competition will prevail:

> 'We win because we hire the smartest people,' Bill Gates said, explaining his company's (Microsoft's) competitive advantage over firms like IBM, Oracle, Sun, Lotus, Netscape. 'We improve our products based on feedback, until they're the best. We have retreats each year where we think about where the world is heading.'[15]

Everyone is involved

The following is an example of a visitor to a plant asking the plant manager to find an example of a defect:

> He'll take me out into the plant and ask one of his QC [quality control] inspectors to show me a part he has rejected. Then I will say to the Plant Manager: Wait a minute. Before we entered the plant, we walked through the executive offices, accounting, engineering and marketing. Don't they make any defects back there?[16]

In fact, everyone is involved in producing defects. In the conventional approach to quality an accusing finger was pointed at the shopfloor. Two-thirds of the workforce was excluded from quality concerns. In TQM everyone is involved in the process from the managing director down the ranks of management to the junior office clerk, the labourer, the canteen and janitorial staff. Everyone in the company is responsible for producing quality goods and services and cutting the 'cost of quality'. In one year Toyota employees made 687,000 suggestions for improving their products and processes, most of them through quality improvement teams (Toyota has less than 40,000 employees).

Every employee has internal customers – someone who receives his or her work – and should discuss with these internal customers their requirements as a first step towards fully satisfying them. This comprehensive approach to total quality can capture the creativity and energy of the entire workforce. Usually this is done in teams – people are given some total quality training in their natural work groups and then unleashed in quality improvement teams.

In 1979, Konosuke Matsushito spoke of how Japanese firms gained competitive advantage over the West precisely because they involve everyone in the company in the quest for quality. He predicted his country's business supremacy in the following terms:

> We are going to win and the industrial West is going to lose out – there is nothing much you can do about it, because the reasons for your failure are within yourselves.
>
> For you, the essence of management is getting the ideas out of the heads of bosses into the hands of labour. For us, the *core of management is precisely the art of mobilising and pulling together the intellectual resources of all employees in the service of the firm*. Only by drawing on the combined brainpower of all its employees can a firm face up to the turbulence and constraints of today's environment.
>
> That is why our large companies give their employees three to four times more training than yours. This is why they foster within the firm such intensive exchange and communication. This is why they seek constantly everybody's suggestions and why they demand from the educational system increasing numbers of graduates as well as bright and well-educated generalists, because these people are the lifeblood of industry.
>
> Your socially minded bosses, often full of good intentions, believe their duty is to protect the people in their firms. We, on the other hand, are realists and consider it our duty to get our people to defend their firms which will pay them back a hundredfold for their dedication. By doing this we end up being more social than you.[17]

Few objective observers of the quality scene would disagree with his prediction.

J.E. Steinhager, director of General Motors' North American sales in Japan, gave a rather wry example of competitive benchmarking when he quoted what

Japanese consumers say when asked their impression of American cars: 'It's as big as two rooms, needs a fuel station every kilometre, costs a lot of money – and you had better watch your rear view mirror because you may see the fender falling off.'[18]

One person's view of how shoddy American manufacturing has become is that of someone who has benefited from the situation. As co-author of *The Japan That Can Say No*[19] Akio Morita, chairman of the board and chief executive officer of the Sony Corporation, offers a sorry history of American decline in meeting customer requirements. His own instincts as an entrepreneur exploited that decline and has helped give his firm and his country the competitive edge in electronics. He was one of the first Japanese to attend Deming's lectures, on 13 July 1950, along with the presidents of 21 leading companies, including Nissan, Mitsubishi and Toyota. When Morita visited the West in the 1950s he was deeply humiliated to learn that Japan had a reputation for producing junk. He returned to Japan with a mission to change it and after 40 years he has the deep satisfaction of having done just that. 'We have been striving to be the Picassos and Beethovens of electronics', Morita said.[20]

Shintaro Ishikara is the other author of *The Japan That Can Say No*. He is an ultranationalist member of the Japanese parliament and has published a sequel, *The Japan That Can Really Say No* (with Jun Eto)[21] in which he boasts of Japan's involvement from a distance in the Gulf War. 'What made the Americans' pinpoint bombing so effective', he writes, 'was PTV, a high-quality semiconductor used in the brain part of the computers that control most modern weapons. There were 93 foreign-made semiconductors in the weapons used by the United States. Among them 92 were made in Japan.' Competitive benchmarking extends, in his view, to America's dependency on foreign technology to carry out its war strategy.

Synergy in teamwork

The Japanese are great believers in synergy. There are no status differences between the engineers with theoretical knowledge and workers with practical knowledge. Both types of knowledge are essential for progress. Therefore, the holders of each type of knowledge consider themselves partners depending on one another for effective management of industrial projects. Engineers, technicians and workers look upon themselves as equals and communicate easily as they work side by side. They create what Professor Okuda has called a 'synergetic partnership'. This enables them to get on well with their continuous improvement. They know how to combine day-to-day modifications to the process and innovation. Their shared decision-making process facilitates change.

A 'rising dynamism' emerges from the shopfloor where people instigate improvements daily. New ways of doing things are proposed by the work group to the team manager who accepts them or rejects them after consultation with technicians responsible for the work processes. Supervisors, therefore, spend a lot of time articulating and harmonizing and consulting over decisions. Eventually from everyone's ideas and feelings about matters they build an unshakeable consensus.

The origin of the word 'synergy' is in dispute with some saying it is an old medical term used to describe the way parts of the body work harmoniously together, while others argue that it is a made-up word from the ancient Greek 'syn' meaning together and 'ergy', a corruption of the word energy, meaning therefore 'energy together'. Its meaning, in management parlance, is clear – synergy is the result of teamwork in which the output is greater than each of the inputs taken separately and also greater than the sum total of the inputs. Two plus two equals five or seven or nine or fifteen in synergy. Watching the indomitable New Zealand All-Blacks triumph over other rugby teams including the Barbarians and the British Lions, as they did in the autumn of 1989, is an object lesson of synergy in teamwork. As a team they were invincible in the autumn of 1989, stretching their impressive record of victories. In the previous decade the All-Blacks had only seven losses and four draws, yet the All-Blacks had no outstanding star players and man for man were outweighed by the Barbarians and the British Lions. What they had was phenomenal teamwork fuelled by fantastic commitment and training. In short they were dedicated to total quality rugby. Before leaving the stadium after every game, they reviewed their major mistakes with a view to preventing them in the future. They were inventive and creative in changing their style of rugby without ever losing sight of their familiar urgency and efficiency in play.

The All-Blacks, under the captaincy of David Kirk, showed amazing team work in their total quality preparation for the inaugural World Cup in 1987. 'The leadership challenge was now different: the team was the overwhelming favourite to win. The All-Blacks were *beyond* wanting to win, and *knew* they were good enough. The task was to prevent complacency,' wrote Robin Young.

> The All Blacks achieved this by setting their own standards: they sought not to win but to play the perfect game. Practice sessions were short but intense. Everything was done at top speed with the aim of producing a completely error free session. The dictum was *'perfect practice makes perfect'*. The team visualised a staircase, where every stepwise advance was only a preparation for the next step. During matches they focussed on incremental improvement: even if a move produced a try, they would attempt to find a small fault in the timing which needed improvement. This could represent the ultimate in TQM's thrust for perfection.

The overall responsibility for physical preparation for the World Cup was shared between the captain, the coach and various specialist trainers. Mental preparation was the sole responsibility of Kirk, as captain.

> He [Kirk] imposed his style on the traditional pre-match routine. . . . On Friday nights pre-match, the captain led a team meeting. Opposition strengths and weaknesses were analysed and individuals' strategies finalised. The team was so confident of its own strength, that little attention was paid to neutralising the opposition. The spotlight was on domination strategies and reinforcing confidence.
>
> On matchday, a light morning training session was held during which each player was encouraged to talk individually about his own opponent: what to expect, how to cope with threats, how to gain advantage. At one o'clock, the captain gave a final ten minute team talk. This covered broad game plan and then sought from each player, in sequence, a comment on the key skills for his personal success.
>
> From the end of the meeting, through the journey to the ground and in the changing room, there was complete silence except for the quiet confirmation of calls. Each individual concentrated calmly on his individual duties.
>
> A last minute injection of fire was gained through ritual. Out on the pitch, before kick off, the team performed the Haka, a Maori war dance. Some individuals found this extremely important, but Kirk himself preferred to remain slightly disengaged, calm and analytical throughout. He found his performance was impaired by over-motivation.[22]

One of the keys to such intense preparation is individual involvement in the team effort as Young pointed out. Individuals were treated as world experts in their positions and never dictated to, either in training or on the pitch. Each player developed and reviewed his own tasks until they became second nature. Solutions to problems were developed by each individual, either in training or during a match. This theme was reinforced in post-match celebrations when each player was asked to summarize the game in five words.

Kirk summarizes his personal leadership strengths as analytical ability, articulateness, perfectionism, dedication and extroversion. He was also young and aloof, both of which he regards as weaknesses although he believes that some distance must be maintained between leader and troops. Kirk's key points for success in teamwork are the following:

- Team members need to be valued as individuals.
- Individuals need to feel integrated within a team.
- Captains must be fair to all team members and treat them equally.
- The team must be confident.
- Individuals must enjoy themselves.

Today the All-Blacks teamwork still serves as a shining example. They lost the final of the 1995 World Cup to the South Africans in extra time. The following year the All-Blacks won the inaugural Tri-nation series against South Africa and Australia. They then went on to win, for the first time, a test series in South Africa (the South Africans, at the time of writing, are yet to win a series in New Zealand). Said Jamie Burrows:

> The All-Blacks 1996 team are the vanguard of a new rugby era marked firstly by several rule changes and professionalism. They still have no stars and were outweighed by the South African forward pack, but the All-Blacks play an exhilarating expansive game that has set the game alight. Each man on the field can run and attack with ball in hand, in the tackle possession is retained and the ball recycled, without infringement. This was best illustrated in the Tri-nation against Australia in Wellington, New Zealand. The rain was horizontal and the ground slow, muddy and sodden. The electric All-Blacks played like the Fijians at the Hong-Kong Sevens. The handling, speed and skill was an illustration of a complete team striving for the perfect game.[23]

In All-Black terms, Sean Fitzpatrick achieved the ultimate one August day in 1996 by leading his country to a first Test series victory on South African soil; a nectar-sweet experience that had eluded an entire pantheon of legends who participated in the five previous 'great treks' between 1928 and 1976. It was entirely typical of the man that he should have risked life and limb to make the final tackle in the final second of an epic contest.

> 'I've had 30 years playing the game I love and the last 12 of those playing for the greatest team in the world. I've had some fantastic coaches and I've played with some fantastic players. I just want to thank them all.'[24]

The idea of synergy in teamwork, where the whole is greater than the sum of its parts, is a key concept in TQM where it is used to promote collaboration, consensus, 'creative conflict' and team winning. These are detailed as follows:

1 *Collaboration* in planning quality improvements, new systems, the documentation of processes, or problem-solving. This approach is more effective than dysfunctional competition which promotes win–lose scenarios where the losers have a way of making the price of winning very high for the winners. A win–win focus prevails.

2 *Consensus* in dealing with conflicting views. Reaching substantial agreement – if not a unanimous view – is better than splitting the group into majority and minority camps.

3 *'Creative conflict'* – conflict can have both positive and negative consequences. It can encourage organizational innovation and creativity.[25] Differences of opinions in management teams, if handled sensitively, can lead to effective and exciting decisions. Many of the best advertisements come out of a great

conflict of ideas, for example the tag line 'Pure Genius' to advertise Guinness. Although some amount of creative conflict is beneficial, too often conflict produces poor consequences. If a board of directors disagrees too radically on the future strategy of the company, divisive action and the ousting of key members can follow, as when Steve Jobs (the co-founder of Apple Computer) was removed from his power base by the board led by John Sculley whom Jobs had recruited. From a synergistic point of view, conflict is an asset not a liability. It can lead to tremendous group creativity.

4 *Team 'winning'* – rather than an individual accolade, winning becomes a group achievement. Recognition for the team and its members is built into the quality improvement projects.

As in all group work, quality improvement team efforts pay attention to the two major components – content and process. Content concerns are about the task or the subject of quality improvement projects to which the groups turn their attention. Process issues have to deal with how the group is working – how decisions are reached, how leadership is handled, how people interrelate, how conflict and competition are dealt with, group morale and so on. If they are to survive as continuous improvement groups, quality improvement teams have to attend to process issues with as much energy as they use attacking the tasks.

In maintaining and fostering quality improvement teams managers analyse group behaviour with regard to involvement, influence, styles of influence, decision-making, task functions, maintenance functions, group atmosphere, membership, feelings and establishing group norms. They sometimes play the facilitator role with their teams and offer feedback on group behaviour following classic behavioural analysis.

Behavioural analysis (BA) of their performance in groups is also helpful for quality improvement teams. There are eleven behaviours exhibited in groups, as shown in Figure 2.10 and detailed as follows:

1 Proposing is behaviour which puts forward a new suggestion, proposal or course of action.
2 Building is behaviour which usually takes the form of a proposal, which extends or develops a proposal made by another person.

   (Items 1 and 2 are called initiating behaviours and are always actionable. They put forward ideas, concepts, suggestions or courses of action.)

3 Supporting is behaviour which makes a conscious and direct declaration of agreement or support.
4 Disagreeing is behaviour which states a direct disagreement, or which raises obstacles or objections.

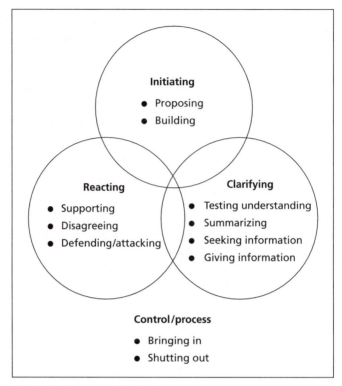

Fig. 2.10 Groups of behaviour

5 Defending is behaviour which attacks another person, either attacking directly or by defensiveness, in terms which usually involve value judgements and emotional overtones.

(Items 3, 4 and 5 are called reacting behaviours and put forward an evaluation of others' contributions.)

6 Seeking information which is a behaviour which seeks facts, opinions or clarification.

7 Testing understanding which is behaviour which seeks to establish whether or not an earlier contribution has been understood.

8 Summarizing is behaviour which restates, in a compact form, the content of previous discussion or events.

9 Giving information is behaviour which offers facts, opinions or clarification to others.

(Items 6, 7, 8 and 9 are called clarifying behaviours and involve the exchange of information, facts, opinions and clarifications.)

10 Bringing in is a behaviour which directly attempts to involve another person or to increase his or her opportunity to contribute.

11 Shutting out is a behaviour which excludes another person or reduces his or her opportunities to contribute. Most commonly it takes the form of interrupting.

(Items 10 and 11 are examples of two behaviours which control the opportunity to contribute.)

By giving quality improvement team members personal and direct feedback on how they relate in groups through behavioural analysis, done in training sessions, they are alerted to their own strengths and weaknesses in group work. Attention to individual behaviour in the quality improvement teams is a *sine qua non* condition of a TQM programme that actually achieves long-term benefits and corporate culture change.

One of the strengths of using teams for TQM is that they can combine the mutually exclusive individual qualities needed for running businesses today. For example, the qualities that lead to creative and inventive ideas are quite opposed to the qualities that prompt a person to check on the smallest detail which may mar the finished product. Whereas an individual is unlikely to possess these opposing qualities, a team can encompass the full range of characteristics needed for effective work.

Hence, TQM in the West taps into all the relevant research on teams. This includes the seminal work of Meredith Belbin. The nine team types that Belbin has identified in his research, which began at the Administration Staff College at Henley in 1969, hold significance for quality improvement teams, by giving team members an awareness of the complementary and divergent roles they play in group work. Belbin's self-assessment questionnaire gives team members feedback on the characteristic behaviours of the roles they normally assume and helps them appreciate the contribution of other team members. It underscores the core principles of synergy in teamwork and the advisability of involving everyone in projects.

Managers who doubt the importance of effective teamwork can find a powerful case study in the work of William Shockley who invented the transistor at Bell Telephone Laboratories in 1947. The US Army wanted to exploit the new technology for weapons and in space exploration, but the early germanium transistor ceased to operate when it got as warm as a cup of coffee. The Army gave Shockley $15 million to invent a better transistor out of silicon. He left Bell in 1955. He chose eight of the top scientists for the project and based it at Stanford University in California. But after two years the group found it impossible to work with Shockley and pushed him out. The team kept together under a new leader, Robert Noyce, and a new sponsor, the Fairchild Camera Company, and moved the operation to bean fields at the south end of the San Francisco Bay area. Together they invented the silicon chip and created Silicon Valley. Shockley got a Nobel Prize for his invention but his failure in teamwork won him exclusion from a process that made all the other team members multi-millionaires.

Being a team leader is a challenge in any sphere of endeavour. Leading an Aerobatic Team adds a visible dimension of hazard to the challenge.

> What I have here are nine very, very talented pilots and some very, very talented engineers . . . everyone can see the goal is outside every day. The aeroplanes sit on the line and they see them fly. The team is very much aware of what it is trying to achieve and they see the results.   Red Arrows Team Leader[26]

After over two years of studying the spectacular teamwork of the Royal Air Force's Red Arrows aerobatic team. Hilarie Owen developed her theory of the synergy chain. A big mistake many teams make at the outset is to assume that team members know the objectives and are committed to them. Objectives and goals must be explicit and teams should incorporate participative goal settings on the part of all members. Ideally these overall objectives should encompass individual or personal goals. So begins a team building process, the first of ten links of the 'synergy chain' (see Figure 2.11).

Rolls-Royce Motor Cars (Vickers Plc): a quality team solution to a crisis

'Strive for perfection in everything you do. Take the best that exists and make it better. When it does not exist, design it. Accept nothing nearly right or good enough.' Henry Royce was ahead of his time. He even had a mission statement to match his precocious quality philosophy: 'To build the finest motor cars in the world'. That was in 1904. These quality statements still hang in the Rolls-Royce car factory at Crewe.

Yet despite its legendary link with the top end of quality products and services for nearly a century, Rolls-Royce Motor Cars found itself in crisis in 1991. A world-wide recession and other exigencies of the market-place combined with the car company's own quality failures to drive it to the brink. From a record high sales of 3,300 cars in 1990, the global market fell to 1,200. The decline called for drastic action. The workforce of 5,000 was cut to 2,300. Design engineers were shifted from comfortable offices in their own separate building to integrated teams on the shopfloor and quality teams took shape. In the restructuring programme, multifunctional project teams were created and the old engineering tradition and job guarantees withdrawn by the struggling company.

Under the leadership of the then Managing Director, Peter Hill, and the then Quality Director, Bernard Preston, who today is Director-Associate and Dealer Programmes, the car factory at Crewe became a dynamic workshop in change management. Ten manufacturing zones were set up as business units to match the ten selling regions. On the industrial relations front, the company cancelled all of its trade union agreements and quit the Engineering

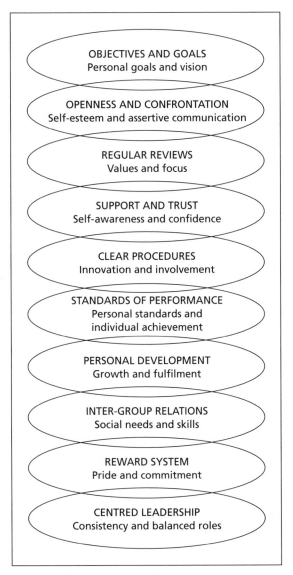

Fig. 2.11 The synergy chain process

Employers' Federation. It then negotiated what amounted to a single union agreement. Signed in 1991, this new agreement was called 'The Green Book'.

A key statement in the document eliminated traditional trade union demarcations. It read:

> To support this approach it is agreed that all the unions party to this Agreement will end any restrictions to the demarcations based on union spheres of influence. Full flexibility and mobility of employees will be needed to ensure full use of

resources and to support the team approach. Accordingly, employees will undertake any work which is within their capabilities, irrespective of grade or specialism anywhere within the Crewe site or off-site as required by the Company and undertake any training necessary to achieve this.

'The Green Book' also opened the way to the introduction of teamwork, skill-broadening, customer focus, empowerment, new training opportunities and a new approach to health and safety which was integrated into the teamworking structure. Out went the inspection and the quality assurance departments as these functions were now entrusted to the teams with the quality specialists being made team members. As Bernard Preston put it: 'Our results have proved the point, our "right first time" quality has improved dramatically.'[27]

The team concept became the vehicle for major and minor improvements. The teams were small groups with working team leaders that had clear accountabilities and responsibilities. They delivered on critical success factors. They dealt with customers and suppliers, measurements of performance, continuous improvements and their own work processes. They knew they were not necessarily permanent. Some national work teams (NWTs) were brought together for specific, short-term projects.

> We use NWTs for almost everything we do. We will bring a cross-functional group of people together to get all the skills in you need, create a vision and objectives for the team activity, set out some deliverables and go for it. There is a lot of empowerment. But teams are not formed for the sake of it and our requirement is that the team has got to add some value to the business.
>
> Bernard Preston[28]

The benefits of the restructuring around quality teams led by a remarkable top management team have been great. They include:

- quality improved by 25 per cent;
- warranty down by 30 per cent;
- cycle time down from 52 days to 30 days;
- inventory down from £29m to £19.1m – much more to go;
- absenteeism – 6 per cent to 2.5 per cent;
- productivity – 84 per cent (start 1993) to 92 per cent (end 1993);
- a close contact between the customer and shopfloor workers.

In addition, 1996 sales increased to beyond 1,700 cars. The Bentley Azure was such a successful new model that waiting lists stretched to six months, despite its £222,500 price tag. The Bentley Continental T, with its distinctive turned aluminium dashboard and impressive speed (nought to 60 in 5.8 seconds) and handling, was becoming the ultimate sports car. 'Bentley erupts with afterburners aglow, accelerating, gathering momentum like a tidal wave on wheels', said motoring correspondent Gavin Green on his road test of the Continental T.

Yet there is nothing crude about the performance. The engine and automatic gearbox combine to form a seamless source of urge; I have never driven an automatic car in which the acceleration is delivered so immediately and, when you're under way, with such smoothness and strength. The handling is indecently agile considering the massive bulk and the high seating position.[29]

A top team, headed by Chris Woodwark as Chief Executive, provides a role model for teamworking at all levels in the company. Joint collaborators with BMW on engine development and heavy investment in new plant which saw a new assembly line installed at Crewe for the 1998 Rolls-Royce and Bentley models, continued to hold out promise of more creative change in Rolls-Royce Motor Cars' quality future. The new assembly line means that the company will no longer buy-in car bodies from Rover in Cowley. Instead they will be made in-house.

Chris Woodwark, however, does not see the change as a move to mass production. 'In fact, our cars will become more bespoke,' he said. 'My goal is for no two Rolls-Royce cars to be the same. We'll achieve this differentiation through a variety of paint colours, trims, specifications, wheels, tyres, carpets and wood finishes.'[30]

Technically Rolls-Royce cars, which go back more than a decade and a half, do not match up to the latest hi-tech BMW, Mercedes or Lexus luxury cars.

Part of the company's strategic decision to source Rolls-Royce and Bentley engines from BMW is an admission of BMW's superior engine build. A BMW modified V12 has been designed for a Rolls and a BMW twin-turbo V8 engine for a new four-door Bentley. A new two-door model, scheduled for the early 2000s, will use a BMW engine. Currently the Continental T and other two-door Bentley models continue to use a V8 engine which is practically hand-built at Crewe.

That hand-built aspect of the cars will continue at Crewe among the carpenters who apply the fine veneer strips of walnut, elm, mahogany, redwood, bird's-eye maple (or whatever woods the customer wants) to the dashboards and doors, and among the leather workers who stitch the elegantly upholstered seating and trim of the cars. A development which has gained momentum at the Crewe factory is this attention to the hand-made luxury touches that can involve direct contact between customers visiting the factory and the skilled workers who explain all the options and possibilities to meet their exact requirements.

Ownership and elements of self-management

It is rare for a person to do home improvements or repairs on a house they are just renting. The DIY business would vanish overnight if home ownership disappeared. One of the causes of the sudden collapse of communism in parts of Eastern Europe had to do with ownership. Few people felt they owned any-thing in the old system. Parallels in industry are obvious – people care mostly and almost exclusively about things they own. For example, the purpose of the John Lewis Partnership as cited by Spedan Lewis, the founder, is all about ownership. He said: 'The Partnership's supreme purpose is to secure the fair-est possible sharing by all its members of the advantages of ownership – gain, knowledge and power; that is to say, their happiness in the broadest sense of that word so far as happiness depends on gainful occupation.'

It may not be possible for most people to have commercial ownership of the firm they work in but they can at least enjoy psychological ownership at work. Total quality programmes are founded on the principle that people want to *own* the problems, the data-driven investigations, the processes, the solutions, the recognition and ultimately the success associated with quality improvement.

By advocating psychological ownership TQM ties in with developments in organizational design away from traditional models of imposing management control over employees' behaviour. Professor Richard E. Walton, at Harvard University, argues for a change:

> Today, in response to massive evidence that control-oriented management models can produce outcomes that subvert the interest of both organisation and the people who work for them, a new workforce management model is appearing. The premise of the emerging model is that organizations must elicit the commitment of their employees if they are to achieve a sustainable competitive advantage in contemporary markets.[31]

The change from a control to a commitment organizational model, Walton argued, announces a radical change in how organizations are designed and governed. Instead of depending on management controls to produce employee cooperation and compliance, companies in the future will rely mostly on mem-ber self-management to achieve common goals. Total quality management is being used as the vehicle for eliciting greater employee commitment through shared decision-making in problem-solving quality-improvement teams. Some companies take it further and use the employee involvement aspects of total quality management strategically to introduce forms of self-management.

J. Richard Hackman, a Harvard Professor of Organizational Behaviour, estab-lishes four separate functions for work to be carried out in a company in terms of the allocation of organizational authority. First, people execute the work. Whether it is physical or mental work people expend energy to do the tasks. Second, a person must monitor and manage the work process. This person or group gathers data about the progress of the work and interprets the data, taking corrective action wherever it is required. Third, a person must design the performing unit, sort out the necessary resources for the work, structuring

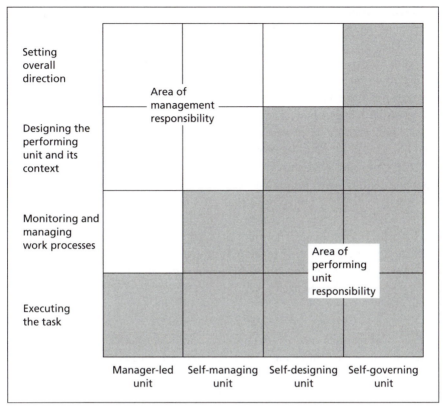

Fig. 2.12 Hackman's authority matrix: four characteristic types of performing units

tasks and assigning personnel to them and establishing norms for the work groups. Fourth, a person must set direction for the organizational unit and determine the collective goals and mission of the organization.[32] Hackman then identifies four types of performing units based on the separate functions (*see* Figure 2.12).

The continuum runs from a management-led unit (the traditional form in the United Kingdom) to a self-managing unit (the unit most suited to TQM programmes) to a self-designing unit (as in top-management task forces) to a self-governing unit (as in a corporate board of directors).

Total quality management programmes encourage work groups to take on the functions of a self-managing unit. Members of work groups are asked to take greater personal responsibility for their outputs in terms of meeting internal and external customer requirements. The emphasis is on personal accountability for the quality of the work they do. They are also taught to measure the quality of their outputs against standards like zero defects, continually monitoring their own performance, collecting data, using competitive benchmarking, actively seeking feedback on how well they are achieving their tasks. They are persuaded to problem-solve and to take their own corrective action to improve their performance. If they do not have the help or resources needed to do their jobs well they are prompted constructively to demand what they need. All this is done with a chain of quality in mind so that people are aware of the linkages between their performance and that of their co-workers – a helping culture is developed. While the emphasis is on getting one's own house in order first, the responsibility is fostered for reaching out to help other work groups with interface problems. Dialogue around agreed internal customer requirements serves this helping function.

Groups that Work (and Those that Don't)[33] is a collective effort by doctoral students from the University of Michigan and Yale University, edited by J. Richard Hackman. The links detailed descriptive accounts of specific work of 27 task-performing teams with theoretical ideas on teamworking to generate action points for practical application and further research. The main findings of the research given below are pertinent for quality improvement teams.

1 Temporal features such as time limits, deadlines, cycles and rhythms had a significant impact on group working. They also created group climate and contributed greatly to the quality of group experience.
2 Groups experience self-fuelling downward (unsuccessful and negative) spirals or upwards (successful and positive) spirals. Those groups that found themselves performing badly got worse over time, while those groups that got themselves in a high performance groove got better. A lot had to do with how the groups were structured and how they were perceived by those outside the group whose praise (or negative comments) labelled the group and contributed to its confidence and success or negative self-image.
3 Dealing with the dynamics of authority held great consequences for effective teamwork. Four authority issues were salient to how the teams handled their task:
   (a) the amount of authority the group had to manage itself;
   (b) the stability of the authority structure;
   (c) the timing of intervention by those in authority, the best time for intervention being at the group's start-up;
   (d) the substantive focus of those interventions. A poorly focused intervention directly into a group's processes, for example, can destroy the group's sense of responsibility for the outcome of the work.
4 The context of a group's work – the stuff they work with – shapes the emotional lives of the members and their interactions in teams. For

example, top-management teams dealt with the issues of strategy, power and influence, while production teams focused on technology in their work context and human service teams dealt with people's needs.

5 Teams have specific risks and special opportunities open to them. For example, a top-management team has the risk of the absence of supportive organizational context, but the opportunity of designing themselves as they see fit and having influence over their own conditions required for team effectiveness. (They control the resources needed and 'call the shots'.) The main risk for customer service teams is to get so involved with the client's needs that they neglect those of the parent company. Its opportunities include being a bridge between the company and its customers, the primary link between the organization and its environment.

In a discussion of 'trip wires' that cause teams to fail, the research illustrated one such 'trip wire' that is frequently set off in quality programmes: 'specify challenging team objectives, but skimp on organizational supports'.[34]

When a quality improvement team is given a clear engaging direction and an appropriate structure, it can fail to achieve its aim or reach its full potential if it is not well supported. Main supports include:

1 a reward and recognition system that recognizes and reinforces superior *team* performance and achievements;
2 an educational system that supplements the members' own knowledge and expertise with whatever training or consultancy inputs they feel they require;
3 an information system that provides the team with the data, forecasts and research they feel they need to achieve their objectives;
4 the material resources – staff, money, working space and meeting room, tools technology, equipment, travel budgets, etc. – needed to attain their aim.

When a quality improvement team is well-directed, well-structured and well-supported, its potential for synergetic outcomes can be boundless.

Managers as role models

The almost religious fervour of Philip B. Crosby's exhortation and his zero defect pledge is part of his style. But it is not exclusively his. Most TQM experts get evangelical about their message. The parallels between the wrenching of oneself away from one way of behaviour and then applying oneself to another quite different form of behaviour in the pursuit of goals of perfection in total quality has a monkish ring to it. The *metanoia* or conversion to total quality and zero defects is both personal and public as it is supported by the band of brothers (and sisters) at all levels in the company. There is also an element of personal witness and leading by good example: 'I learned even though I had been preaching this for years, that when it comes to quality, the witness of management is more important than anything else,' Crosby said.

The parallel with what is expected of total quality managers in terms of behaviour that they personally live out, the messages they proclaim, and what people expect of religious and political leaders draws itself.

Revelations about the hypocrisy of President John F. Kennedy have been given historical status with the publication of an academic study of the life of Kennedy.[35] The realities are deeply disturbing to his countrymen and admirers around the world, for the book substantiates the spate of wild articles in the popular press about the president's immorality over the years. Events leading up to the impeachment of President Bill Clinton have further discredited the United States presidency in the role of moral leadership. The American president is supposed to combine the role of king and prime minister, and therefore the public rightly expects the president to set a moral example and to support 'traditional values', as well as to keep out of danger of blackmail. Kennedy failed on all counts, despite his ability to enthral his listeners with his eloquence and to project an image as a stylish, caring, family man. Like-wise Clinton scandalized millions and lost respect for himself and for his office on a global scale. Although total quality cannot be achieved by exhortation by senior managers, like organized religion and politics, it needs to be led from the top by genuine role models.

At all levels managers need to be conscious that they are role models for total quality. What they say about total quality is important. What they do is absolutely critical. 'Teaching people, leading people, showing people, provid-ing tools – everything loses meaning', Crosby says, 'if employers, customers and suppliers feel that management is not walking like they talk.' A BBC series, written and presented by Charles Handy, was called *Walk the Talk* and included a TQM case study, 'B. Elliott Expects', which focused on two companies, MTE and Russell Castings.[36]

The very best TQM programme accordingly builds in a system of manage-ment feedback so that managers get some idea of how they are doing as role models for quality.

Management role feedback

Performance feedback is vital to enable managers at all levels to improve their contribution to the business. Feedback provides information on where a man-ager is today and gives an indication of the level of improvement compared with previous feedback.

There are two types of feedback that are relevant here. The first is the tradi-tional performance review. The work group managers should have a formal

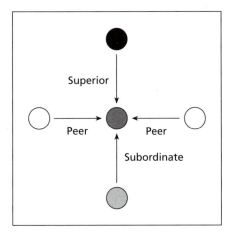

Fig. 2.13 The three directions of managerial style feedback

discussion with each work group member individually at least once a year. The review should cover the following items:

- individual performance against key business objectives;
- personal strengths and areas for improvement;
- training needs over the next 12 months;
- future career aspirations;
- individual's and manager's comments on the performance review.

The second is managerial style feedback. Before managers change the way they manage, they should know what improvements are needed in their current management style. They should also know what aspects of their style should not be changed. The starting point for improving management style, therefore, is an honest assessment of managers' current behaviour by people who are familiar with it. There are three directions of feedback (*see* Figure 2.13) as follows:

- work group manager to work group member (superior feedback);
- work group member to work group manager (subordinate feedback);
- work group member to work group member (peer feedback).

There are six general management areas where feedback is important in the total quality process as follows:

1 Leadership (directive/supportive): task management; delegation; decision-making.
2 Teamwork: interactive behaviours; participation.
3 Communications: active listening; two-way information sharing; personal rapport.

4 Motivating: presence (visibility/accessibility/encouragement/interest); recognition; reward.

5 People development; personal performance reviews; career development; succession planning.

6 Commitment to the total quality process: use of a quality delivery process, TQM system; quality improvement projects/application of the problem-solving process.

An appropriate feedback questionnaire should be designed to be completed by one's manager, his or her peers and his or her own work group members at least once a year so that the manager can analyse and measure progress and understand perceived strengths and weaknesses.

Leadership

John F. Kennedy was a US President enjoying power and prestige in 1962 when he ordered the removal of US missiles from their locations in Turkey. He took the decision after reviewing alternative plans prepared by many government agencies. The Joint Chiefs of Staff, the State Department and the National Security Council had carefully co-ordinated the alternative plans and added their views. But President Kennedy himself made the decision and his written orders went spiralling out from the Oval Office of the White House to American military bases in Turkey. Yet months later, at the height of the Cuban missile crisis, Kennedy was shocked to learn from the Soviet head Nikita Krushchev that the missiles remained in their silos – his orders had not been carried out. His leadership had not been effective in this critical area of foreign policy.

Leadership is what leadership *does*. Fans of British football were amazed in the 1997/98 season to see the transformation of Arsenal, the famous North London football club, under the leadership of their new manager, Arséne Wenger. Within 18 months the quiet French manager had turned the faltering football club into Premier League champions and FA Cup winners. Yet he refused to be drawn into the media maze of prediction. He kept reassuring his team and their supporters that the title was 'within our own hands, but we must not become over-confident.'

Gianluca Vialli, the new player/manager for Chelsea, the West London football club, was thrust into his role during a crisis toward the end of the 1997/98 season, and soon proved to his supporters the key role of leadership in changing the fortunes of his football team. Vialli's engaging, energetic leadership style – at times leading from the front in crucial games, at other times leaving himself on the bench in equally important matches – has led his club to the European Cup-Winners Cup Championship.

The two football club managers, Arséne Wenger and Gianluca Vialli, have very different leadership styles, yet both achieved remarkable results. What elements in sports leadership are common to success in business and translate into leading total quality management programmes?

Leadership in management has always been a difficult challenge, which is why it is the most researched aspect of managerial behaviour. The appropriate style of leadership for total quality management is not self-evident. Yet in any TQM programme the question of leadership style is a crucial matter.

The first studies of leadership were one-dimensional. They looked to the traits or personal qualities of the man or woman, as if there were a magic mix of traits that were simply waiting to be discovered. The difficulty with this approach was that it implied – since most of the traits were inborn, part of one's genetic package – that leaders were *born* and not *made*. A further difficulty with this approach was identifying and agreeing the actual traits themselves necessary for leadership success. For example, is 'honesty' such a leadership trait, or does a leader have to be 'devious' and 'Machiavellian' to achieve his or her goals? Surely a leader today would need to be 'well read' and 'intellectually curious', one might think, yet Lech Walesa, an electrician at the Lenin Shipyard in Gdansk, was neither. It did not stop him from being a superb leader as a brash union organizer with a charismatic personality, quick wit and the gift of the gab, who stood up to the Kremlin and dealt the Eastern bloc a fatal blow. His progress from leader of Solidarity in 1980 to elected president of Poland in 1990 earned him a place among *Time Magazine*'s top 100 leaders of the twentieth century.

A second wave of leadership research avoided the traits trap and focused instead on the behaviour of leaders. A leader is what a leader does. Two leadership behaviours – directive behaviour and supportive behaviour – were well researched. Directive behaviour includes one-way communication from the leader to his followers. Whenever the leader tells people what to do, sets targets and deadlines and closely supervises their work or colours in their vision for them in vivid detail, he or she is engaging in directive behaviour. Supportive behaviour is about the leader's relationship with his or her followers. It is about two-way communication in which the leader asks for inputs from the followers, listens to them, shares decision-making and is supportive with feedback, encouragement and praise. Extensive research – much of it done at Ohio State University – on these two leadership behaviours concluded that they were both equally important to a leader's effectiveness. This two-dimensional model of leadership dominated management thinking until the writers Ken Blanchard and Paul Hersey added the third dimension by including the follower in the model. To answer the question, which leadership behaviour is appropriate, directive or supportive, the leader must consider the situation and the situation

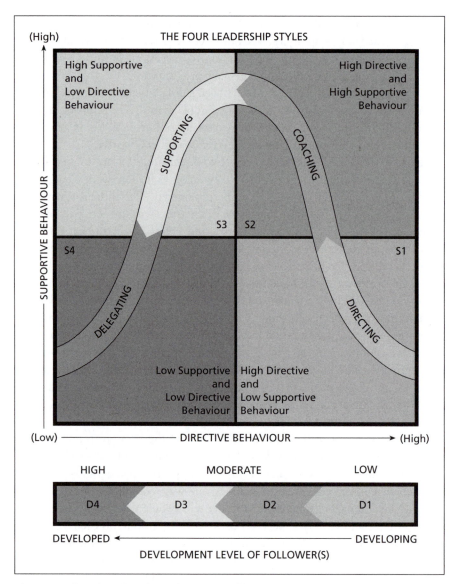

(High) THE FOUR LEADERSHIP STYLES

High Supportive and Low Directive Behaviour

High Directive and High Supportive Behaviour

SUPPORTING

COACHING

S3 | S2

S4

S1

SUPPORTIVE BEHAVIOUR

DELEGATING

DIRECTING

Low Supportive and Low Directive Behaviour | High Directive and Low Supportive Behaviour

(Low) ———— DIRECTIVE BEHAVIOUR ————→ (High)

HIGH   MODERATE   LOW

D4 | D3 | D2 | D1

DEVELOPED ←——————————————————— DEVELOPING

DEVELOPMENT LEVEL OF FOLLOWER(S)

Fig. 2.14 The Situational Leadership Profile II: The Model

is defined by the follower's competency and willingness to achieve the task. This preparedness of the follower can be plotted from low to moderate to high (*see* Figure 2.14). The mix of directive and supportive styles used by the leader depends, then, on the readiness and motivation of the follower and this is task-specific.

Within the 'situational leadership' model the manager's goal must be to engage in empowering behaviours. He or she does so whenever the manager:

- listens to the problems of subordinates;
- praises subordinates for task accomplishment;
- asks for suggestions or input on task accomplishment;
- encourages or reassures subordinates that they can do the task;
- communicates information about the total organization's operation;
- builds a subordinate's self-esteem;
- facilitates subordinates problem-solving or decision-making;
- acknowledges subordinates' contributions;
- enthuses subordinates about a project.

The aim of leadership in a TQM programme then is to empower employees to engage in continuous improvement. Empowered individuals take more risks, learn more skills and knowledge, grow and develop, are responsible and accountable for their work, choose from options and make decisions, are creative and innovative and are entrepreneurial. It would be difficult to find a better model for empowerment in a TQM enterprise than that of Rank Xerox shown in Figure 2.15.

Recognition and rewards

Owen Edwards, a writer and critic, commented on an interview he had with General Robert H. Barrow, the Commandant of the Marine Corps. He said '. . . my eyes were drawn to a rainbow array of ribbons above the general's left jacket pocket . . . at a glance, I knew quite a lot about General Barrow: that he had been in combat in far-flung places, had been wounded, and at least once displayed great valour in battle.'[37]

He added: 'The rectangular patch of color and its silent proclamation of experience, accomplishment and fortitude impressed me.' Next to the general Owen Edwards, a former Marine himself, felt he had nothing palpable to show for his life achievements. He wished that 'civilians who . . . endure their share of mental and physical ordeals, might have some equivalent way to make their victories instantly visible to others.'

The need for recognition is a deep-seated one as testified to by another former Marine who set up an exemplary TQM programme at Paul Revere Insurance and argued for symbols of recognition and reward throughout. Making the case for bronze, silver and gold lapel pins linked to levels of achievement against the view that 'nobody would wear them', Patrick Townsend argued that they would wear them if the organization imbued the awards with meaning and value citing his own experience as an officer in the US Marine Corps.'[38]

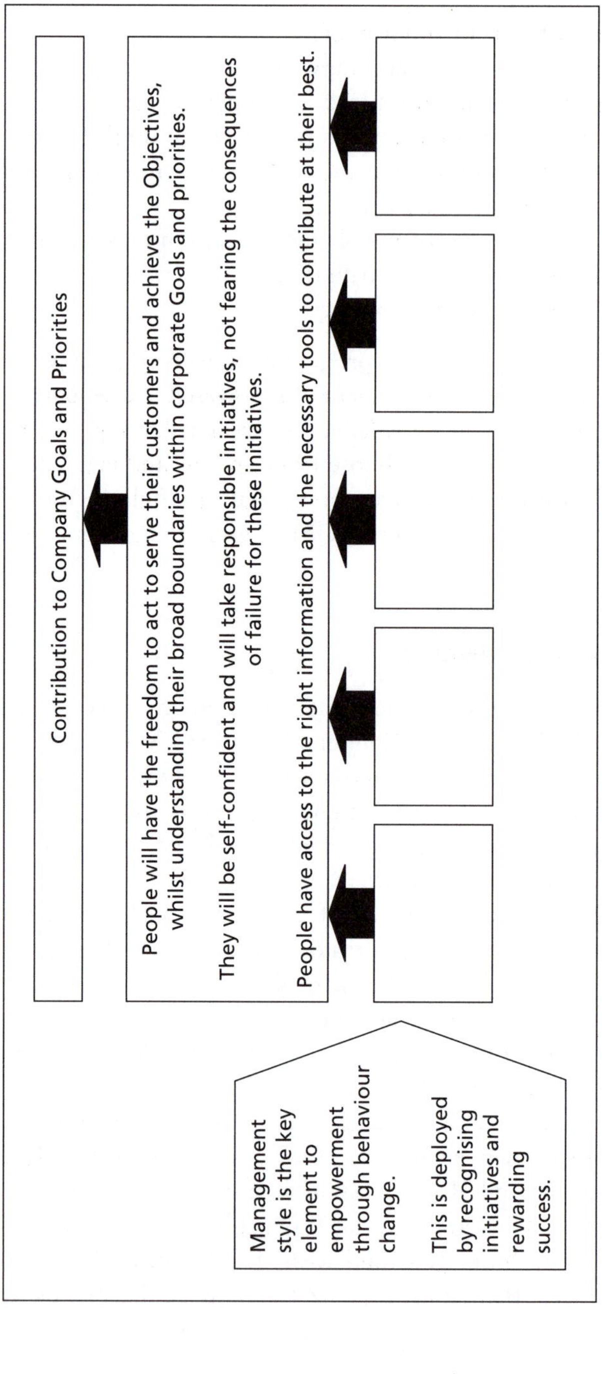
Contribution to Company Goals and Priorities
People will have the freedom to act to serve their customers and achieve the Objectives, whilst understanding their broad boundaries within corporate Goals and priorities.
They will be self-confident and will take responsible initiatives, not fearing the consequences of failure for these initiatives.
People have access to the right information and the necessary tools to contribute at their best.
Management style is the key element to empowerment through behaviour change.
This is deployed by recognising initiatives and rewarding success.

Fig. 2.15 Empowerment – the Rank Xerox model

Source: Lecture by Clare Harding, Xerox Quality Department to Cranfield School of Management MBA, 17 March 1995.

An appropriate system of recognition and reward is critical to any company's TQM programme, particularly as the quality improvement process offers greater involvement to ordinary working people. Positive reinforcement through recognition and reward is essential to maintain achievement and continuous improvement through participative problem-solving projects. People work for many reasons – for achievement, advancement, increased responsibility, recognition, job interest as well as money.

Although the words are often used together, recognition and reward are quite distinct concepts. Recognition from its Latin root *cognoscere* means 'to know again'. It is a means of encouraging individuals and groups by acknowledging their achievements. It also serves as a spur to further efforts through appreciating contributions already made. There are both formal and informal ways of giving recognition. Some examples of formal recognition are presentation of their accomplishments at management reviews, publication of achievements in company media, a letter of thanks and commendation, lunches or dinners, award certificates, plaques and other tokens. Informal recognition includes words of thanks, gestures of appreciation and favourable comments made to others about the individual or group.

Reward is the giving of financial benefits linked to performance, further reinforcing the day-to-day recognition processes. Two examples are merit-based increases in earnings resulting from performance appraisal, and the promotion of an individual who contributes in a major way to quality improvement.

Both recognition and rewards have a powerful motivating effect on people at work. They enhance a person's awareness of self-worth and self-esteem. The giving of recognition and rewards are gestures that recognize a person's uniqueness and human dignity. They also have a social value since they are often given in the presence of colleagues. The way recognition and rewards are perceived, administered and received are an important part of the change process stimulated through quality management. Managers have a key role in this process.

The following are recognition and rewards guidelines for managers:

1 Managers should look for positive behaviour to recognize and reward rather than for negative conduct to criticize. It is a question of emphasis – applauding success rather than always berating failure.
2 Managers should give recognition and rewards in a public way to maximize their impact and effectiveness.
3 Managers should strive to be open and genuine in the process of recognition and reward-giving. A single word of sarcasm or cynicism can ruin a recognition programme, so can being 'over-the-top' or too slick about it.
4 Managers should have a wide range of recognition and reward options to allow them to match the recognition or reward to the individual or special group involved.

5 Managers need to develop a sense of timing about recognition and rewards. Recognition should be continual and rewards should follow hard on the heels of achievement.

6 Managers must remain impartial and even-handed in giving out recognition and rewards. They should also be able to communicate exactly why individuals and groups are receiving awards. Ambiguities in this area create hard feelings and can be destructive of the very participative process they are intending to foster.

The quality delivery process

Total quality management is not just about awareness of quality. TQM demands the implementation of new systems: 'the quality delivery process' is a generic name for such a system.

The purposes of the quality delivery process are to:

1 Ensure that everyone works on those activities which are most important for the success of the business by fulfilling work group missions.
2 Improve the quality of work delivered (outputs) to the customers – internal customers, the next person down-the-line, who receives the work.
3 Eliminate work that is wasted because people do not do it right the first time.
4 Harness the combined skills, ideas and experience of the work group members to improve the business continuously through teamwork.
5 Satisfy the external customers.

A work group comprises a manager in the company and all the staff who directly report to him or her. These are the people who can significantly affect the quality of the work they do each day. The work group manager leads the team. The work group produces outputs which are delivered to either external or internal customers. Usually, there are only a few (five to ten) outputs that really matter and these must be identified and measured for quality.

Quality improvement is achieved through projects which are 'owned' by the work group. The project team comprises two to ten people who can best contribute to the solving of business problems resulting in the improvement of outputs. A project team will continue to work on the problem(s) until the customer is satisfied with the output. To satisfy customers, work groups must determine customer requirements. This will involve members of the work group in discussions with customers, or a sample of them if there are many for the same output, to be sure the work is designed in such a way that they will be capable of delivering the quality required by the customers. Customer satisfaction should be measured by interview/questionnaire (direct means) or by counting/analysing the number of complaints and returns received (indirect means).

The target is for every work group in the company to work on at least one improvement project at any one time. There will always be room for further improvement.

There are ten steps in the quality delivery process, as follows:

1 Create mission statement – a mission statement is a sentence that defies the work group's activities. It is focused on the end objective rather than the means of achieving it.
2 Determine the outputs of the work group and check that they fulfil the mission.
3 Identify the customer(s), both internal and external, who receive the outputs.
4 For each output, define agreed customer requirements which must be met in order to achieve customer satisfaction.
5 Develop the work group's output specification for each output.
6 Determine the group's work processes, including the identification of inputs, which will deliver the outputs to the customer(s) at the lowest internal cost.
7 Identify the measurements of each output which will compare the 'actual' quality level delivered with the output specification.
8 Identify any problem caused by a measured 'shortfall' to target (or identify an 'opportunity' to exceed target at no additional cost; or an 'opportunity' to meet customer requirements at a lower internal cost).
9 Establish a project team to solve the identified problem which will improve the 'actual' quality level delivered to the customer (or capture the 'opportunity' in step 7).
10 Measure customer satisfaction against the agreed customer requirements.

Review of quality delivery process

The following checklist can be used to review whether each of the ten steps has been fully covered. A little time spent at this stage will avoid having to repeat some of the steps in the process (*see* Figure 2.16).

Step 1: Create mission statement
- Does the mission statement define the main purpose for which the work group exists?
- Is it focused on the end objective rather than the means of achieving it? (It should not contain lengthy statements on the 'why' and 'how' of achieving the mission.)
- Has it been agreed with the next higher manager?

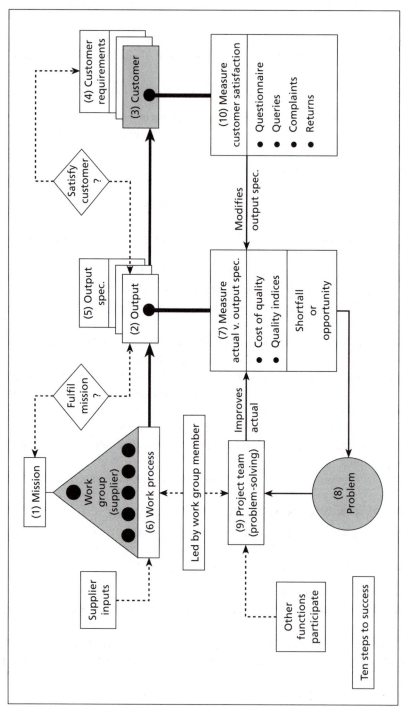

Fig. 2.16 The quality delivery process

Step 2: Determine the outputs

- Is the output described clearly, so that there is no doubt about what is being produced?
- Is the output tangible – something that can be touched, seen or measured?
- Will the internal customer for the output find the description acceptable?
- Is the work group really the supplier for this output?

Step 3: Identify the customers

- Is there agreement about the identification of the customers for this output?
- If multiple customers have been identified for this output, have they agreed that they are all customers?
- Has the end user been identified where the 'output' is incorporated by other work groups for another customer down the line?
- Have the customers been named – specific individuals who can explicitly identify requirements?
- Does the customer feel that the work group is the appropriate supplier?
- Has the work group confirmed its role with the customer?

Step 4: Define customer requirements

- Did the customers themselves define these requirements?
- Are the requirements, as now stated, clear enough to be translated into output specifications?
- At this point, can the customer requirements be met?
- Was discussion with the customer successful in agreeing customer requirements?

Step 5: Develop the output specification

- Is there a clear relationship between customer requirements and output specifications?
- Are the specifications measurable? If not, can they be made measurable?

Step 6: Define group's work process

- If this is a new output, has a work process to produce it been identified?
- Will the steps in the work process deliver the output to the customer at the agreed quality level?
- Have work group responsibilities been identified for each step to ensure the process is carried out satisfactorily?
- Has the in-process measurement been identified that will be used to ensure the work process is 'in control' (i.e. capable of producing outputs at the right quality consistently)?
- Is the work process adding value at the lowest internal cost?
- Are there any unnecessary or rework/correction activities in the work process?
- Is anyone checking/inspecting the work produced and how can this be eliminated?

Step 7: Identify measurements of output
- Have measurements to determine the delivered quality level been selected?
- In general, will the selected measurements provide early indications of any possible problems or errors?
- Will the measurements indicate whether the output conforms to the output specification?
- If you were the customer, would you be satisfied that these measurements ensure the quality of the output?

Step 8: Define the problem
- Is there a shortfall between 'actual' and 'target' (output specification) quality levels when measuring the output?
- Is there an opportunity to achieve better than target at no additional cost?
- Does the target level reflect competitive best practices?
- Has the problem statement been written down?

Step 9: Establish a project team
- Who is going to lead the project team?
- Have the team members been identified?
- Can everyone on the team positively contribute to the solving of the problem? (No room for passengers or cynics!)
- When will the first project team meeting be held?

Step 10: Measure customer satisfaction
- Have the key measures of customer satisfaction (or dissatisfaction) been identified?
- Have customers (or a sample of them if there are many customers receiving the same output) been asked whether they are satisfied with the output(s)?
- Have the customer's requirements changed (reflecting a need to change the output specification)?
- How frequently has the work group planned to measure customer satisfaction?

Quality measurements

There are seven generic ways (in addition to the cost of quality) in which the quality of outputs can be measured:

1 Defects (work not to specification).
2 Rework (work requiring correction).
3 Scrap (work thrown away).
4 Lost items (work done again).
5 Backlogs (work behind schedule).
6 Late deliveries (work after agreed time).
7 Surplus items (work not required).

The above measurements apply to office 'outputs' (such as paper, electronic data, telephone calls, etc.) as well as to the outputs of production/laboratories/warehouses (such as parts, tools, finished products, etc.).

There are five key measurements for each 'output'.

1 Target: the budget or target level of performance to be achieved.
2 Forecast: the forecast level of performance which may be better or worse than the target depending on current business situation. The forecast also shows when the target will be reached.
3 Actual: the actual level of performance achieved to date.
4 Problem: the difference between the actual and target level of performance where 'actual' is worse than 'target'.
5 Opportunity: the opportunity for improving quality better than target at no extra cost.

A paradigm shift to quality

The legacy of Thomas Kuhn who died in the summer of 1996 includes a thin book entitled *The Structure of Scientific Revolutions*. His book explored the difficulties of creating new thinking patterns in the scientific community. The name he gave to the new mental models that create change is 'paradigms', which he defined as: 'A constellation of concepts, values, perceptions and practices shared by a community which forms a particular vision of reality that is the basis of the way a community organizes itself.'[39]

Kuhn found that scientists changed their paradigms with great difficulty. The patterns were so entrenched, these scientists were often blinded to the incoming data of the new paradigms. Kuhn's central view on the resistance of scientists to change their views was well illustrated in the medical world where new ideas are often fought against. Until late 1997, all sufferers from stomach ulcers in the UK were treated by traditional methods and medicines. Their treatment was based on the wrong medical conclusion that nothing could grow in the stomach. However, two Western Australian doctors, Dr Robin Warren and Professor Barry Marshall in 1983 found that 70 per cent of gastric and 90 per cent of duodenal ulcers were caused by bacterium in the stomach. Their research on the bacterium called helicobacter pylori has led to a breakthrough in the treatment of stomach ulcers. The Australian researchers from Perth gave themselves the infection and cured themselves. For over a decade and a half they have traveled to medical conferences around the world to present their findings. But it has taken a global campaigning to have their research finally accepted by the medical world. Thanks to the eventual acceptance of their new paradigm most of Britain 200,000 stomach ulcer suffers can be cured of their illness within 10 days by taking a course of medicine to stop the infection. The two Australian doctors have been jointly awarded the inaugural Faulding Florey Medal for medical research and have been nominated for a Nobel Prize. Their concern now is that the take-up on the cure is still too slow. Professor Marshall estimates that only one in five people with ulcers has used the new treatment. Debunking the long-held myths that ulcers are principally caused by stress, spicy food and alcohol has been difficult. 'Once the germ has been eradicated it is usually a permanent cure,' Dr Marshall said . . .[40] In medicine the paradigm shifts are irrevocable, but they take time to implement.

Management trainer Joel Barker helped popularize the paradigm concept in management circles over the last twenty years. He defines a paradigm 'as a set of rules and regulations that establish boundaries, and tell us what to do to be successful within those boundaries.'[41]

Within one's own paradigm many things are possible to achieve which would be impossible outside the paradigm. Barker gives the colourful example of the Tara-Jumaran Indians of Northern Mexico who run seventy miles as part of a religious festival. But, while they enable, paradigms also have the power to block incoming data that is not in sync with the paradigm. Because Chester Carlson's new electrostatic photography (the Xerox process) was outside the photographic paradigms of the 1930s, his invention was turned down by major photographic companies who 'passed' on one of the best business ideas of the century.

Likewise the Swiss watchmakers were blind to the impact of the quartz movement watch which represented a new paradigm in watch making and had been invented by Swiss researchers in their laboratories in Neuchatel, Switzerland in 1967. Because the electronic watch was battery powered and did not have any bearings, gears or a mainspring, it was dismissed as a fad. The Swiss did not even patent it and gave the idea away free to the Japanese and Americans at the annual Watch Congress that year. Ten years later the quartz watch had proved itself as the new paradigm of watches and the Swiss saw their world market share fall from 65 per cent of sales (80 per cent of profits) to below 10 per cent, losing 50,000 jobs in the watch industry out of the 65,000 they once had.

Partly as a result of such vivid illustrations of the importance of recognizing paradigm shifts, the word 'paradigm' has been one of the most overused words of the last two decades. Academic writing, business news stories and popular articles are littered with the words 'paradigm' and 'paradigm shift'. Yet there is no more accurate way to describe the sudden change from the outdated idea that quality is an entitlement of the wealthy who can afford to pay for it to the new belief that everyone has a right to quality goods and services without exception than to call it a paradigm shift. Take the example of how this paradigm shift altered forever the American car industry.

Apart from the popular Volkswagen Beetle, the mass car market in the early 1970s in the United States was supplied by American car manufacturers. In 1954, for instance, of the 7.2 million new cars sold in America, only 50,000 – well under 1 per cent – were imports.[42]

The paradigm shift was away from the unreliable, fuel-inefficient, oversized US models to the cheaper, better designed and lower-cost in maintenance foreign imports. By 1992 the US car industry was losing $700 million a month. 'Made in Japan' had gone from being a sign of shoddiness to a proud emblem of the highest quality – a paradigm shift with consequence to Japan's balance of trade with the West.

Standards, quality accreditation and quality systems

Standards are appropriate specifications against which something can be measured to see if it meets the standard. A wide range of industrial, business and related activities in the UK are governed by standards established by the British Standards Institute (BSI), an organization set up in 1931 whose roots go back to the Engineering Standards Committee established about a hundred years ago.

BS 5750 is a *capability* (not a *product*) *standard*. Established by the BSI, BS 5750 was developed by the Quality, Management and Statistics Committee with the help of the Technical Committee (QMS/2) which was made up of about fifty representative organizations from government, industry and other interested parties. Most British Standards are product standards. The key parameters for a certain product are defined in a published document and are awarded a Kitemark from BSI as assurance to both the buyer and the seller that the product conforms to the established standard.

Capability standards differ from product standards. The driving test a learning driver takes is a capability standard. BS 5750 is, likewise, a capability standard. It is the standard for quality systems and it measures *how* a product or service is produced rather than *what* is produced.

To qualify for BS 5750 a company must agree to third-party or independent assessment of its processes and quality systems by BSI assessors or other accredited assessors.

Established in 1979 and revised in 1987 to be more comprehensive in scope, BS 5750 aims to have universal application. BS 5750 is actually a series of published standards in separate documents, Part 0 to Part 13 (with Parts 5 and 6 left out since their currency has lapsed). Each Part sets out requirements that must be met. Parts 1, 2 and 3 deal with the quality systems requirements themselves. Then follows the stockist schemes. The second category of Parts to BS 5750 (Parts 0 [01/02] 4, 8 and 13 are not requirements but rather provide guidance and advice. Figure 2.17 illustrates the common management system principles between BS 5750 and BS 7750.

A cell containing a ● represents a connection between the relevent clauses of the two standards.

Requirement of BS 5750: Part 1 subclause	Requirement of BS 7750 subclause										
	4.1 Management system	4.2 Environmental policy	4.3 Organization and personnel	4.4 Environmental effects	4.5 Objectives and targets	4.6 Management programme	4.7 Manual and documentation	4.8 Operational control	4.9 Records	4.10 Audits	4.11 Reviews
4.1 Management responsibility	●	●	●							●	
4.2 Quality system	●						●				
4.3 Contract review				●	●	●					
4.4 Design control						●	●	●			
4.5 Document control							●				
4.6 Purchasing				●				●			
4.7 Purchaser supplied product				●							
4.8 Product identification									●		
4.9 Process control								●			
4.10 Inspection and testing								●			
4.11 Inspection, measuring and test equipment								●			
4.12 Inspection and test status								●			
4.13 Control of non-conforming product								●			
4.14 Corrective action								●			
4.15 Handling, storage, packaging and delivery				●				●			
4.16 Quality records									●		
4.17 Internal quality audits										●	
4.18 Training			●								
4.19 Servicing				●				●			
4.20 Statistical techniques								●			

Fig. 2.17 The links between BS 7750 (1992) and BS 5750: Part 1

Source: BS 7750: 1992 (British Standards)

To obtain BS 5750, a company must:

1 design and implement a quality system;
2 meet all the *requirements* of the Standard (also taking on board the suggestions and advice in the Standard is usually helpful);
3 pass an assessment conducted by an authorized assessor.

The quality *policy* a company adopts needs a quality *system* to bring it about. The International Standards Organization (ISO), based in Geneva, Switzerland, has developed the so-called ISO 9000 series which sets out methods by which a system can be implemented to ensure that the specific requirements are fulfilled. It is the same as BS 5750 on which it was modelled – an identical international standard. (Successful assessment for BS 5750 also gives a company the right to use the equivalent ISO or EN standards' mark.[43]

A quality system includes all the various components – organizational structure, responsibilities, procedures, processes and resources – needed to delivery quality products and services. It is necessary for quality systems to interactively encompass all an organization's activities, which include processing, controlling and communicating. All of these activities are documented in a quarterly manual. The quality system should proceed according to Deming's PDCA cycle, i.e. beginning with documentation, implementation, audit and review.

The ISO-based standards encompass the following general categories:

- Management responsibility
- Quality system
- Contract review
- Design control
- Document control
- Purchasing
- Customer supplied products or services
- Identification and traceability process control
- Checking/measuring/inspecting of incoming materials or services
- Measuring/inspecting/test equipment
- Inspection/test status
- Non-conforming products and services
- Corrective action
- Protection of product or service quality
- Quality records
- Quality system audits and reviews
- Training
- Servicing
- Statistical techniques.

Marketing Quality Assurance (MQA)

The field of public relations and areas of marketing, sales and customer services can benefit from a third-party certification agency, MQA, which provides assessment services to organizations which want to develop quality systems. If the company achieves the quality assurance specification set out by MQA, they are awarded a certificate of excellence and the right to use the MQA mark.

MQA offers registration to ISO 9001, EN 29001 and BS 5750 (Part 1) for a company's marketing, sales and customer service activities. The specification sets out a marketing audit, marketing strategy, customer assurance, a code of conduct, and a marketing and sales quality system. The specification is made up of 58 requirements, which are ordered under 15 headings and related directly to the ISO 9000 series. These are:

- Quality policy
- Business plans
- Organization
- Management representatives
- Management review
- Quality system
- Marketing and sales plans
- Code of conduct
- Marketing and sales operations
- Customer assurance
- Purchasing
- Resources, personnel, training, organizational structure
- Controls and procedures
- Records
- Quality audits.

State of the Quality Organization

On a global basis there are about 70 organizations supporting national quality award programmes and over 70 organizations promoting national ISO and quality management programmes. The forecast is that these organizations will continue to grow and will contribute to their national economies. The conclusion of a recent, comparative, world-wide study of these organizations stated: 'There continues to be a strong demand for the products and services of the various National Quality Organizations. And that with time, the infrastructure that supports the improvement of organizations and their products and processes can and will be diffused in all corners of the world.'[44] The reasons for the predictions are many and varied; however, they include the trends in world trade and global marketing activity which show evidence of an ongoing need to work on quality issues. While the momentum to eliminate trade barriers increases, so also does the need for standardization and harmon-ization of organization activities and standards. Whether for reasons of continuous improvement, benchmarking, quality award competition, customer requirements, leadership or new products or production certification require-ments, quality organizations plan to grow and expand into new markets. Their efforts will be matched by the leadership efforts of the top management of major companies and the mushrooming initiatives of governments to make their countries and regions more competitive. The range of activities from governments include enabling decrees, grants to quality groups, financial incent-ive schemes, the allocation of research resources, support for benchmarking activities, participation in promotional events and information sharing. Consequently the future of quality organizations should look bright as their purposes and philosophies meet continuing needs on a local and global scale.

Notes

1 Tom Stoppard, *The Real Thing* (London: Faber & Faber, 1986), p. 52.
2 John Harvey-Jones (with Anthea Massey), *Trouble Shooter* (London: BBC Books, 1990), p. 99.
3 E.J. Kane, *Quality Progress*, April 1986.
4 IBM Annual Report, 1986.
5 Peter W. Moir, *Profit by Quality, The Essentials of Industrial Survival* (Chichester: Halstead Press (John Wiley), 1988), p. 7.
6 Andy Serwer, *Fortune*, no. 9, May 1998, pp. 27–31.
7 Ibid., p. 28.
8 Jim Lovell and Jeffrey Kluger, *Apollo 13* (London: Hodder & Stoughton, 1995), pp. 351 and 352.
9 Philip B. Crosby, *Quality is Free* (New York: Mentor, 1980), p. 24.
10 H. James Harrington, *The Improvement Process: How America's Leading Companies Improve Quality* (New York: McGraw-Hill, 1987).
11 'Brussels faces fresh charges of BSE cover-up', *The Financial Times*, 3 September 1996.
12 Dr Tony O'Reilly, Chairman, President and Chief Executive Officer of H.J. Heinz, quoted in Andrew Kakabadse, *The Wealth Creators* (London: Kogan Page, 1991), p. 19.
13 *See* BBC, *Benchmarking for Competitive Advantage*, a practical guide video package from BBC for Business, 80 Wood Lane, London W12 OTT, 1995.
14 Mark Skipworth and Christopher Lloyd, 'British Rail pulls a fast one', *Sunday Times*, 15 September 1991.
15 Walter Isaacson, 'In search of Bill Gates', *Time*, 13 January 1997.
16 'Quality control eludes the grips of profit erosion', *Iron Age*, 3 October 1977, p. 48.
17 The quote is from an interview with Konosuke Matsushito in 1982. He established an electrical goods firm famous throughout the world.
18 *Newsweek*, 15 July 1991, p. 5.
19 Shintaro Ishikara and Akio Morita, *The Japan That Can Say No* (London: Simon & Schuster, 1991). *See also* Akio Morita and son, *Made in Japan* (London: Fontana/Collins, 1988).
20 Charles Garfield, *Peak Performers, The New Heroes in Business* (London: Hutchinson Business, 1986), p. 267.

21 Shintaro Ishikara and Jun Eto, *The Japan That Can Really Say No* (London: Simon & Schuster, 1991).

22 Robin Young, 'The role of involvement in leadership and motivation of world-class sports team' (unpublished MBA paper, Cranfield School of Management, 1991), based on interview with David Kirk.

23 Jamie Burrows, 'The All-Blacks: a superb team' (unpublished MBA paper), 1997, Cranfield University.

24 'Fitzpatrick the fabulous All-Black bids farewell', *The Independent*, 28 April 1998.

25 For a current, well-argued case for creative conflict, *see* Richard Pascale, *Managing on the Edge: How Successful Companies Use Conflict to Stay Ahead* (London: Viking, Penguin, 1990).

26 Hilarie Owen, *Creating Top Flight Teams: The Unique Teambuilding Techniques of the RAF Red Arrows* (London: Kogan Page, 1996), p. 85.

27 Brett Whitford and Rebecca Bird, *The Pursuit of Quality: How Organisations in the United Kingdom Are Attaining Excellence Through Quality, Certification and Total Quality Management Systems* (London: Kogan Page, 1996), p. 270.

28 Ibid.

29 Gavin Green, 'Road test Bentley Continental', *The Independent*, 4 January 1997, p. 18.

30 Gavin Green, 'Rolls-Royce redux', *The Independent*, 4 January 1997, p. 18.

31 J.R. Hackman, 'The psychology of self management in organizations', in M.S. Pollock and R.O. Perloff (eds), *Psychology and Work: Productivity Change and Employment* (Washington, DC: American Psychologist Association, 1986), p. 90.

32 Ibid., pp. 90–1.

33 Richard Hackman (ed.), *Groups That Work (and Those That Don't): Creating Conditions for Effective Teamwork* (San Francisco: Jossey-Bass, 1990).

34 Ibid., p. 500.

35 Thomas C. Reeve, *A Question of Character* (London: Bloomsbury, 1991).

36 *Walk the Talk*, BBC Education, Scotland, April–May 1991.

37 Owen Edwards, 'A need for medals', *New York Times Magazine*, 14 July 1985, p. 38.

38 Patrick L. Townsend with Joan E. Gebhart, *Commit to Quality* (New York: John Wiley & Sons, 1990), p. 85.

39 Thomas Kuhn, *The Structure of Scientific Revolutions* (Chicago: University of Chicago Press, 1970), p. 175.

40 Wendy Pryer, 'Easy cure proves hard to sell', *West Australian*, 2 October, 1998.

41 Joel Arthur Barker, *Discovering the Future: The Business of Paradigms*, Video Training Package (Burnsville, Maine: Charter House, International Learning Corporation, 1990).

42 Bill Bryson, *Made in America* (London: Secker & Warburg, 1994), p. 413.

43 EN 29002 is the SGS Yarsley Quality Assured Firm mark.

44 Sari Scheinberg and Anna Korsoun, *State of the Quality Organization: A Comparative Review of the Organizations, Their Products and Services and Quality Award Programs*, sponsored by the Swedish International Development Agency (SIDA), the Swedish Institute for Quality (SIQ) and Xerox Corporation (Göteborg: Recomate AB, October 1998), pp. i and ii.

Chapter 3

....

Learning from the quality gurus

A leader's main obligation is to secure the faith and respect of those under him. The leader must himself be the finest example of what he would like to see in his followers.   Homer Sarasohn in Japan, 1948

A prophet is not without honour, save in his own country, and in his own house.
                                                                      St Matthew, 13: 57

Following the Second World War, General Douglas MacArthur as commander of the American forces in occupied Japan decided to dismiss all the country's senior and middle management of large companies as a punitive measure for their part in the war. In a closed society where old age was revered and where management hierarchies were respected, MacArthur had set in motion a revolution. Men in their mid-30s were thrust into leadership roles which would transform Japan from a largely illiterate, semi-industrialized country turning out cheap and unreliable copies of Western products, into today's nation with the world's highest per capita income and a producer of best quality goods. These men searched for products and ideas and asked for help from the West. They ran with the advice they were given, particularly on the quality front.

W. Edwards Deming (1900–93)

As someone who learnt a great deal from Dr Deming, I should like to express my heartfelt sorrow at his passing. One of the major reasons why Toyota is now well-known throughout the world of quality is because of the quality control procedures taught by Dr Deming. We will keep Dr Deming's concepts and spirit alive. As manufacturers it is our mission to produce good products efficiently, based on the principles of high quality.[1]

Dr W. Edwards Deming was the first American quality expert to teach Japanese managers methodically about quality. He first arrived in Japan in 1947 wearing his statistician's hat to help General MacArthur's government of occupation prepare for a census. At the time Deming was head mathematician and adviser in sampling at the US Bureau of Census. At the Bureau, Deming taught staff the use of sampling methods and statistical control techniques and achieved fantastic productivity increases and cost savings in taking the 1940 census.

His success at the Bureau of Census led to Deming being asked to teach his quality method courses for US industrialists, engineers and inspectors. Deming's methods were credited with better quality products, a higher volume of production, and reduction in scrap and rework, all of which became important in America's war effort. Reflecting on those days, Deming said:

> The courses were well-received by engineers, but management paid no attention to them. Management did not understand that they had to get behind improvements of quality and carry out their obligations from the top down. Any instabilities can help to point out specific times or locations of local problems. Once these local problems are removed, there is a process that will continue until somebody changes it. Changing the process is management's responsibility and we failed to teach them that.[2]

Three years later he was doing in Japan what he did so well in America during the war – talking to people about quality and productivity. His sponsor was the Union of Japanese Scientists and Engineers (JUSE), an organization started four years earlier to set about restructuring the country's war-torn industry. This time at his insistence managers became a separate key group. He based his early messages in 1950 on advanced statistical quality control techniques. He reached over a hundred industrial leaders in 1950 and four hundred more the following year. Leaders of companies that were to become household names in the West attended – including Sony, Nissan, Mitsubishi and Toyota. He won from the Japanese business community and the government a national commitment to his quality messages.

It is easy to generalize and to overstate Deming's role in rebuilding Japan's industry. As David Hutchins wrote:

> Dr Deming did not, as many Westerners think, introduce the Japanese to statistical quality control. These concepts and their importance were well known to the Japanese long before he even went there. However, the Japanese were struggling with the problem of conveying the mathematical concepts to their people . . . Dr Deming's contribution was to help them cut through the academic theory, to present the ideas in a simple way which could be meaningful right down to production worker levels.[3]

Yet Deming's work was significant and very visible. Since 1965, the most fiercely fought for and coveted award in Japan has been the Deming Award, given annually to chosen Japanese companies, worker groups and individuals who have distinguished themselves in the area of total quality.

Deming's contribution to Japan is certainly a substantial one. His role as a key player in the Japanese turn-round was recognized in 1980 when NBC television broadcast a documentary *If Japan Can, Why Can't We?*, which pegged

Deming as the 'father of the third wave of the industrial revolution'. Since then his influence has spread – first across America, with Deming users groups dedicated to understanding and promoting Deming's approach to quality, and then globally. For example, there is the MANS foundation in Holland, the British Deming Association[4] and the W. Edwards Deming Institute of New Zealand. The chief executive officer of the Ford Motor Company announced that he was 'proud to be called a Deming disciple'.

In the United Kingdom, the Department of Trade and Industry published a technical brief by Henry R. Neave entitled *The Deming Philosophy* which it sends out free to British companies. In the autumn of 1988, the work of Dr Deming and its application in the United Kingdom was the subject of a Central ITV documentary.[5]

Deming had all the academic credentials needed for an international teacher which included a masters degree from the University of Colorado, a PhD in Mathematical Physics (1928) from Yale University and about two hundred publications. He retired from his position at New York University in 1975 to become Professor Emeritus. At the age of 91, he was still writing and publishing articles and books and holding research seminars, and still operating as an individual, with a business card with the job title 'statistician'. In the 1980s he ran four-day quality seminars about twice a month for managers who numbered in the hundreds. He had forty such seminars booked for 1992.

'If I had to reduce my message to managers to just a few words, I'd say it all had to do with reducing variation,' Deming said. He believed that quality and productivity always increased as variability decreased. Statistical methods of quality control kept a check on variable matters. Neave wrote:

> Interpreting quality in terms of reliability, dependability, predictability and consistency of product and service, it is clear that quality improvement is analogous to reduction of variation. As Deming argued decades ago, what makes this approach to quality so valid is that improved quality in this sense is generally accompanied by improved productivity and lower costs – unlike traditional approaches in which quality improvement generally implies lower productivity and higher costs.[6]

Deming's approach to quality built on Shewhart's work and aimed at understanding the causes of two types of variation:

1 Uncontrolled variation which is due to assignable or special causes. For example, change of operation, procedures or raw materials and breakages are all outside influences on a process which interrupts its normal pattern of operation.
2 Controlled variation which is due to unassignable, chance, random or common causes. For example, all of these causes are due to the process itself, its design and installation.

Thus quality improvement for Deming must begin with an accurate identification of the two types of variation. If one finds a great deal of deviation from the normal operation of a system due to special causes (unassignable, chance or random causes) it is quite impossible to evaluate those changes management might make in the system attempting to improve it. 'Process capability' in these circumstances loses its meaning.

Once special causes of variation have been eliminated and only common causes are left, quality improvement can come about only by management reworking or redesigning the system. If a manager wrongly identifies the cause of the variation, getting one type of cause mixed up with the other, the action taken by the manager to improve things can, in fact, make them worse.

In an effort to explain this central concept, Myron Tribus, a director of Exergy Inc. based in California and the director of American Quality and Productivity, advanced 'the germ theory of management'. In it he gives a good example of what Deming and others were about, based on the earlier work of Walter Shewhart, the originator of the concepts of statistical control of processes, known today as SPC, and of the control chart.[7]

> Shewhart discovered what, in retrospect, ought to have been clear to everyone. When you assemble a vacuum tube, if every component that goes into the vacuum tube is the same as in every other vacuum tube and if each tube is put together precisely the same way and each is free of contamination, and if each is subjected to exactly the same load conditions, then each will live the same life. The problem is that not all vacuum tubes can be made the same. There are small variations in the chemical composition of the materials. There are small variations in the assembly process. There is always a small amount of dirt that falls by chance in different places. In short, there is always variability and this leads to uncertainty in how long the vacuum tube will last. If the process of assembly is sufficiently out of control, it is almost certain that some of the vacuum tubes will have very short lives. The tubes are victims of the virus of variability. This was Shewhart's discovery.
>
> Shewhart's investigations lead to the concepts of statistical quality control and in terms of our analogy, his work, like Pasteur's has laid the foundations for the 'germ theory of management'.
>
> Few people understand what uncontrolled variability does to the cost of doing business. Fewer still understand what can be done about it and what is the management's role.
>
> Just as Lister understood the broader significance of Pasteur's work in the field of medicine, so it was that Dr W. Edwards Deming understood the significance of Shewhart's work to the general theory of management. Deming was not alone. There were other pioneers, such as Homer Sarasohn and J.M. Juran who also saw the broader implications of Shewhart's work to management. These men realized that the key to better management was the study of the *processes whereby things get done*. If you remove the sources of variability from any process, you make it

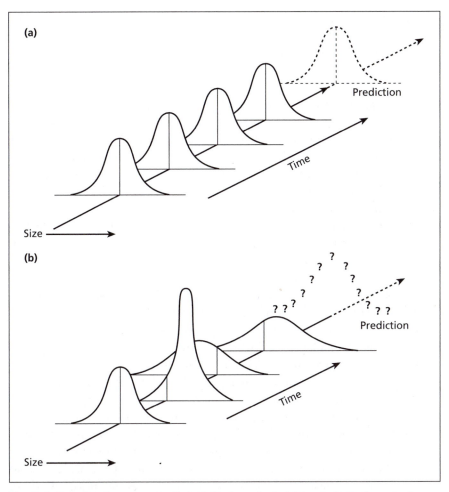

Fig. 3.1 Shewhart's concept of statistical control: (a) in statistical control; (b) out of statistical control

more predictable and therefore more controllable. You can schedule activities closer together and eliminate waste and delay.

The key idea is the elimination of the virus of variability.[8]

Figure 3.1 illustrates the idea of statistical control. The behaviour of the process remains the same over time with controlled or stable variation (Figure 3.1(a)). In contrast, the behaviour of the process is subject to change, usually in unpredictable ways and at unpredictable times with uncontrolled or unstable variation (Figure 3.1(b)).

Deming states that 94 per cent of all quality problems are down to management. But in addition to setting up better processes and systems they should involve employees in participative decision-making. He is positively hostile to inspection. Deming set out his approach to total quality in his now famous 14 points. Two of the points – the elimination of numerical targets and performance appraisal – are logical consequences of his teaching on reducing variation.

Targets can be set which are beyond the capability of a system to achieve. To attempt to reach the target managers push the system out of shape and cause 'knock-on' problems in other parts of production. Likewise, performance appraisal becomes manifestly unfair if there is a great deal of common cause variation which effectively hampers of eclipses an employee's personal contribution. In general, workers work *in* the system, not *on* the system, which remains a managerial activity.

Taken together Deming's 14 points, in addition to promoting product or service quality and more efficient business processes, give industry a human face. In brief, the points are as follows:

1 Be constant and purposeful in improving products and services. Allocate resources to provide for long-term needs rather than short-term profitability. Aim to be competitive, to stay in business and to provide jobs.
2 Adopt the new philosophy. We are in a new economic age begun in Japan. Commonly accepted delays, mistakes and defective workmanship can no longer be tolerated; a transformation of Western management approach is needed to stop the downward spiral of decline in industry.
3 Stop depending on mass inspection as a way to achieve quality; build quality into the product in the first place. Demand statistical evidence of quality being built into manufacturing and purchasing functions.
4 End the practice of awarding business on the basis of price alone. Instead require other meaningful measures of quality beyond price. Work to minimize total cost not just initial cost. Move towards a single supplier for any one item on a long-term relationship of loyalty and trust. Make sure purchasing managers realize they have a new job to do.
5 Find problems. It is management's job to improve the system continually, make better every process for planning, production and service to improve quality, increase productivity and decrease costs.
6 Institute modern methods of on-the-job training. Include management in the training to make better use of all employees. New skills are required to keep up with changes in material, methods, product design, machinery, techniques and service.
7 Set up new ways of supervising production workers. Front-line supervisors should help people produce quality products, forgetting about the numbers game. Improvement of quality will automatically improve productivity. Management should initiate action in response to reports of

inherited defects, maintenance needs, bad tools, confused operational definitions and other things that lead to poor quality.

8 Drive out fear, so that everyone may work effectively for the company.
Encourage top-down and bottom-up communications.

9 Break down barriers between departments. People in research, design, sales
and production should work as a team to deal effectively with problems
with products and service.

10 Eliminate numerical goals, slogans, exhortations (like zero defects) and
production targets for the workforce since most quality problems have to
do with processes and systems which are created by managers and are beyond
the power of the employees. Such exhortations are simply a source of
aggravation.

11 Eliminate work standards that prescribe numerical quotas for both the
workforce and for managers. In their place put useful aids and supportive
supervision. Use statistical methods for continuous improvement of quality
and productivity.

12 Remove barriers that impede hourly-paid workers and managers from
enjoying pride of workmanship. Abolish performance appraisal and
management by objectives.

13 Institute a vigorous programme of education and retraining. People should
be improved with ongoing education and self-improvement. Competitive
advantage is always rooted in knowledge.

14 Structure top management to empower them to achieve the above 13 points.
Push every day to progress the 13 preceding points and take action to make
the total transformation happen.

Implementation

There are major obstacles to implementing the Deming philosophy. Deming
discusses these in Chapter 3 of his book *Out of Crisis* under the unfortunate
label of 'deadly diseases'. The major barriers (*see* Figure 3.2) are lack of
constancy, preoccupation with short-term profits, the many forms of performance appraisal, the mobility of management and their reliance on only visible
figures as a criteria for success. Lack of constancy is Deming's phrase for it,
but other writers have indicated that there is a great fickleness in management
today embracing one theory after another with alacrity. The valid aspects of
each of the management ideas get rendered invalid and pointless because they
are implemented in a piecemeal way with frequent shifts from one idea to another
giving the impression of fad, fashion or flavour of the month.

The lack of management constancy over the idea is revealed when managers
fail to make the cultural or organizational changes required for the new idea
to flourish. It is also unmasked when managers pay only lip-service to the
new idea and push faulty products out the door when under pressure. (The

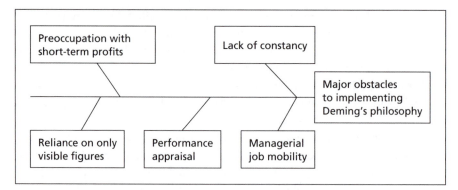

Fig. 3.2 Major obstacles to implementing Deming's philosophy

contradiction here to a sound quality philosophy speaks volumes to those who witness the reversal.)

Deming sees inconstancy as a lack of commitment on the part of managers to stay in business by planning to provide products and services in the future that will help people live better materially, succeed in the market-place and be a source of steady jobs.

Preoccupation with the need to generate short-term profits is another obstacle to implementing Deming's approach. Short-term profits are seen as the enemy of management constancy of purpose to stay in business and generate long-term growth. Deming scorns the banks who share in the preoccupation with quarterly dividends and short-term profit, instead of helping with the long-term planning which is the best way to protect investments.

Performance appraisal in the shape of personal review systems, annual review, merit rating and evaluation of performance are, in Deming's view, formidable obstacles to his message on total quality.

Management by objectives (MBO) is likewise a roadblock. Deming equates it with 'management by fear'. The negative results that follow include:

1 MBO fosters short-term performance, rivalry and political behaviour. It annihilates long-term planning, engenders fear and destroys teamwork.
2 MBO leaves people bitter and twisted, bruised, despondent, depressed and dejected – unfit for work weeks after receiving the rating on their work. The report card approach gives them an inferior mark ascribing to the people in a work group differences which may be totally accounted for by the system in which they work.

Another major obstacle in implementing Deming's methodology is the practice of management mobility or 'job-hopping'. It all causes instability and results in managers making decisions without having an in-depth understanding of the business. In the crunch of the decision-making process, managers may draw on their experience in other jobs which are simply not relevant.

Deming argues wisely that it takes time to become embedded in any organization, to really get to know its business, problems, employees and customers. While experience gained elsewhere may be brought to bear profitably on current problems, unless a manager has had time to become part of the new company, he or she will not be able to test the validity of the application of previous experience.

Deming rails against the practice in the United States of boards of directors bringing in new managers to improve the quantity of dividends and letting them go having done the nasty work.

By using only visible figures a company creates another serious obstacle to implementing Deming's approach to quality. Figures are important and accounts do matter and employees and suppliers have to be paid. But focusing on visible figures alone is a quick route to failure. The end-of-quarter panic leads managers to manipulate everything to get the 'numbers'. Other important things like quality, research and education are pushed aside by the numbers game.

Joseph M. Juran

Dr Joseph M. Juran is a Balkan-born American in his nineties who operates his quality consultancy business, the Juran Institute, from offices in the United Nations plaza in New York City. He was an inspector at the Western Electricity Company and a professor at New York University. His reputation as perhaps the top quality guru rests on the publication in the 1950s of his massive book, *Quality Control Handbook*, which is still the standard reference book on quality world-wide.

Juran developed his TQM message around the following ten steps:

1 Create awareness of the need and opportunity for quality improvement.
2 Set goals for continuous improvement.
3 Build an organization to achieve goals by establishing a quality council, identifying problems, selecting a project, appointing teams and choosing facilitators.
4 Give everyone training.
5 Carry out projects to solve problems.
6 Report progress.
7 Show recognition.
8 Communicate results.
9 Keep a record of successes.
10 Incorporate annual improvements into the company's regular systems and processes and thereby maintain momentum.

Shortly after publishing the book he went to Japan to build on Deming's work there. His main message to Japanese managers was that quality control is an integral part of management at all levels, not just the work of specialists in quality control departments. Juran's series of lectures to top Japanese management were cascaded throughout their companies to other levels of managers down to the shopfloor by the same organization that sponsored Deming's talks – the Union of Japanese Scientists and Engineers (JUSE) which had many senior executives as members – and the Japanese Standards Association.

Large companies had already started in-house literacy programmes for their workers on the shopfloor led by foremen who held 'reading circle' meetings. Juran's quality messages and techniques were translated into reading materials for these groups and sold at newspaper kiosks and even broadcast on radio. It was a short step from the 'reading circle' becoming problem-solving quality improvement meetings – quality circles were created and grew under JUSE's sponsorship to their present level. Juran, speaking about quality circles in the late 1960s, said: 'The quality circle movement is a tremendous one which no other country seems able to imitate. Through the development of this movement, Japan will be swept to world leadership in quality.'[9]

November 1960 was designated as the first 'quality month' in Japan. Nearly forty years of quality months – always November – have given companies, and the nation as a whole, the opportunity to stage local, regional and national quality events and conventions. 'As a result the Japanese have become the best trained managers on earth in quality,' Juran said.[10]

Juran's teaching on quality continues today through quality training and seminars and the production of training materials. Juran defines quality as 'fitness for use or purpose' and argues for that definition instead of 'conformance to specification'. In Juran's view a dangerous product could conform to all specifications but still be unfit for use. His biggest contribution was to take quality beyond the technical aspects of quality control which were well developed in the 1940s to the management arena.

Juran believes that quality happens only through projects – quality improvement projects established in every part of the company. Addressing the Rank Xerox 1985 Mitcheldean Quality Convention, Juran outlined his basic approach which matched exactly what Xerox had been doing – the Juran trilogy – quality planning, quality control, quality improvement. He outlined his basic approach as first set up a quality council, and second identify projects, the more, the better. 'There is no such thing as improvement in general,' he said; 'it all takes place project by project and in no other way.' Perhaps Juran is open to criticism here implying as he does that virtually all quality improvement is achieved through a project-by-project method. In reality projects are only part, however important, of a TQM process.

The Juran trilogy

Juran expresses his essential message to managers through the three basic quality-related processes: quality planning, quality control and quality improvement which has become known as the Juran trilogy (*see* Figure 3.3). His starting point is quality planning for a process. This could be any process – an office process for producing invoices, a product development process for generating new products, or a factory process for cutting gear wheels.

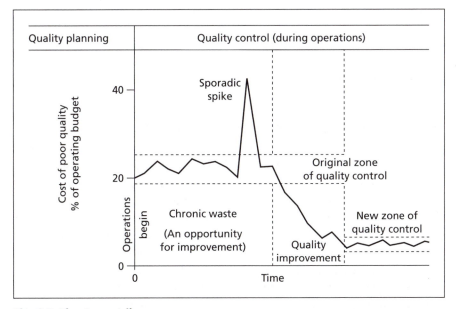

Fig. 3.3 The Juran trilogy

After the planning, the process is turned over to the operators whose job it is to run the process at optimal effectiveness. But due to deficiencies in the original planning, the process runs at a high level of chronic waste – a waste that has been planned into the process in so far as the planning process failed to eliminate it. Because the waste is inherent in the process, the operators are unable to get rid of it. Instead they set up a quality control system to keep it from getting worse. If it does get worse, a firefighting team is thrown together to sort out the cause of this abnormal variation, this increase in waste, and corrective action is taken so that the process again falls into the zone defined by the 'quality control' limits.

Juran draws a fine parallel between his trilogy processes and financial processes in which quality planning equates to budgeting, quality control to cost control or expense control, and quality improvement to cost reduction or profit improvement. What should happen under Juran's quality improvement

Table 3.1 The end results of Juran's trilogy processes

Trilogy process	End result
Quality planning: the process for preparing to meet quality goals	A process capable of meeting quality goals under operating conditions
Quality control: the process for meeting quality goals during operations	Conduct of operations in accordance with the quality plan
Quality improvement: the process for breaking through to unprecedented levels of performance	Conduct of operations at levels of quality distinctly superior to planning performance

process is quite different from what normally happens in companies (*see* Table 3.1).

How does Juran's trilogy relate to performance?

Juran's vast consultancy experience gives him a database on the topic which is impressive. The data takes shape in the following patterns of priorities and assets devoted to the three processes within the trilogy (*see* Table 3.2).

Juran, like Deming, believes in statistical quality control. He estimated that about 15 per cent of quality problems (variation) in a company are due to special causes which means they may involve the workers. In his view 85 per cent or more are down to management dealing with the system.

Summing up the Juran message, Junji Noguchi, an executive director of the JUSE, said: 'He taught us that the most important thing to upgrading quality is not technology, but quality management.' In 1969 Juran turned down a request from JUSE to allow them to use his name for their national quality awards and the honour went to his rival consultant Deming. Juran, however, was himself awarded Japan's highest honour for foreigners, the Second Class Order of the Sacred Treasure and he got it for quality. He was a one-man-show until 1980 when he established Juran Institute Inc., at first in Wilton, Connecticut, and now in New York City.

Table 3.2 Juran's trilogy related to performance

Trilogy processes	Self-assessment by managers	Prevailing processes
Quality planning	Weak	Limited priority
Quality control	Very strong	Top priority by a wide margin
Quality improvement	Very weak	Very low priority

Kaoru Ishikawa (1915–89)

Professor Kaoru Ishikawa is known as the 'Father of Quality Circles' for his role in launching Japan's quality movement in the 1960s. In the late 1950s he articulated the philosophy which led to the development of quality circles in the early 1960s. In a series of articles in 1960 in a prominent Japanese magazine, entitled 'Gemba to QA', he argued that the American management style whereby 'management manage and people do' could not be grafted onto Japanese work practices. He suggested a blend of the best of the American practices, such as the American flowline production techniques, and Japanese practices be fused with traditional European craftsmanship. He developed the idea of bringing craftsmanship back to groups rather than to individuals. His 'fishbone' diagram, which bears his name as the Ishikawa diagram, was invented in 1943 as a management problem-solving tool. It is used by quality circles and quality improvement teams world-wide.

His quality circles were first piloted at the Nippon Telegraph and Cable Company in 1962. By 1978 there were one million quality circles with 10 million employees mostly in manufacturing. Today there are 2 million quality circles involving 20 million members and extending into the service sectors of Japan.

In his book *What is Total Quality Control?*[11] Ishikawa said that seven basic tools were 'indispensable for quality control'. These are Pareto analysis, fishbone diagrams, stratification, tally charts, histograms, scatter diagrams and control charts. With these tools, Ishikawa argued, managers and staff could tackle and solve the quality problems facing them.

His writings on quality control won him many accolades including the Deming prize, the Nikon Keizai Press Prize and the Industrial Standardization Prize. He won the Grant Award (1971) from the American Society for Quality Control for his educational programme on quality control. One of Professor Ishikawa's books available in English entitled *Guide to Quality Control* was first published in 1974, revised twice and has been reprinted over a dozen times.[12] The book is based on his original Japanese book which had become a handbook for Japanese quality circles. In a straightforward manner and an open learning style, Ishikawa teaches quality circle members about data collection, histograms, cause and effect diagrams, check sheets, binomial probability and sampling.

Philip B. Crosby

As a popularizer of TQM Philip B. Crosby is less academic than Dr Deming, Dr Juran or Professor Ishikawa in his approach to total quality but just as effective. He is well known in the United Kingdom. Lee Iacocca wrote of him in *Talking Straight*:

> For my money nobody talks quality better than Phil Crosby. . . . We thought enough of it [Crosby's quality college] that we established our own Chrysler Quality Institute in Michigan, modelled after his operation – our company's put about twenty thousand of our people through it – they're going back to school at a rate of nearly two thousand a month – and I admit they do return with QUALITY stamped on their foreheads.[13]

Crosby has spent nearly the last fifty years working in the quality arena, 14 of those years for ITT where in one year ITT saved $720 million using Crosby's own TQM programme. He got his business education in quality as he came up through the ranks from inspector to tester to assistant foreman to junior engineer to section chief to manager to director and finally to corporate vice-president. Today he is chairman of his own quality college and consultancy firm called Philip Crosby Associates (PCA) Inc., which he started in 1979 and is based in Winter Park, Florida.

Crosby has written six books during this time, of which *Quality is Free* is the most popular, having sold over a million copies. The books are part autobiographical tracing his career as a quality expert, as they also show the progression of his thinking on quality matters.

He rightly ranks himself with Deming and Juran and he writes:

> It is not possible to take people with as much experience as Dr Deming and Dr Juran and I and put us in boxes with clear labels like in a zoo.
>
> We all believe that the problem of quality belongs to management. We all believe that prevention is the way to get it. And we are all impatient that everyone is not leaping into what we see as a sensible mature philosophy of doing things.
>
> Dr Deming has emphasized statistics over the years and has brought that approach to thousands of people. Dr Juran is known for his engineering methods. If you do what they teach, you will do very well. They are dedicated people and worthy of respect. Dr Deming and I write notes back and forth. Dr Juran seems to think I am a charlatan and hasn't missed many opportunities to say that over the years.[14]

Crosby then differentiates himself from the other two citing his zero defects goal as something practical, reasonable and achievable. Crosby prefers to target his training on managers rather than on quality control people. Finally, as a practitioner, he presents his shopfloor-to-boardroom credentials – from inspector to chief executive officer for more than 28 years.

Crosby lists four new essentials of quality management which he calls 'the absolutes':

1 Quality is defined as conformance to requirements, not as goodness.
2 Quality is achieved by prevention not appraisal.

3 The quality performance standard is zero defects (a concept he invented in the 1960s when he worked for the Martin company on missile projects) and is best known for no acceptable quality levels.

4 Quality is measured by the price of non-conformance, not by indexes.

Crosby's definition of quality is 'conformance to requirements'. He discusses conformance and non-conformance rather than low and high quality. He has developed 14 steps to a quality improvement programme and these are set out as follows:

Step 1 is to make clear management's commitment to quality. This step starts with a policy statement on quality and Crosby's suggested form of words for the policy is: 'Perform exactly like the requirement . . . or cause the requirement to be officially changed to what we and our customers really need.' Such a short statement captures Crosby's definition of quality based on conformance and avoids the elephant traps senior managers fall into in trying to frame a quality policy – writing a treatise instead of a short statement, allowing for non-conformance with an accepted quality level (AQL) built into the policy, indicative statements on how to deviate from the policy, a delegation of the responsibility for evaluating the policy away from the chief executive.

Step 2 is to set up quality improvement teams with representatives from each department. Before this can happen the main messages of TQM have to reach everyone in the organization. Crosby has developed a ten question 'true or false' test to measure employee/manager thinking on total quality (*see* Table 3.3, and *see* Note 15 for Crosby's answers). Crosby considers these improvement teams to be part-time involvement for the members, but a

Table 3.3 Crosby's 'true or false' questionnaire to measure employee/manager thinking on total quality[15]

1 Quality is a measure of goodness of the product that can be defined in ranges such as fair, good, excellent.	True/False
2 The economics of quality requires that management establish acceptable quality levels as performance standards.	True/False
3 The cost of quality is the expense of doing things wrong.	True/False
4 Inspection and test operations should report to manufacturing so they can have the tools to do the jobs.	True/False
5 Quality is the responsibility of the quality department.	True/False
6 Worker attitudes are the primary cause of defects.	True/False
7 I have trend charts that show me the rejection levels at every key operation.	True/False
8 I have a list of my ten biggest quality problems.	True/False
9 Zero defects is a worker motivation programme.	True/False
10 The biggest problem today is that the customer doesn't understand our problems.	True/False

full-time job for the chairperson, who has to be a manager who has the confidence of his or her staff and is a true believer in the need to improve quality and achieve zero defects and defect prevention.

As Crosby sees it, the responsibilities of the team members are the following:

1 To lay out the entire quality improvement programme.
2 To represent their departments on the team.
3 To represent the team to their departments.
4 To carry out the decisions of the team within their own department.
5 To make creative contributions to quality improvement.[16]

Step 3 is to set in place quality measurement to provide a display of current and potential non-conformance problems. The measurement should facilitate objective evaluation and corrective action. Most companies already have established a quality control department which measures reject rates. The task is to communicate the information in a way that is understandable and useful to employees using terms such as 'defects per unit' or 'percentage defective' and by displaying trend charts. Frequent defects should be classified as to seriousness, cause, and responsibility to prepare for corrective action.

Step 4 is to determine the 'cost of quality' and explain how to use it as a management tool. Crosby's components of the overall cost of quality are: scrap; rework; warranty; service apart from regular maintenance; inspection labour; engineering changes; purchase order changes; software correction; consumer affairs; audit; quality control labour; test labour; acceptance equipment costs; and other costs of doing things wrong. Crosby argues that the cost of quality should be no more than 2.5 per cent of sales. The best way to reduce the cost of quality is through prevention.

Step 5 is to raise the level of quality awareness and the personal concern for the company's quality reputation for all employees. The quality awareness programme is run by the improvement team with the help of the professionals in public relations, personnel, quality, etc. The programme should have a low-key start and be ongoing. The idea is to have a two-pronged approach using both the regular meetings between management and employees to discuss non-conformance problems, and company-wide communications with posters, newsletters and special events.

Step 6 is to take corrective action on the problems raised in the previous steps. Crosby recommends four levels of activities to attack the problems and to obliterate them. These are daily, weekly and monthly meetings between rising levels of managers focused on eliminating the critical main problems first. Corrective action is also initiated through task forces.

Step 7 is to plan a zero defects programme. Crosby offers the following seven suggestions for doing so:

1 Get the message out through all supervisory people that there is going to be a zero defects approach.
2 Determine what materials are needed and secure them.
3 Choose a launch that has a good fit with your company culture.
4 Spell out the functions that will be accomplished.
5 Design some system of recognition for improved performance.
6 Set up a detailed time schedule for the programme and rehearse people who will take part.
7 Identify the error-cause removal process and make plans to set it in motion.

The theme of zero defects is to do it right the first time. It is a performance standard. Crosby's enthusiasm for zero defects has led him to recommend that employees actually sign a zero defects pledge:

> Most human error is caused by lack of attention rather than lack of knowledge. Lack of attention is created when we assume that error is inevitable. If we consider this condition carefully, and pledge ourselves to make a constant conscious effort to do our jobs right the first time, we will take a giant step towards eliminating the waste of rework, scrap, and repair that increases costs and reduces individual opportunity. Success is a journey not a destination.[17]

Step 8 is to train supervisors actively to carry out their part in the total quality improvement process. By supervisor Crosby means all managers from the chairman on down the line. The training he offers starts with a six-hour blitz on quality awareness and is followed by a specialized training session on zero defects scheduled about four weeks before zero defects day. The aim is to make the supervisors confident in the messages and able to explain the new systems such as the error-cause removal system. He recommends that a handbook be prepared by the company with the key messages in it. To show that he believes in the old axiom that 'repetition is the mother of learning', he recommends that the entire training programme be repeated.

Step 9 is to hold a zero defects day to create an event that will let all employees know through a personal experience that there has been a change. The idea here is to commit the company and its employees in public to the new deal and to show some style and celebration in doing so. He recommends a large open gathering and a bit of 'show biz' to have fun as well as to demonstrate commitment to the total quality ideas from the top down.

Step 10 is goal setting and encouraging individuals and groups to set improvement goals. Supervisors should lead the groups to set about two firm goals for each work area that are specific and measurable and that do not duplicate the scheduled improvement goals that flowed from the zero defects day. For example, to reduce defects per unit by 20 per cent in one month, or to win the good housekeeping award next month.

Step 11 is to encourage employees to communicate to management the difficulties they have in achieving their improvement goals in the error-cause removal campaign. One of Crosby's suggestions here is to set up a suggestion box into which workers can pop a one-page error-cause removal form. He claims that 90 per cent of these forms are acted on. In the forms the employee need not know the answer, as in traditional suggestion boxes. The following are his suggested rules for such a scheme:

1 Everyone who submits an error-cause removal form receives an immediate personal thank you note. The form is forwarded to the department that has responsibility for the problem. A further acknowledgement is sent to whoever submitted the form once a decision is made about it.
2 Every error-cause removal form is taken seriously.
3 If someone decides to do nothing about an error-cause removal form, he or she should clear this decision with at least one but preferably two levels of supervision.

Step 12 is to recognize and appreciate all those who participate in the programme. Step 13 is to establish quality councils to communicate on a regular basis. And step 14 is to do it all over again to emphasize that quality programmes never end and that they are indeed a journey not a destination.

C.J. Ham, Senior Director of Corporate Organization and Efficiency at Philips' Eindhoven (Netherlands) headquarters, has said: 'Some of our national organizations are using Crosby or Deming approaches; others are using Juran. The point here is that there is no one single "right" way to improve quality – indeed, all the quality "gurus" are right each within his own terms of reference.'

John S. Oakland

John Oakland has done more to further the philosophy of total quality management and its practical implementation in companies on a world-wide basis than any other academic or consultant in Britain.

He heads the European Centre for TQM at the University of Bradford Management Centre, where he is also EXXON Chemical Professor of Total Quality Management. He and his team have helped thousands of companies undertake company-wide quality programmes, as well as conducting research in the area of quality implementation and evaluation.

Quality consultants tend to come from either the operations management/quality control side of industry or from the Human Resources function. Oakland comes from the nuts and bolts, no nonsense operations management perspective. His early career in research and production management and a PhD in Chemistry have given him a grounding in industry that shines through his pragmatic approach to implementing TQM and his writings about quality theory. His book *Total Quality Management* appeared in 1989 and quickly became the standard, seminal British book on TQM. The new edition of this book appeared four years later and was accompanied by a companion book, *Cases in Total Quality Management*, co-authored with Leslie J. Porter, a Bradford colleague.[18] The book of case studies illustrates one of Oakland's best contributions to the TQM movement – his ability to first clearly explain the theory and then to translate that theory into practice. The case study book shows how this has been done in 17 different actual companies. These cases show what actually occurred in the complicated business of installing TQM programmes and each case illustrates different aspects of company-wide quality improvement efforts. Taken together the cases provide a compendium of TQM practices. The cases, of course, follow the TQM methodology developed by Oakland and his Bradford cohorts.

Oakland's *Statistical Process Control*[19] consolidated his reputation in the field. He is a fellow of the Institute of Quality Assurance, the Royal Statistical Society and the Association of Quality Management Consultants. He has worked closely with the British government in researching quality and helping companies understand and implement total quality systems and concepts by writing booklets, appearing in videos and giving presentations on quality topics. His influence across Europe has been substantial and the global dimension of his work is reflected in his own research projects on quality implementation and his membership of the American Society for Quality Control.

Oakland's recent contribution to the quality field is to further integrate TQM into a company's strategy. 'TQM should not be regarded as a woolly-minded approach to running an organisation,' Oakland writes. 'It requires a carefully planned and fully integrated strategy, derived from the mission.'

Oakland defines total quality management as 'a comprehensive approach to improving competitiveness, effectiveness and flexibility through planning, organising, and understanding each activity, and involving each individual at each level.'[20]

His model can be summarized in five points (*see* Figure 3.4):

1 First one must identify customer–supplier relationships.
2 Then set up a system to manage processes.
3 Change the company culture from what it was to a TQM culture.
4 Improve communications company-wide.
5 Demonstrate commitment to quality.

Oakland's implementation plan for TQM involves 14 steps, and, although he does not explicitly make the biblical allusion to building a house on firm rock, he implies it. Understanding quality, commitment and leadership are for him the solid foundation of a company-wide TQM programme (*see* Figure 3.5). Everything else in the quality edifice is built upon it. Policies, plans, actions,

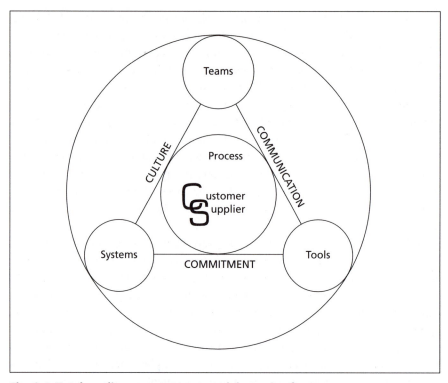

Fig. 3.4 Total quality management model – major features

Source: Oakland, J.S. (1994) *Total Quality Management: the Route to Improving Performance*, Oxford: Butterworth-Heinemann, p. 40.

systems and measurements follow and these require competency in the mechanics of quality management.[21]

Measurements are then put in place followed by an analysis of the 'cost of quality' together with a strategy for reducing it drastically. Tools and techniques required for improvement are introduced at this stage of implementation.

Capability and control are crucial to a programme's start up as are organization for quality and a communications effort. The requisite company culture change through continuous improvement is accomplished by teamwork and ongoing training rather than a one-off effort.

> Designing and planning improvement should be the job of all managers, but a crucial early stage is putting quality management systems in place to drive the improvement process and make sure that problems remain solved forever, by means of structured corrective action procedures and techniques.[22]

Oakland's highly prescriptive work is full of flow charts and diagrams, checklists and questions, caveats and exhortations, similies and simple examples,

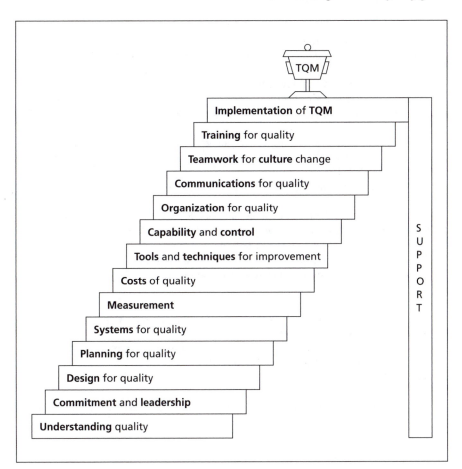

Fig. 3.5 The steps to TQM
Source: John S. Oakland, p. 425, Figure 15.7

and comparisons with the work of the originators of total quality that reveal him to be a patient teacher of quality improvement rather than a fiery prophet with a message of cataclysmic change.

Notes

1 The President of Toyota Motor Co. (Worldwide), *Nikkei Industrial Newspaper* (Tokyo), December 1993.
2 Henry R. Neave, *The Deming Philosophy*, Management into the '90s series (London: Department of Trade and Industry, 1989), p. 4.
3 David Hutchins, *In Pursuit of Quality* (London: Pitman, 1990), pp. 76–7.
4 British Deming Association is located in Salisbury. It is a not-for-profit organization formed in 1987 to promote awareness in Britain of the Deming philosophy. It attempts to help both individuals and organizations to understand Deming's approach. (Telephone: 01722 412138.)

5 *Doctor's Orders*, ITV Venture series, 7.30 pm, 18 October 1988.

6 Henry R. Neave, op. cit., p. 6.

7 Walter Shewhart, *Economic Control of Quality of Manufactured Product* (Van Nostrand, 1931). Reprinted in 1980 by the American Society for Quality Control, and reprinted in 1986 by CEEP Press, Washington, DC.

8 Myron Tribus, 'The germ theory of management' (Boston: Massachusetts Institute of Technology Center for Advanced Engineering Studies, undated series of articles).

9 David Hutchins, op. cit., p. 81.

10 Christopher Lorenz, 'Learning from the Japanese', *The Financial Times*, 3 February 1981.

11 Karou Ishikawa, *What Is Total Quality Control – The Japanese Way* (Englewood Cliffs, NJ: Prentice Hall, 1985).

12 Karou Ishikawa, *Guide to Quality Control* (Tokyo: Asian Productivity Organization, 1983).

13 Lee Iacocca, *Talking Straight* (London: Sidgwick & Jackson, 1988), pp. 256–7.

14 Philip B. Crosby, *Let's Talk Quality: 96 Questions You Always Wanted to Ask Phil Crosby* (New York: McGraw-Hill, 1989), p. 79.

15 From Philip B. Crosby's *Quality is Free* (New York: McGraw-Hill, 1979), p. 158. Answers: question 3 is true, question 7 should be true and the rest are false.

16 Ibid., p. 232.

17 Ibid., pp. 200 and 201.

18 John S. Oakland and Leslie J. Porter, *Cases in Total Quality Management* (Oxford: Butterworth-Heinemann, 1994).

19 J.S. Oakland, *Total Quality Management: The Route to Improving Performance* (Oxford: Butterworth-Heinemann, 1994), p. 40.

20 Ibid., p. 425.

21 Ibid.

22 *Statistical Quality Control A Practical Guide* (1990) Oxford: Butterworth-Heinemann.

Chapter 4

· ·

Cutting the cost of quality

Flight controllers here looking very carefully at the situation. Obviously a major
malfunction.[1]   NASA Mission Control

Case study of the space shuttle *Challenger* accident

The 'cost of quality' is a shorthand formula for all the business costs incurred
in achieving quality. Specifically it includes prevention, appraisal, internal
failure, external failure, exceeding requirements and lost opportunity. This
key concept of the cost of quality can be illustrated by the space shuttle
Challenger accident on 28 January 1986.

It should have taken eight minutes to put the 2,000 ton space shuttle
Challenger into space. (In its ascent it burns 10,000 tons of frozen gases and
solid fuel each second.)[2] The flight of space shuttle *Challenger* on mission
51-L lasted just 73 seconds. It burst into a fireball of hydrogen and oxygen
propellants hurtling the crew compartment, made fireproof to withstand the
heat of re-entry into the earth's atmosphere, into a three-minute freefall. Some
of the astronauts – perhaps all seven – were conscious until it hit the sea at a
speed of 140 miles per hour. All seven were killed.

The loss of the space shuttle *Challenger* was caused by a failure in the joint
between the two lower segments of the right solid rocket motor. The specific
failure was the destruction of the seals called O-rings that are intended to prevent hot gases from leaking through the joint during the propellant burn of
the rocket motor. Like a blow torch the hot gases shot out of a hole less than
an inch in diameter and melted the struts that held the booster rocket to the
spacecraft. The booster rocket swivelled into the main fuel tank and ruptured
it causing the fireball.

The findings of the Presidential Commission appointed to investigate the
accident led it to conclude that the failure of the pressure seal in the aft field
joint[3] of the right solid rocket motor 'was due to a *faulty design* unacceptably
sensitive to a number of factors. These factors were the effects of temperature,
physical dimensions, the character of materials, the effects of re-usability,
processing, and the reaction of the joint to dynamic loading.'[4]

But the cause of the accident was not just poor engineering. The Commission devotes about forty pages to laying a large portion of the blame for the accident to NASA's management, which it cites as 'the contributing cause of the accident'.[5]

In the words of the Presidential Commission:

> The decision to launch the *Challenger* was flawed. Those who made that decision were unaware of the recent history of problems concerning the O-rings and the joint and were unaware of the initial written recommendation of the contractor advising against the launch at temperatures below 53 degrees Fahrenheit and the continuing opposition of the engineers at Thiokol after the management reversed its position. They did not have a clear understanding of Rockwells' concern that it was not safe to launch because of ice on the pad. If the decision makers had known all of the facts, it is highly unlikely that they would have decided to launch 51-L on January 28, 1986.[6]

The faulty design of the booster rocket by an outside contractor and NASA's own management failures in communication and decision-making make the space shuttle accident a classic case study in how *not* to manage a complex technological project.

A detailed analysis of that flawed process might well fit into a total quality management training session. Videos and written materials are available that reconstruct the dramatic events the day before the launch of the *Challenger*.[7] But that level of detailed analysis lies outside the scope of this chapter.

The costs associated with the space shuttle *Challenger* accident were staggering. First of all there were the lives of the seven astronauts so spectacularly and needlessly lost by the failure of the shuttle. While the loss of any human life is inestimable in value, the legal profession attempts to establish claims to money damages due to accidents based on loss of earnings, bereavement, human suffering, etc. All seven astronauts' families have settled their legal claims against NASA and Morton Thiokol, the producer of the booster rockets, out of court. Of lawsuits brought by the families of four victims of the 1986 *Challenger* tragedy, a total of $7.7 million in tax-free annuities will go to the survivors of Astronauts Francis Scobee and Ellison Onizuka, Payload Specialist Gregory Jarvis, and schoolteacher Christa McAuliffe who had planned to teach from space. Suits brought by relatives of Crew Members Judith Resnik and Ronald McNair were also settled out of court. The suit against Morton Thiokol by the family of *Challenger* Pilot, Michael John Smith, was settled in August 1988. It was the last claim against the company by the estates of each of the seven *Challenger* astronauts to be settled. Details of the settlement remain confidential but must have amounted to several million dollars.

In losing the astronauts, NASA lost the millions of dollars invested in their training. Five of the seven astronauts Francis R. Scobee, the Commander, Michael

John Smith, the pilot, Ellison S. Onizuka, Mission Specialist One, Judith Arlene Resnik, Mission Specialist Two, and Ronald Erwin McNair, Mission Specialist Three, were career astronauts and had many years of training. Christa McAuliffe, Payload Specialist One, and Gregory Jarvis, Payload Specialist Two and one of NASA's customers, had comparatively brief training as astronauts, but were, of course, accomplished in their own careers.

The second largest cost of the accident was the lost opportunities that occurred during the nearly three years' downtime for the American space programme. When NASA could not launch satellites, its foreign competition moved in. Arianespace, the commercial satellite launch consortium set up by the European Space Agency (ESA) had always been a formidable competitor for satellites. Launching from the equatorial site at Kowrou in French Guyana, Arianespace needed less thrust to put a satellite in orbit round the earth. It also used unmanned, expendable booster rockets which meant it was a very much smaller and cheaper operation than NASA's Kennedy Space Center.

With ESA subsidies Arianespace was able to gain competitive advantage over NASA offering cheaper launch fees to an expanding international clientele. Before the accident Arianespace advertised dual-communication satellite launches for a total mission cost of $58 million. Compared with NASA's charge of $34 million per satellite on a fully commercial shuttle flight, Arianespace was offering its customers a saving of ten million dollars. NASA's miscalculating of its competitive position can be traced back to August 1983 when it made its first official statement of objectives. Twenty-one launches were targeted for fiscal years 1984 and 1985 at fees per payload expected to capture 75 per cent of commercial payloads world-wide. In those fixed periods the shuttle flew four and then eight missions. The overall goal of flying 500 missions by the end of the 1980s was wildly 'out of sync' with reality. On 23 July 1999, space shuttle Columbia was launched to deploy 'Chondra' – the latest and most powerful of NASAs X-ray observatories, 20–50 times more sensitive than the other X-ray observatories. The flight was the 95th shuttle mission and the first to be commanded by a woman, Colonel Eileen Collins.

Space competitors to the United States all increased their threat during NASA's three years of inactivity due to the accident. Europe, Japan, India and China continued to carve out niches in the space market. Developing nations are getting into the act because installing a satellite-based communications network is far cheaper than laying land-based cables, especially in a country with few rural roads. Many developing nations are to follow Indonesia's lead, who in 1977 bought communications satellites to link the scattered islands of the Indonesian archipelago. They also use the remote sensing satellite, America's landsat, to locate potential oil and water-bearing rocks and to monitor crop growth, pollution and fisheries. Ten nations now have satellite launch facilities.[8]

To keep the confidence of its commercial, civil, government and military customers NASA agreed to an increasingly ambitious schedule of flights. In 1986, three launches were scheduled for scientific missions:

1 ASTRO-1 (March, survey of Halley's Comet).
2 The Ulysses (15 May, international solar-polar flights).
3 The Galileo Jupiter Orbiter (25 May, another deep space probe of the solar system).

All three scientific missions had tight launch 'windows'. In fact, the Halley's Comet launch window would have been lost if the *Challenger* flight had been delayed further. In the end, with the destruction of *Challenger*, a case was made to take away the deep space probe launches from the shuttle programme. The Galileo mission suffered repeatedly from what people began to call NASA's 'great white elephant'. Originally for launch in 1982, the Jupiter-bound orbiter was launched into Earth orbit by the shuttle in October 1989 after which its own rocket stage propelled it away from Earth toward Jupiter.

The Huygens/Cassini mission, which is to investigate the giant planet Saturn and its largest moon, Titan, in meticulous detail, was withdrawn from the shuttle programme due to its seven-year delay on launching the Galileo mission. (In business terms the shuttle programme lost the order due to unreliable delivery dates.) It was sent to Saturn using a tried and proven expendable booster rocket, a Titan 4, when the spacecraft was finally launched on 6 October 1997 from Cape Canaveral. Cassini is due to reach Saturn in July 2004. After entering orbit around the ringed planet, Cassini will make detailed observations of Saturn, its largest moon, Titan, and some smaller icy moons, and study the magnetic environment surrounding the planet over a four-year period. The mission is an international effort of NASA, the European Space Agency (ESA) and the Italian Space Agency.

The cancellation of scientific missions over the early part of the three years' downtime period had serious commercial and political consequences from which NASA has not recovered. Military missions in space came to a standstill as attempts to use Saturn rockets failed during the downtime period.

A third major cost of quality for the shuttle programme was the cost of appraisal and prevention, the cost of finally putting it right. $2.4 billion was spent redesigning and replacing crucial components of its shuttle fleet. NASA implemented over 400 design changes including a redesign of the O-ring seals and the addition of a third O-ring as a further safety measure (*see* Figure 4.1).

Astronauts now wear space suits and carry their own individual oxygen supplies, a parachute and an inflatable raft. A new emergency escape system was designed to give the astronauts a chance to leave the orbiter quickly in the event of a 'benign disaster' after the boosters had fallen away. In such a crisis, the crew would jettison the huge external fuel tank and stabilize the

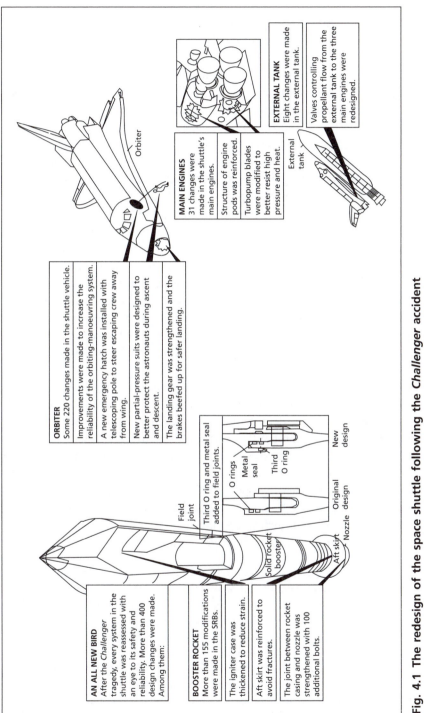

ORBITER
Some 220 changes made in the shuttle vehicle.

Improvements were made to increase the reliability of the orbiting-manoeuvring system.

A new emergency hatch was installed with telescoping pole to steer escaping crew away from wing.

New partial-pressure suits were designed to better protect the astronauts during ascent and descent.

The landing gear was strengthened and the brakes beefed up for safer landing.

Orbiter

MAIN ENGINES
31 changes were made in the shuttle's main engines.

Structure of engine pods was reinforced.

Turbopump blades were modified to better resist high pressure and heat.

External tank

EXTERNAL TANK
Eight changes were made in the external tank.

Valves controlling propellant flow from the external tank to the three main engines were redesigned.

Field joint

Third O ring and metal seal added to field joints.

O rings

Metal seal

Third O ring

New design

Original design

Solid rocket booster

Aft skirt

Nozzle

AN ALL NEW BIRD
After the *Challenger* tragedy, every system in the shuttle was reassessed with an eye to its safety and reliability. More than 400 design changes were made. Among them:

BOOSTER ROCKET
More than 155 modifications were made in the SRBs.

The igniter case was thickened to reduce strain.

Aft skirt was reinforced to avoid fractures.

The joint between rocket casing and nozzle was strengthened with 100 additional bolts.

Fig. 4.1 The redesign of the space shuttle following the *Challenger* accident
Source: Time Magazine, 10 October 1988.

winged orbiter into a downward glide. Then, when the craft descended to an altitude of about 30,000 feet, the astronauts would set off explosive bolts, blowing a newly installed hatch off the ship, and extend the 12-foot telescoping escape pole, which is positioned to guide them away from the orbiter's wing and tail. One by one, each would slip a ring attached to his or her suit around the pole and would slide off into the thin air, deploy the parachute and drop into the ocean, where the astronaut's radio transmitter would guide rescuers. The escape procedure would work, of course, only under circumstances that leave the vehicle intact and under control.

Part of 'putting it right' was the cost of the inquiry into the accident. On 3 February President Reagan issued Executive Order 12546 setting up the Presidential Commission on the Space Shuttle Accident. The 13-person commission held hearings from 6 February to 2 May 1986 and published its five-volume report on 6 June 1986. Their hearing involved national television coverage.

The Commission was chaired by William P. Rogers, former secretary of state and a lawyer by background. Neil Armstrong, the first man on the moon, was vice-chairman and present as an aeronautical engineer along with three other engineers. Sally Ride, another astronaut and the first American woman in space, was one of four physicists. There was another lawyer and an editor, and General Kutyna, with a science degree from the Massachusetts Institute of Technology.

The Commission was given 120 days to do the investigation with a brief to: review the circumstances surrounding the accident and establish the probable cause or causes of the accident; and develop recommendations for corrective or other action based upon the Commission's findings and determinations.

Dr Richard P. Feynman, a Nobel Prize winning nuclear physicist, a member of the Commission, was very quick to focus on the O-ring problem. In a private briefing before the hearing opened at NASA's Jet Propulsion Laboratory in Pasadena, California, he heard of the design problem of the O-rings – which are about a quarter of an inch thick and lie on a circle 12 feet in diameter. He explained the special quality problems with its design:

> When the seals were originally designed by the Morton Thiokol Company, it was expected that pressure from the burning propellant would squash the O-rings. But because the joint is stronger than the wall (it's three times thicker), the wall bows outward, causing the joint to bend a little – enough to lift the rubber O-rings off the seal area. Mr Weeks (a seals expert) told me this phenomenon is called 'joint rotation', and it was discovered very early, before they ever flew the shuttle.
>
> The pieces of rubber in the joints are called O-rings, but they are not used like normal O-rings are. In ordinary circumstances, such as sealing oil in the motor of an automobile, there are sliding parts and rotating shafts, but the gaps are always the same. An O-ring just sits there, in a fixed position.

But in the case of the shuttle, the gap *expands* as the pressure builds up in the rocket. And to maintain the seal, the rubber has to expand *fast* enough to close the gap – and during a launch, the gap opens in a fraction of a second.

Thus the resilience of the rubber became a very essential part of the design.

When the Thiokol engineers were discovering these problems, they went to the Parker Seal Company, which manufactures the rubber, to ask for advice. The Parker Seal Company told Thiokol that O-rings are not meant to be used that way, so they could give no advice.

Although it was known from nearly the beginning that the joint was not working as it was designed to, Thiokol kept struggling with the device.

They made a number of makeshift improvements. One was to put shims in to keep the joint tight, but the joint still leaked. Mr Weeks showed me pictures of leaks on previous flights – what the engineers called 'blowby', a blackening behind an O-ring where hot gas leaked through, and what they called 'erosion', where an O-ring had burned a little bit. There was a chart showing all the flights, and how serious the blowby and erosion were on each one. We went through the whole history up to *the* flight, 51-L.[9]

At one of the Commission's first meetings, Professor Feynman asked Lawrence Mulloy from NASA's booster rocket division at the Marshall Space Flight Center in Huntsville, Alabama, about the seals:

Feynman: During a launch, there are vibrations which cause the rocket joints to move a little bit – is that correct?

Mulloy: That is correct sir.

Feynman: And inside the joints, these so-called O-rings are supposed to expand to make a seal – is that right?

Mulloy: Yes sir. In static conditions they should be in direct contact with the tang and clevis and squeezed twenty-thousandths of an inch.

Feynman: Why don't we take the O-rings out?

Mulloy: Because then you would have hot gas expanding through the joint.

Feynman: Now in order for the seal to work correctly, the O-ring must be made of rubber – not something like lead, when you squash it, it stays.

Mulloy: Yes sir.

Feynman: Now if the O-ring weren't resilient for a second or two, would that be enough to be a very dangerous situation?

Mulloy: Yes sir.[10]

Professor Feynman then took a piece of the rubber O-ring which he placed in a C-clamp and dropped it in a glass of ice water for a while. When he took it out and removed the C-clamp, the rubber didn't spring back. It had lost its resilience in the cold water. The simple little experiment showed the viability of the rule that the shuttle should not have flown at temperatures below the specified 53°F. On the morning of the launch of *Challenger* temperatures were 28–9°F. Professor Feynman's overall conclusions for NASA were all pointed powerfully in the direction of establishing total quality for the future.

The conclusions of Richard Feynman were as follows:

If a reasonable launch schedule is to be maintained, engineering often cannot be done fast enough to keep up with the expectations of the highly originally conservative certification criteria designed to guarantee a very safe vehicle. In such situations, safety criteria are altered subtly – and with often apparently logical arguments – so that flights can still be certified in time. The shuttle therefore flies in a relatively unsafe condition, with a chance of failure on the order of a percent. (It is difficult to the more accurate.)

Official management, on the other hand, claims to believe the probability of failure is a thousand times less. One reason for this may be an attempt to assure the government of NASA's perfection and success in order to ensure the supply of funds. The other may be that they sincerely believe it to be true, demonstrating an almost incredible lack of communication between the managers and their working engineers.

In any event, this had had very unfortunate consequences, the most serious of which is to encourage ordinary citizens to fly in such a dangerous machine – as if it had attained the safety of an ordinary airliner. The astronauts, like test pilots, should know their risks, and we honor them for their courage. Who can doubt that McAuliffe (a school teacher) was equally a person of great courage, who was closer to an awareness of the true risks than NASA management would have us believe?

Let us make recommendations to ensure that NASA officials deal in a world of reality, understanding technological weaknesses and imperfections well enough to be actively trying to eliminate them. They must live in a world of reality in comparing the costs and utility of the shuttle to other methods of entering space. And they must be realistic in making contracts and in estimating the costs and difficulties of each project. Only realistic flight schedules should be proposed – schedules that have a reasonable chance of being met. If in this way the government would not support NASA, then so be it. NASA owes it to the citizens from whom it asks support to be frank, honest, and informative, so that these citizens can make the widest decisions for the use of their limited resources.

For a successful technology, reality must take precedence over public relations, for Nature cannot be fooled.[11]

More costs of the *Challenger* accident

Perhaps one of the greatest and unquantifiable costs of the accident was the *image damage* it did to NASA. The agency's reputation had been built up from the Apollo Moon landings onwards. It was one of the most respected government organizations in the world. NASA, famous for its care of its astronauts and its shining technological competence, had its image shattered in 73 seconds. Since the *Challenger* disaster, 'NASA bashing' has taken its toll. But the public memory of the technological compromises it made in the design of the space shuttle and the managerial incompetence that contributed to the disaster will not easily be erased. Whenever a nation's policy fails spectacularly as it did in America's intervention in Vietnam or in the space shuttle disaster, the people, the politicians and the press look for scapegoats and perhaps go overboard with criticism. Yet public accountability is the price of living in an open democratic society for government agencies and companies. Any failure of confidence for a governmental agency usually results in the penalty of further cut budgets and reduced funding – a classic case of lost opportunities.

The failure of NASA's *Challenger*, at the time, had geopolitical consequences which were deadly serious then, although with the collapse of the Soviet Union and the ending of the cold war three years later, have naturally diminished in importance. The geopolitical effects of the *Challenger* accident included a weakening of America's credibility over the Strategic Defense Initiative, the so-called Stars Wars deterrents with its technical problems of unprecedented complexity. Could an agency that got its rocketry wrong for the space shuttle be a potent power in creating space umbrellas to catch oncoming nuclear missiles? While the American space programme was on hold in the aftermath of *Challenger*, the former Soviet Union won propaganda points in the space rivalry stakes by creating its own space shuttle. The Russian shuttle looked like the USA shuttle, but was actually safer as it used proven liquid fuel rocket boosters, not solid fuel ones. The Russian orbiter had a small, air-breathing engine for greater manoeuvrability on re-entry. But by then the Soviet Union was on the brink of bankruptcy and its space shuttle flew only twice. Before the collapse of the USSR, the Soviets launched many satellites, sent two scientific probes to Mars and ferried a stream of cosmonauts between earth and its old space station Mir – using old-fashioned, but high-quality, expendable rockets, and outstripping US scientists in learning about the effects of extended space flight on people. America was forced for a few years at least to play a catch-up game in the space race.

The replacement shuttle for the *Challenger*, named *Endeavour*, took nearly four years to build and cost $1.8 billion. Although at one time NASA boasted it would have seven shuttles in its fleet, it now admits that *Endeavour*, the fourth shuttle, may be the last. There are no funds in the government's budget for a fifth shuttle. NASA's own advisory panel believes the agency should concentrate its scarce resources on creating a more powerful unmanned rocket for future space missions.

As a result of the Commission's critical report many key managers, including the head of NASA, lost their positions. Almost all the managers of the upper echelon involved with the shuttle have been replaced since the accident.[12] At the Marshall Space Flight Center, Dr William R. Lucas, the official in charge, retired two months after the report was published. Lawrence B. Mulloy, George Hardy and Stanley Reinzartz, all from the top team, also left.

Part of any total quality management process is having the right people. There is a new director of NASA and new managers for the shuttle project office, the booster rocket project, and science and engineering, as well as a new official for safety and quality assurance. But they have all worked at Marshall a long time. They represent the traditional NASA manager – the same breed of manager who launched *Challenger* – which may not be good for the organization.

John Pike, space policy analyst for the Federation of American Scientists, while conceding that NASA had solved some of its technical problems with the shuttle, said: 'They have fundamentally failed to fix the political and managerial problems that led to the technical problems.'

One of the managerial problems has to do with the type of manager NASA employs. Two American academics, Kenneth A. Kovach and Barry Render, with experience in the defence and aerospace industries, drew on a database on 'management style' at NASA over five years to profile the NASA manager and offer some insight into the decision-making process that led to the accident.[13] Their evaluation of results was produced by standardized tests.[14] They emerge from the battery of tests as a group of inbred managers with similar characteristics. They have a strong preference to gather and evaluate information by thinking and sensing, rather than by using intuition and feeling. They showed strong masculine decision-making traits making them unlikely to change their minds. They revealed a set of needs (on Maslow's hierarchy) which adequately fulfilled lower-level needs, but unsatisfied ego/status and self-actualization needs, making them unlikely to yield to outside intervention. They had strong desires to control others and to be a part of their inbred, homogeneous management team.

This management profile produces decision-makers who are reluctant to act on the advice of anyone outside the group or to change an existing decision or patterns of behaviour. To expect them to place supreme importance on diminishing human risks at the cost of sacrificing their mission and goals is to expect the group to act out of character. Kovach and Render argue that since people do not and cannot be made to change their management profile substantially NASA needs to change its collective profile by recruiting from outside the agency managers with different profiles who would give a better balance to the decision-making teams.

Eight months after the disaster Dale H. Myers, NASA Deputy Administrator, announced a new management and operations structure for the National Space Transportation System (NTSTO – the space shuttle programme). The new structure was designed to prevent both internal and external quality failures by improving communication, decision-making, systems of managerial control and accountability.

Diane Vaughan's[15] account of the space shuttle accident was published on the tenth anniversary of the disaster. Written from the perspective of the sociology of mistakes, the book explored the inner workings of the space programme, focusing on the human drama and the institutional causes of the accident. It described the impact of budget cuts in NASA during that time and how key engineering decisions were made.

This account offers a very different emphasis from the Presidential Commission and the report of a bipartisan investigation by the US House of Representatives Committee on Science and Technology, published in October 1986, which agreed with many of the findings of the Presidential Commission. Whereas the White House Commission found fault principally with the managerial decision-making process to launch, the House Committee laid blame on people making poor technical decisions about the O-rings over a period of years. The blame was placed on senior NASA managers/engineers and contractors who 'failed to act decisively to solve the increasingly serious anomalies in the solid Rocket Booster joints.'[16]

Vaughan summed up this historically accepted explanation of the accident as 'production pressures and managerial wrongdoing'. She tabled the unasked question 'why the NASA managers, who not only had all the information on the eve of the launch but also were warned against it, decided to proceed?'[17]

> This question was never directly asked and therefore never answered. In this vacuum, the conventional explanation was born and thrived: economic strain on the organization together with the safety rule violations suggested that the production pressures caused managers to suppress information about O-ring hazards, knowingly violating safety regulations, in order to stick to the launch schedule.'[18]

Her sociological explanation, by contrast, showed how

> mistakes, mishap and disaster are socially organized and systematically produced by social structures. No extraordinary actions by individuals explain what happened: no intentional managerial wrong doing, no rule violations, no conspiracy.
>
> The cause of the disaster was a mistake embedded in the banality of organizational life and facilitated by an environment of scarcity and competition, an unprecedented, uncertain technology, incrementalism, patterns of information, routinization, organizational and inter-organizational structures and a complex culture.[19]

US privatizes space shuttle programme

Since the loss of *Challenger*, NASA has launched 70 successful flights for a total of 95 in all. But twenty-five years old and in need of replacement, America's shuttle fleet is supplied by a new generation of privately operated orbiters. The new mission is to take pay loads into space more efficiently and at less cost than is possible with the existing NASA shuttle fleet. On 2 July 1996, the US government sidestepped the NASA space agency, which has maintained complete control over the US space programme since 1958, and turned to private industry by awarding a $941 million contract to develop a simple prototype of the new space craft to Lockheed Martin.

In October 1996 NASA took its first real steps towards privatizing space shuttle operations despite growing concerns over safety. The American space agency gave over the operation of the shuttle to the United Space Alliance, a consortium of American aerospace companies headed by Rockwell and Lockheed Martin. However, NASA will keep its fingers on the final launch button, own the shuttle orbiters and employ the astronauts.

NASA hopes to save $750 million from its annual $3.2 billion space shuttle operations budget by the year 2000 by bringing all shuttle operations under one contract. NASA is also under instructions from the White House to cut its overall $14 billion annual budget by a third by 2001. As part of the privatization efforts, there are fewer NASA employees looking over the shoulders of contracted technicians and, according to NASA press officer Joel Wells, further reductions of NASA personnel will continue through natural attrition. The total head count at Kennedy has fallen from 14,686 in 1997 to 11,984 in 1998.

Many experts including Bryan O'Connor, a former shuttle commander and NASA director of the programme, think that the privatization programme is premature and dangerous. The Aerospace Safety Advisory Panel which oversees NASA's operations argues for a slow down in the privatization programme to avoid 'unacceptable safety risks'.[20] However, the United Space Alliance consortium will be penalized for failing to meet safety and mission objectives, but will have a share in all savings *after* meeting a target of $400 million a year. It will keep 35 cents out of every dollar saved once the target has been achieved. The privatization process was gradual, first 16 and then another 70 shuttle operation contracts were merged into the United Space Alliance operation.

It is all an effort by the US to regain a greater share of the world market for rocket launchings. During the decade following the *Challenger* disaster, the US has watched nearly two-thirds of the global rocket launchings market slip away to other competitors, particularly the European Ariane space programme. Part of the drive to privatize shuttle production comes from NASA's own realization of how far it has fallen behind. NASA's head Daniel Goldin testified to Congress that the entire US space community should 'hang its head in shame for losing the lead'. Congress is also driven to cut the cost of the space shuttle programme which has risen sharply due in part to the overriding concern for safety following the 1986 disaster. Current shuttle launches cost about $500 million; this translates to about $10,000 per pound. The new shuttle will be expected to achieve a $1,000 per ton target.

The new orbiter has to be totally reusable and be able to go from Earth into orbit in a single-state launch without shedding any of its parts. (The current space shuttle sheds both its booster rockets and its fuel tank.) It will have to move as fast as a rocket and manoeuvre like a jet. The new orbiter is scheduled for tests in early 2000.[21]

Cost of quality

The impact of quality on any business can be measured in terms of 'the cost of quality', a shorthand phrase for total business cost in achieving quality. As much as 20 to 30 per cent of a company's revenue can be absorbed by quality costs as illustrated in Figure 2.7 (*see* p. 41). The goal of TQM is to halve the cost of quality and to halve it again over time (*see* Figure 4.2).

There are three main areas of cost to be identified, measured and improved. These are:

1 cost of conformance
2 cost of non-conformance
3 cost of lost opportunities.

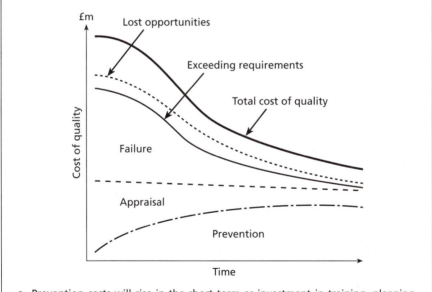

- Prevention costs will rise in the short term as investment in training, planning, processes and systems sets the foundation for the future.
- Appraisal costs gradually reduce as inspection, the checking of others' work and progress chasing late deliveries are no longer necessary.
- Internal and external failure, exceeding requirements and lost opportunities will dramatically reduce as the 'prevention' activities take effect.

Fig. 4.2 The effect of halving the cost of quality

The cost of conformance has two aspects – cost of prevention and cost of appraisal. Cost of prevention is the cost of activities that prevent failure from occurring. Examples include training employees, quality awareness programmes, planning, and quality workshops or quality circles. Cost of appraisal is the cost incurred to determine conformance with quality standards. Examples include inspecting, checking, auditing and expediting because parts or reports are not delivered on time.

Cost of non-conformance encompasses three aspects. First there is the cost of internal failure. This is the cost of correcting products or services which do not meet quality standards prior to delivery to the customer. Examples include scrap and rework. Secondly there is the cost of external failure – correcting products or services *after* delivery to the customer. Examples include warranty costs, installation of field retrofits, customer invoice errors/adjustments and unplanned field service costs.

Third, there is the cost of exceeding requirements. This is the cost incurred providing information or services which are unnecessary or unimportant, or for which no known requirement has been established. Examples include redundant copies of documents, reports which are not read, detailed analytical effort when generalized estimates would suffice, and sales calls which are not required by the customer.

An example of this is the case of the senior manager of an information technology company with its headquarters in New York City. As is the custom with many American multinationals, he had a title of vice-president in charge of manufacturing for 'the world'. He made the mistake of telling one of his staff that he had to 'know what was going on over there' (meaning in Europe) for a meeting in two days' time. The overly zealous staff member drew up 200 questions and faxed them to five operating sites in the United Kingdom and on the continent. Everyone worked flat out to provide the information in such a short time frame. A massive document resulted from the query which cost about $200,000 to produce and gave the senior manager thousands of times more data than he wanted for his meeting, while creating maximum aggravation in the European operations.

Perhaps the most difficult cost of quality to quantify is the cost of lost opportunities. This is the lost revenue resulting from the loss of existing customers, the loss of potential customers and the lost business growth arising from the failure to deliver products and services at the required quality standards. Examples include cancellations due to inadequate service response times, ordering of competitors' products because the company's products are not available, the intangible cost of a demoralized workforce and the wrong products offered for the specific customer's application.

A reduction of the cost of quality offers many benefits, but they are not immediate. It may take two to four years to halve the cost of quality and

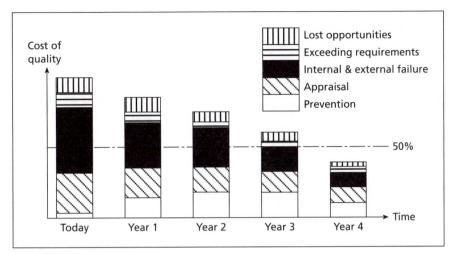

Fig. 4.3 Reducing the cost of quality

'prevention costs' may rise during the first year to two. Eventually all of the costs (even prevention) can be taken down to half of what they originally were. Then they can be reduced by half again repeating the process again and again (*see* Figure 4.3).

Cost of quality examples

This section of the chapter presents real-life examples of the cost of quality. These recent examples are in the form of extracts from newspapers and magazines and cover prevention costs, appraisal costs, internal failure costs, external failure costs, exceeding requirement costs and lost opportunities costs.

Prevention costs

These are all the costs associated with trying to prevent failure from happening. Training and education programmes are costs of prevention.

Judges' mistakes

In a recent statement from the Law Society, judges are to receive training to avoid mistakes which could cost a minimum of £10,000 for an appeal to be heard to correct the error.

BT seminars on line in Wales

Keeping senior managers in British industry and commerce abreast of the rapid changes in communications – and how such changes can secure competitive edge

121

– is the keynote of a programme of nationwide seminars organized by British Telecom as part of its Information Exchange initiative.[22]

Passive smoking

Smokers can threaten the life of an unborn baby simply by lighting up a cigarette near a pregnant woman. Two government reports on passive smoking – where non-smokers inhale other people's cigarette fumes – show that a healthy mother-to-be spending just two hours a day in a smoky atmosphere doubles the risk of having a low weight baby.

One of the reports by medical experts found that:

- An unborn child absorbs more nicotine than the smoking mother-to-be.
- There is a direct link between smoking and low birth weight.
- An embryo can be seriously damaged, even before a woman realizes she is pregnant.[23]

'Knee-jerk' law reduces pit bull terrier menace[24]

The much maligned Dangerous Dogs Act 1991, often held up as the worst example of knee-jerk legislation, has largely succeeded in eliminating the menace of pit bull terriers, an all-party group of MPs said yesterday.

About 430 pit bulls have been destroyed under the legislation and vets believe that thousands more have died.

The MPs say the 'largely unsung' success of the legislation, introduced by Kenneth Baker when he was Home Secretary, means it is time to relax some of its harsher measures such as its mandatory death penalty, and introduce 'bail' for dogs awaiting trial.

The MPs on the Commons Home Affairs Select Committee claim the maximum estimate for the number of pit bull terriers in Britain was 10,000 when the law was introduced after a spate of highly publicized attacks by pit bull terriers on children.

The law, put on the statute book within four weeks, was supposed to eliminate the ownership and breeding of pit bulls used 'for criminal or anti-social purposes'.

It led to the registration of 8,500 dogs which have to be muzzled and leashed in a public place, neutered, tattooed and insured. Unregistered dogs must be destroyed.

In their inquiry report, MPs say the number of registered dogs had fallen to 3,500 by October this year. 'These figures suggest clearly that the act has been instrumental in reducing the population of pit bull terriers very substantially.'

The Metropolitan Police said officers now rarely faced a menacing pit bull when carrying out a drugs raid. Vets and the RSPCA said in their evidence there had been a dramatic fall in the number of dogs being attacked by pit bulls.

'We are in no doubt that the protection of the public requires strong legislation to govern the ways that dogs may behave and to force owners to control their dogs,' the MPs conclude.

Appraisal costs

There are costs to determine conformance with quality standards. Measurement systems include inspection, checking, auditing, surveying, inquiries, etc.

The ruthless killer in the ranks

More soldiers die from smoking-linked heart attacks than from wounds . . . When all causes of death are added together a smoker's chance of dying as a direct result of their tobacco habit is one in four. And soldiers who are super fit are no exception. Since the Falklands War more serving soldiers have died of heart attacks caused by smoking cigarettes than have died of wounds from smoking guns.[25]

Surgeons' errors result in 1,000 deaths per year

The 1,000 deaths a year due to surgeons' errors are to be investigated in the most searching inquiry into operating-theatre procedures. The £250,000 inquiry, funded by the Department of Health, follows publication of a pilot study last December.

The study disclosed a disturbing catalogue of errors and surgeons admitted 'a falling off of adequate standards which rests on the shoulders of the profession'.

Among the worst cases were two in which surgeons operated on the wrong part of the body and another in which the surgeon awarded himself 10 out of 10, but removed the wrong organ.

Giving details of the Project, which will end in October 1989, Dr John Lunn, consultant anaesthetist, said: 'We are going to put our own house in order.'

The three-region study showed that many deaths resulted from ambitious young persons tackling operations beyond their capabilities.

The Project announced yesterday, which has no parallel in the world, will be conducted under full anonymity, so erring doctors will never be brought to account.

He [Dr Lunn] said it should result in saving life and avoidance of errors which have serious consequences for the patient.[26]

Internal failure costs

Internal failure costs are those which occur within the organization before delivery to the external customer. In manufacturing this would include scrap and rework, design changes during production and surplus goods or obsolete inventory. Software errors detected before a computer program is despatched to the customer would also be an example.

Nuclear submarine at Vickers Shipbuilding

A section of nuclear submarine being built at Britain's leading warship yard has been welded into the hull upside down, it was disclosed yesterday.

Officials at Vickers Shipbuilding at Barrow-in-Furness admitted the mistake had been made and said an urgent internal inquiry was now under way.

Workers say a cylindrical hull section, measuring 20 ft by 30 ft, of the Trafalgar class submarine *Triumph* has been welded in completely the wrong position. It will now have to be ripped out and re-welded which would take several weeks.

One tradesman who has worked in the yard for 15 years said: 'It's what you might call a classic cock-up. I don't think anyone can remember quite such a blunder. The management are trying to keep it very quiet.'

In a curt statement, the Ministry of Defence said the problem was Vickers' 'contractual responsibility', adding: 'The Company has quality control and inspection arrangements to ensure that problems are identified and rectified at the earliest possible time.'

Vickers refused to comment except to confirm there had been a 'welding error' and to say it did not expect the building programme to be disrupted seriously.[27]

Three Mile Island

According to the President's Commission on the accident at Three Mile Island, technicians described the control room at the Pennsylvania power plant as an intimidating place, with panels of red, green, amber and white lights and alarms that sound or flash warnings many times each hour. When the first alarm of the meltdown incident went off it was followed by a cascade of about 100 alarms within a few minutes. 'I would have liked to have thrown away the control panel. It wasn't giving us any useful information,' one of the operators said.[28]

Stephenson Rocket burns Bank's pocket

More than £25 million of the Bank of England's new £5 notes, due to be issued next month, have had to be pulped in a controversy over the portrayal of George Stephenson, the pioneer rail engineer famed for building the *Rocket*.

It was stated on the original notes that he died in 1845 – three years before the correct date.[29]

San Juan Ixhuatepec: risk factory – an internal failure that reaches out into the local community

People in this impoverished industrial suburb of Mexico City have complained for years about a dangerous neighbour: a gasoline-storage complex run by the state monopoly, Pemex. The company, which has a long history of fatal accidents, added a new chapter last week when three gasoline tanks exploded after a faulty valve began to spurt fuel. Four people died in the ensuing two-day inferno. Twelve years

▶

ago, a series of gas explosions at the same complex killed about 500 people. Pemex has promised to make a thorough investigation into last week's disaster, but many people here just wish the behemoth would move away. 'We're not asking for much, just to live without constant danger,' says Rebecca Lira, 42, a mother of six. 'If I don't die in an explosion, I'll die of a heart attack just worrying about when the next accident will happen.'[30]

An internal failure creates every pilot's nightmare

It was the moment every pilot dreads, the controls on Flight AIH 838 – a Boeing 757 carrying 241 passengers and crew – became jammed soon after takeoff from Fuertenventura in stormy conditions, bound for East Midlands and Newcastle. Unknown to the flight crew, Captain Ray Cockerton and First Officer Andrew Redknapp, a torch had been left in the right-hand wing. During takeoff which, unusually, was at full power because of the poor conditions, the torch lodged in the aileron, the flap which is used to turn the plane.

It had been left there by an engineer at Luton the day before and had not caused any problem in three previous flights.

After landing, according to the CAA's report, 'the crew demonstrated the problem, at which point a large metal torch was forced through the wing below the righthand aileron'.

The passengers were never told about what had caused the incident, but 30 refused to take the plane provided by Airtours to take them back to East Midlands and travelled by land.

At his home in the East Midlands, Captain Cockerton wrote a four-page report and was told by the company there there would be a debriefing session with all the crew. This never materialised.

Apart from a thank you letter from Airtours managers, the incident was barely mentioned again and within a week he was back on duty.

Captain Cockerton said that was a mistake: 'I felt occasionally tearful but otherwise I was apparently fine for three or four months, then I started getting flashbacks, insomnia and irritability.'

Eventually, in June, he felt that his mental state warranted reporting sick and he sought medical advice. He was diagnosed as suffering from post-traumatic stress syndrome and referred to a specialist for successful counselling sessions. Captain Cockerton resigned a few days later and now flies for another leading airline.

As for the engineer who left the torch, he put up a big notice in his mess at Luton asking if anyone had seen his torch. Last night, Monarch refused to comment on whether he was disciplined.[31]

External failure costs

External failure costs occur when the product or service is offered to the customer and found defective. These costs include returned products and rejected services or unhappy customers. For a humerous example, *see* Figure 4.4.

Suddenly, a heated exchange took place between the king and the moat contractor.

Fig. 4.4 External failure costs

Source: Gary Larson, *The Far Side Gallery 4* (London: Warner Books, 1993), p 125.

Balfour Beatty 'must bear greater responsibility' for failings

A catalogue of failings during the construction of tunnels on the Heathrow Express project was listed by the HEX trial judge Mr Justice Cresswell, as he sentenced main contractor Balfour Beatty and subconsultant Geoconsult on Monday [*see* Table 4.1].

The 'hands-off' role of BAA's HEX team, unfamiliar duties accepted by Balfour Beatty, Geoconsult's design and monitoring, Balfour Beatty's construction quality control and the contractor's failure to investigate allegations of defects, he said, were all factors contributing to the collapse of tunnels in October 1994.

'Balfour Beatty must bear the greater responsibility for the collapse,' said the judge. 'Balfour Beatty fell seriously short of the "reasonably practicable" test. It was a matter of chance whether death or serious injury resulted from these very serious breaches.'

He added: 'Balfour Beatty put their concerns about the fact that the tunnels were markedly behind schedule above proper action to protect employees and the public.' He added that an aggravating feature was the contractor's 'failure to heed warnings'.

However, he said that he gave 'full credit' to the contractor for its early guilty plea. The judge commended both companies for their 'exemplary steps' after the disaster.

Balfour Beatty pleaded guilty after an expert report carried out for the contractor in 1998 showed that a weak tunnel invert resulting from poor construction caused the collapse.

'Knowing that we could have taken more care with the construction of the invert we pleaded guilty,' said Balfour Beatty managing director Andy Rose in a letter that was read out by the judge.[32]

Table 4.1 HEX: the cost

Planned

Balfour Beatty's original tender value:	£60m
Trial tunnel cost	£1.1m

Unplanned

Cost of collapse to BAA	£35m
Cost of collapse to Balfour Beatty	£35m
Cost of collapse to BAA and Balfour Beatty's insurers	£100m
Cost of airport disruption	£50m
Cost of shutting down JLE sites as a safety precaution	£200m
Fine for Balfour Beatty	£1.2m
Fine for Geoconsult	£0.5m
Cost to Geoconsult of expert witness report	£0.125m
HSE prosecution costs	£0.88m
Total extra unplanned cost	**£422.7m**

(Excluding cost of precautionary two-week London Underground Piccadilly line closure, Balfour Beatty's legal costs and Geoconsult's legal costs)

▶

127

Daily Telegraph wrong date

The extent to which *The Daily Telegraph* is our readers' daily compass and guide became apparent to us yesterday.

As a result of a technical error, we caused Thursday February 25 to arrive 24 hours too early for 300,000 readers of the Final edition.

Wednesday's edition of the front page was dated Thursday February 25, although the inside pages were correctly dated Wednesday, February 24.

Throughout yesterday our switchboard was hearing horror stories from readers who took us at our word. One rang from Birmingham to complain we had caused him to arrive there a morning too soon.

Another described a premature visit to the dentist, and yet another set off for Southend. Some elderly readers went to collect their pensions, only to be rebuked by the Post Office for turning up on Wednesday.

But some were very annoyed and upset, particularly those who had travelled all over the place thinking it was Thursday and got there before they found out.[33]

BR fined £1/4m over Clapham train disaster

British Rail was fined £250,000 at the Old Bailey yesterday, after admitting failures in safety measures at the time of the Clapham rail disaster in which 35 people died.

Mr Justice Wright said the British Railways Board allowed safety standards to fall below an acceptable level and that resulted in a situation of 'quite horrifying danger' at Clapham Junction, where two trains collided after a loose wire in a control box led to a signal failure.

The court was told that a signal south of Clapham station which should have displayed a red 'danger' signal was showing yellow. As a result, the 6.14 am Poole to Waterloo train ran into the back of the stationary 7.18 am Basingstoke to Waterloo train.

The judge said that the safe operation of the network required the highest possible standards of installation, repair and maintenance in the signalling system.

'The accident on December 12, 1988, occurred because these defendants allowed those standards to fall below any acceptable level.' The result was a state of affairs in the railway cuttings between Earlsfield and Clapham Junction stations on that morning of 'quite horrifying danger'.[34]

Hospital patients killed by doctors

Doctors at Sudbury General Hospital in Canada after a series of suspicious deaths, discovered that they were administering a lethal nitrous oxide gas to patients in the operating theatre instead of the oxygen they intended to give them. Their investigation revealed that during construction of a new emergency wing, the pipe that carried oxygen from a central gas storage point had been switched with the one that carried nitrous oxide, an anaesthetic that can be fatal unless mixed with oxygen. It took them several months to uncover the mistake, and a Coroner's jury attributed nine deaths to it.[35]

▶

Airline powercage

The lives of 25,000 airline passengers were endangered over a 90-day period because police left six sticks of gelignite behind a seat of a British Airways 747 after an exercise with their dogs to practise detecting explosives. The jet flew the equivalent of 20 world tours with the gelignite on board.[36]

Nuclear power plant still active after all these years

Ten years after the Three Mile Island nuclear plant gave the citizens of Pennsylvania and the American nuclear industry a nasty surprise (the plant was minutes away from meltdown) they are still cleaning up the mess.

So far it has cost $1,000 million, $300 million more than the plant cost to build in the first place. It has employed 1,000 workers, a range of new and ingenious robot tools, and infinite patience to get even this far. But the chances are that nothing can eradicate the fear and suspicion of nuclear power created by the accident.

By the end of 1990, all being well, the mass of melted fuel collected at the bottom of the reactor will have been dug out and carted away. Then the doomed Unit 2 of the Three Mile Island plant will be shut and watched for another 30 years, until Unit 1 next door comes to the end of its life. The two units will then be taken apart together.[37]

Faults on 60% of security video-cameras

As many as six out of ten security cameras installed in Britain may not be working properly or are completely useless, according to security experts.

Many cameras are so badly installed and maintained that they are unable to do the job they were intended for, they say.

A confidential Home Office study, leaked to *The Independent on Sunday*, confirms that cameras used to protect thousands of buildings, including government departments and High Street banks and building societies, are often ineffective.

David Fletcher, the British Security Industry Associations chief executive, said: 'What is the point of a company having an expensive security camera installed if there is no film in it or it is defective because of lack of maintenance?'

Investigations into a spate of robberies at banks and building societies in the City of London have been hampered because security cameras were either defective or switched off. Sir Owen Kelly, Chief Constable of the City, wrote to financial institutions, warning them to take more care of their security equipment.

The Home Office study into the problem concludes that because there are no 'performance standards for CCTV (closed circuit television) security systems installations can be ineffective and poor value for money'.

Common faults discovered by the study included blurred or out-of-focus images. Bad installation meant that people came out too small, too dimly or too briefly on the video tape to be identifiable; sometimes, they could not be seen at all.

Security cameras would give better results, the report says, if they 'had been correctly selected, installed, adjusted and maintained'.[38]

▶

Smear testing riddled with mistakes, says watchdog

Mistakes and sloppiness across the cervical smear testing system are putting women's lives at risk, according to a report from the National Audit Office.

Half of all hospital laboratories that examine smears are not coming close to acceptable accuracy targets and the mistakes are causing 'avoidable harm and death', the head of the public spending watchdog, Sir John Bourn, said. Errors were commonplace throughout the £130 million programme.

A report presented to MPs today says that 13 English health authorities, mainly in London, failed to meet the national target of screening 80 per cent of eligible women every five years. Women who had the test often had to wait six weeks for results rather than the recommended month.

Of women tested, 8.3 per cent – against a target of 7 per cent – had to have repeat smear tests because the first was of poor quality and could not be examined accurately.

About half the laboratories were making too many mistakes when analysing smears.

'Many laboratories will be missing some abnormalities and many may be reporting abnormalities where none exist,' Sir John said.

Even where abnormal smears were properly identified, most patients had to wait at least eight weeks for treatment, and even women showing serious cervical abnormalities had not been seen by a specialist a month after their tests.

The report highlights a string of cases in which mistakes at screening laboratories led to misdiagnoses, hysterectomies and even deaths. The most serious failure, at Kent and Canterbury Hospitals NHS Trust, affected 91,000 tests. Eight women died from cervical cancer.

Other serious failures were recorded by the audit office in laboratories at the Hospital of St Cross, Rugby; Pontefract General Infirmary; the James Paget Hospital, Great Yarmouth; St Peter's Hospital, Chersey, Surrey; and the Merton, Sutton and Wandsworth Family Health Service Authority in London.

Women from ethnic minorities, particularly Bangladeshis, Indians and Pakistanis, were likely to miss out on smear tests, usually because of cultural and religious factors, the audit office found. Women from low income groups were also failing to come forward to be tested.

Sarah Harman, a solicitor representing more than 100 women affected by the Kent mistakes, said the report illustrated a national smear test crisis. 'It is quite clear from this that it is not just a problem at Kent and Canterbury, and labs all over the country are just not up to the standard.'[39]

A flake of film foiled Hubble

A fragment of synthetic film the size of a grain of sand was to blame for the troubles that afflict the Hubble Space Telescope. The fragment broke off a calibrating device during the making of the telescope's primary mirror. As a result the mirror was ground too flat.

▶

The Hubble satellite, a set of eight instruments built around two mirrors, was launched in April. At a cost of $1.6 billion (£800 million), it was to be the ultimate in orbiting optical telescopes. In June, NASA announced that Hubble's first images were blurred. A spherical aberration 10 times greater than tolerable had been ground into the main mirror, NASA discovered. This means that rays of light striking the mirror close to its centre and rays striking around its edges are not focused at the same central point, so causing the fuzziness.

Since July, six experts led by Lew Allen, head of NASA's Jet Propulsion Laboratory in California, have been investigating how that could have happened. Their report published this week describes a chain of errors that began with a small oversight. But Perkin-Elmer of Connecticut, which made and tested the primary mirror, and NASA, which was in charge, missed the mistake because the company's quality assurance team was understaffed and failed to enforce its double-checking procedure.

Meanwhile, behind schedule, the optical systems team building the mirror took short cuts and ignored contradictory findings, the Allen report says. 'The most unfortunate aspect of this . . . failure, is that the data revealing these errors were available from time to time in the fabrication process, but were not recognised and fully investigated at the time'.[40]

Cost of correcting Hubble

On 2 December 1993 the Space Shuttle Endeavour (Mission STS-61) took off for an eleven-day repair mission carrying new equipment and seven astronauts who had trained for over a year using virtual reality technology and a full-sized mock-up of Hubble in a tank of water to simulate weightlessness. The objective was to rendezvous with Hubble and to bring it into Endeavour's cargo bay. Four of the astronauts walked into space and replaced a number of Hubble's instruments. The operation took five space walks in all, totalling 35 hours.

The repair priority was to place into the telescope two special components to compensate for the faulty mirrors; in addition they were to replace the solar panels and a number of broken or malfunctioning components. They could not replace the main mirror without dismantling the telescope and rebuilding it.

The extra mirrors and lenses were inserted to correct for the aberration.

At 1.00 am EST on 18 December 1993, the Hubble science team gathered again to see if the new additions had solved the problem. When the image of a star appeared on the computer screens everyone knew immediately that the repair mission had succeeded. The star's image was a bright pin-point of light no longer spread out by the effects of the spherical aberration.[41]

Rubber from washer caused Lauda disaster

A piece of rubber from a damaged washer became lodged in a hydraulic pipe and triggered, it is now believed, the chain of events which led to the crash of a Lauda Air Boeing 767 jet in which 223 people died.

▶

After months of exhaustive tests, Boeing engineers managed to recreate the conditions which could have led to the crash and immediately informed American safety officials. They then ordered airlines to stop using reverse thrust on 767s until further notice.

For months Boeing engineers had been baffled by the crash which investigators at the scene rapidly established was almost certainly caused by the sudden deployment of the thrust reversers in flight. Repeated attempts to recreate the conditions which led to the reverser suddenly deploying failed and investigators were beginning to believe that such an accident was, in fact, 'impossible'.

Then, late last week, yet another test was conducted at the Boeing headquarters in Seattle in which an 'O' ring seal was deliberately broken to see what would happen. To their astonishment the engineers saw sections of rubber sucked into the pipe containing hydraulic fluid which led to an electrically operated solenoid valve controlling the thrust reverser. As it lodged in the pipe the flow of fluid was blocked and the valve, which should only have opened on the direct instructions of the pilot, reversed itself, allowing hydraulic fluid to activate the thrust reverser.[42]

Concorde mishap caused by paint stripper

Paint stripper used to clean British Airways' Concorde fleet probably caused the aircraft's rudder to disintegrate as it flew the Atlantic at more than twice the speed of sound, air safety experts believe.

Concorde 102 was flying at more than 1,400 mph and at 56,000 ft towards New York with 49 passengers when the crew felt what they believed was an engine surge. As it decelerated and dropped below 41,000 ft 'a more unusual vibration was felt', according to air accident officials. When the aircraft landed it was discovered that part of the lower rudder was missing, as was most of the skin on the right hand side of the tail.

The failure, which happened in January, was kept secret by shocked safety chiefs and BA engineers because it followed a similar incident over the Tasman Sea two years ago.[43]

Airline fined after plane ran out of oil

British Midland was ordered to pay $175,000 in fines and costs for putting at risk the lives of 183 passengers and crew in a case which raises questions about aviation maintenance procedures.

Luton Crown Court heard that both engines of a Boeing 737 on a flight from East Midlands to Lanzarote on 23 February 1996 almost ran out of oil because the gearbox covers had been left off during maintenance the previous night.

The engines had less than 10 per cent of the required amount of oil left, which meant the plane was within minutes of losing all power when it made an emergency landing at Luton airport after a 17 minute flight.

Judge Daniel Rodwell said: 'It is only through the vigilance of the pilot and his crew that the dramatic sudden loss of oil pressure was noticed and the aircraft

▶

was able to land safely. Had they not noticed, the engine very shortly after would have, if not seized, suffered such a dramatic loss of power that the aircraft would have crashed with a very high probability of killing all 189 on board.'

The verdict coincided with the publication of a report by the Air Accident Investigations Branch which linked the airline with two other potential catastrophes caused by faulty maintenance by night staff. In June 1990, the cockpit window of a BAC1-11 fell out and the pilot was almost sucked out. He was only saved by a steward holding on to his legs. The wrong bolts had been installed. And in 1993, flaps on a Virgin A320 were left in the maintenance mode, which meant the aircraft could only turn right.[44]

Department of groundless optimism: IBM's Olympic fiasco

Big Blue screwed up at the Olympics, no doubt about it. IBM invested well over $40 million in labor and equipment to fulfil its role as official Olympic sponsor and MIS Department, but in the opening days of the Games, part of the computer system IBM installed was impossibly slow, garbled data and completely omitted critical information. It showed one pugilist to be 2 feet tall and another as 97 years old. It forced wire services for a few days to input statistics manually from paper forms hand-delivered by runners. The fiasco was reported all over TV, the Web and the papers, and through it all ran IBM's multimullion-dollar Olympic ad campaign that (initially at least) touted bulletproof reliability. If self-parody were an Olympic sport, IBM would have medaled.[45]

Theft embarrasses slack Louvre

The Louvre lost a painting on Sunday and 20,000 people lost their tempers.

It was not the biggest or the most valuable painting in the Louvre – a diminutive landscape by Corot – but it was gone and an embarrassed museum wanted it back. All entrances to the sprawling building were blocked by police for nearly three hours.

Frightening rumours circulated among the large crowd trapped inside: there had been a murder, a bomb, a fire. People fainted, screamed, shouted. But the police insisted on searching the art-lovers' bags – and some of the art-lovers' bodies – one by one.

The tiny 13in-by-19in canvas by the French, pre-Impressionist painter Camille Corot was sliced out of its frame in an obscure, little-visited and unguarded room in the Sully pavilion. Its absence was noticed by an attendant at 1.30 pm on Sunday. It was still missing yesterday.

Five Corots were stolen from French museums – allegedly for Japanese collectors – in the 1980s; all were later recovered.

This is the fourth incident of the kind at the Louvre in the last four years. A religious robe from the 4th century BC disappeared from the collection of ancient Greek artefacts this January; two relatively obscure paintings vanished in 1995 and 1994. There have also been several acts of vandalism.

▶

The attacks have mostly occurred on a Sunday when the museum is most crowded. On each occasion, the Louvre has promised to review its security. Pierre Rosenberg, president-director of the museum, admitted yesterday that the stolen Corot had no individual alarm; it was hung in a room with no permanent attendant and no video surveillance. The thief prised open a glass security case and cut around the painting with a razor, without being noticed.

Mr Rosenberg tried to be philosophical yesterday. 'In my opinion, thefts of this kind are relatively rare. They are part of our sad fate (as one of the most visited art galleries in the world).'

The museum was not so relaxed when the theft was discovered. Visitors complained that they had been squashed for two hours as bags were laboriously checked. No audible explanation was given. Louvre staff explained that they had been asking for a proper system of loudspeakers for years: the authorities had always refused, fearing it would make the place appear 'like a supermarket'.

The missing canvas – *Le chemin de Sèvres* – was painted in 1858–9. Corot paintings fluctuate wildly in price – from £400 to £600,000 – according to their size and subject. A Corot of a similar size and topic was sold recently in New York for just over £70,000.[46]

Exceeding requirement costs

Exceeding requirement costs occurs when you give a customer more than what is required – often this cost takes the form of providing information or services which are unnecessary or unimportant or for which there is no expressed or agreed requirement.

The habit of sending copies of letters or documents to all and sundry instead of only to those who should have copies is an example. Conducting a huge analytical study when a generalized estimate would suffice is another example.

Post Office attacked for 'waste' of £4m ads

The Post Office is to launch a £4m television advertising campaign after market research found that the pubic dislikes the organisation's queues, believes its staff are unhelpful, and associates it with industrial action.

But the nationwide campaign for the counters division, to be launched next week, has angered its staff and Tory MPs. They believe it is wasting money promoting a service which is a virtual monopoly.

The campaign follows the unveiling last week of a new name and logo for the parcels division. It is also due to be advertised with a multimillion pound campaign.

►

Kenneth Warren, chairman of the Commons Select Committee for Trade and Industry, condemned the expenditure as a misuse of money by a public body. 'They are restraining trade while advancing their own interests,' he said.

Gerald Howarth, Conservative MP for Cannock and Burntwood, said yesterday: 'The Post Office does not need to advertise its services and should spend more on sorting out its delivery.'

The Post Office denied yesterday that the counter services were a monopoly and said: 'We are in competition to an extent with banks and building societies.'[47]

Buddhist's pique at RAF rescue

A Buddist who climbed a snow-capped mountain to meditate provoked an air and land rescue operation yesterday. The man, dressed from head-to-toe in saffron robes, climbed Cader Idris, near Dolgellau, in north Wales, to commune with nature for the winter solstice.

His solitude was interrupted by an RAF helicopter and a mountain rescue team, which came to save him after he was seen to be suffering from a head wound.

A team of 20 from the South Snowdon Mountain Rescue Volunteers interrupted their Christmas party to go up the 2,900 ft mountain. They were helped by an RAF helicopter, which used a searchlight to find the man in the darkness.

They discovered him in sub-zero temperatures inside a tent. Far from being grateful, the man, in his fifties, from Milton Keynes, Bucks, said: 'Go away, I'm meditating.'

He told them that he had climbed the mountain to celebrate the winter solstice with meditation.

Barry Skinner, of the search and rescue team, said: 'There were a lot of crossed wires over this incident. He was a bit upset at being disturbed, so we said sorry and left him to it.'[48]

Lost opportunities costs

Lost opportunities costs result in lost revenue due to an erosion of the customer base or the failure to win new customers or to grow the business because of quality failure. An example would be losing a customer to one's competitor over the delivery times.

Chainsaw lost opportunity following hurricane

A chainsaw company was unable to capitalise on the demand for chainsaws following the 'hurricane' in the South East of England in October 1987. It had long lead times for production and could not switch quickly to producing small chainsaws due to inflexibilities in manufacture.

A competitor on the other hand, had Just-in-Time, quality suppliers and was able to offer saws at very short notice, increase sales and capture an additional 22% market share.

▶

£100,000 for blunder over Old Masters

The auctioneers who failed to spot a pair of Old Masters were ordered to pay more than £100,000 damages today to Penelope and Paul Luxmoore-May.

The couple who received a mere £840 for the masterpieces by George Stubbs – which later went for £90,000 at Sotheby's – were awarded the cash by a High Court after a two-year legal fight.

Guildford auctioneers Messenger May Beverstock called themselves 'expert' valuers but they put a £50 price tag on two 'dusty' oil paintings of foxhounds later attributed to the 18th century master Stubbs.[49]

Electronics debacle

Europe's high-tech giants are losing out to U.S. and Japanese competitors.

From the plant gates to the three-storey company headquarters in Eindhoven, a sense of shock hung over N.V. Philips, the largest electronics firm in Europe, in the wake of unexpectedly drastic cutbacks. Nearly 20% of the Dutch multinational's employees expect to lose their jobs by the end of 1991 as part of Philips' plan to slash its worldwide work force of 285,000 by up to 55,000. The layoffs will cut across product lines – from television sets to medical scanners to computers – and effect the shop floor as well as the executive suite. Says Frans van Tilbury, 56, a medical-systems worker who recently celebrated his 40th year with the company: 'Philips used to be a healthy firm, but now it is falling apart'.

The sun has not set on Philips, but its lustre as Europe's high-tech standard bearer against Japanese and American competition is tarnished. The shadows are lengthening as well at other European high-tech behemoths, particularly in the information-technology sector, which includes computers, microchips, consumer electronics and office systems. Philips alone will lose at least $1.2 billion in 1990; France's Groupe Bull faces a severe slump, as do computer divisions at Germany's Siemens Nixdorf Informationsysteme AG and Italy's Olivetti. Says Angela Dean, a London-based technology analyst with Morgan Stanley International: 'the shake-up in Europe is just beginning'.

European governments have generally looked to information technology as a source of new jobs to replace those lost in such dying sectors as coal, steel and ship-building. But subsidizing and protecting manufacturers, if only for reasons of national pride, have left the Continent's high-tech firms fragmented and unable to control more than 25% of the combined $110 billion home market. Siemens Nixdorf, Europe's leader in the category, accounts for only 7% of those sales, followed by Olivetti (3.9%), Bull (3.3%) and Philips (2.4%). Contends Michel Delapierre, an electronics-industry expert at the University of Nanterre: 'Europe's companies are relics from another age that were set up to champion national interests.'[50]

Ozone layer depleting 'at twice rate expected'

The ozone layer over Britain and the rest of Europe is disappearing twice as fast as scientists had expected and worse is in store, an official report warned yesterday, writes Tom Wilkie.

▶

Dr John Pyle, chairman of the Department of the Environment's Stratospheric Ozone Review Group, said that he would not be surprised if the rate doubled again by the end of the decade.

Researchers believe that chlorine accumulating in the stratosphere from chlorofluorocarbons (CFCs) is responsible for the depletion of the ozone layer. Dr Pyle said that, whatever efforts are made to phase out the use of CFCs quickly, chlorine concentrations in the stratosphere will continue to rise at least until 2000.

Thinning of the ozone layer allows more of the harmful ultraviolet light from the sun to reach the surface of the earch. Excessive exposure to ultraviolet light can cause skin cancer and cataracts in humans, and can interfere with the growth of plants.

Dr Pyle, a scientist with the British Antarctic Survey, noted that the decrease in ozone was particularly marked during the months of February and March, the start of the growing season in the northern hemisphere.

'We have no idea what the implications are. The Antarctic ozone hole occurred quite suddenly and it seems prudent not to put the northern hemisphere at risk,' he said.[51]

Brel chief sacked as new trains fall behind schedule

The chief executive of Brel, Britain's biggest railway train manufacturer, has lost his job because of the company's failure to deliver trains to British Rail on time.

Mr Peter Holdstock, 60, who led the management-employee buy-out of Brel from BR in April 1989, has been replaced by Mr Bo Sodersten, a 53 year old Swede with long experience in the railway equipment industry.

Mr Holdstock's departure is understood to have been prompted by Brel's plunge into losses resulting from the company's continuing inability to meet production schedules on new trains for BR.

The most serious delays have been with a new express train called the Class 158 which was supposed to have led to a leap in quality of services on Regional Railways and Scotrail routes from September 1989.

Instead, timetables were thrown into chaos when production difficulties led to a year-long delay in delivery. Teething troubles with the new trains have caused further serious problems since they started entering service.

Brel has also fallen badly behind schedule on the production of a new class of suburban trains called the Class 165, destined for Network SouthEast's Chiltern routes out of London's Marylebone station.

Mr Ian Forrester, Brel's director of personnel and business services, said the delays in deliveries meant sales income was failing to match the company's heavy outgoings on labour and materials for the new trains.[52]

Shoe specialists take backward step

Turmoil in the British footwear market saw the closure of a further 380 shoe shops last year, bringing the overall toll to 3,010 since the recession according to Verdict, the retail consultancy.

▶

Shoe specialists like Clarks, Cable & Co. and Saxone have been heavily punished for failure to respond to customer demand, the report says, and are fast losing market share to Next, Marks & Spencer and clothing chains.

The market for shoes rose by 7 per cent last year to £4.7 billion, according to Verdict – but the share of shoe specialists sunk from 59 per cent to 55 per cent.

However, the quickening pace of shoe shop closures – partly stemming from the break-up of Sears' British Shoe Corporation – has left a £440 million gap in the high street market, it says, mainly at the bottom end of the market. More upmarket retailers such as Church's, where John Church is executive chairman, Bally and Russell & Bromley have been able to maintain their market position thanks to their long tradition of serving their respective niches.

Richard Hyman, chairman of Verdict, said: 'It was the lower part of the market where the reverberations of the break-up of British Shoe Corporation were most keenly felt. In general terms, the lower to mid-market customer is now up for grabs.'

The report criticises shoe specialists for listening too much to manufacturers and not enough to customers.[53]

Notes

1 NASA Mission Control spokesman, Steve Nesbitt on the space shuttle *Challenger* accident, 28 January 1986.

2 Malcolm McConnell, *Challenger, A Major Malfunction* (London: Simon & Schuster, 1987), p. XV.

3 There are two types of joints to hold the 150-feet high booster rocket sections together: the permanent 'factory joints' which are sealed in the Morton Thiokol factory in Utah; the temporary 'field joints' which are sealed before each flight 'in the field' at the Kennedy Space Center in Florida.

4 *Report to the President by the Presidential Commission on the Space Shuttle Challenger Accident*, Vol. 1 (Washington, DC, 1986), pp. 40–72.

5 Ibid., p. 72.

6 Ibid., p. 82.

7 See BBC *Panorama* broadcast, 'The Dream That Fell Out of the Sky', 28 April 1986.

8 'Who's what in the global space club?', *New Straits Times* (Kuala Lumpur, Malaysia), 25 August 1989.

9 Richard P. Feynman, *What Do You Care What Other People Think* (London: Unwin Hyman), pp. 113–237.

10 Ibid., p. 150.

11 Ibid., pp. 236–7.

12 *New York Times*, 29 February 1986.

13 Kenneth A. Kovach and Barry Render, 'NASA managers and Challenger: a profile and possible explanation', *Personnel*, April 1987, pp. 40–4.

14 Ibid., p. 40. The tests were: Leaning Styles Inventory (LSI); Androgyny, Management of Motives Index (MMI); Work Motivation Inventory (WMI); and Fundamental Interpersonal Response Orientation, Form B (FIRO B).

15 Diane Vaughan, *The Challenger Launch Decision: Risky technology, Culture, and Deviance at NASA* (Chicago: University of Chicago Press, 1996).

16 *See* US House Committee on Science and Technology, *Investigation on the Challenger Accident Report* (Washington, DC: Government Printing Office, 1986).

17 Diane Vaughan, op. cit., p. xii.

18 Ibid., p. xii.

19 Ibid., p. xiv.

20 Tim Furniss, 'Shuttle goes private amid safety fears', *Sunday Times*, 6 October 1996.

21 David Usborne, 'US privatises shuttle production', *The Independent*, 3 July 1996.

22 *Western Mail*, 3 November 1990.

23 *Sunday Mirror*, 14 February 1989.

24 ' "Knee-jerk" law reduces pit bull terrier menace', *Guardian*, 19 December 1996.

25 *The Independent*, 4 April 1989.

26 *Daily Telegraph*, 6 April 1988.

27 *Daily Telegraph*, 8 April 1988.

28 John W. Senders, 'Is there a cure for human error?', *Psychology Today*, April 1990.

29 John Merritt, 'Stephenson Rocket burns Bank's pocket', *Sunday Times*, 20 May 1990.

30 *Time*, 25 November 1996.

31 Christian Wolmar, 'Every pilot's nightmare', *The Independent*, 26 November 1996.

32 *New Civil Engineer*, 18 February 1999.

33 *Daily Telegraph*, 25 February 1988.

34 *The Independent*, 15 June 1991.

35 John W. Senders, op. cit.

36 *Today*, 31 March 1989.

37 Nigel Hawkes, source unknown.

38 *Independent on Sunday*, 8 July 1990.

39 Valerie Elliott and Mark Henderson, 'Home News', *The Times*, 22 April 1998, p. 4.

40 *New Scientist*, 1 December 1990.

41 Simon Goodwin, *Hubble's Universe: A New Picture of Space* (London: Constable, 1996), pp. 22 and 23.

42 *The Times*, 19 August 1991.

43 *The Times*, 11 September 1991.

44 Christian Wolmar, 'Airline fined after plane ran out of oil', *The Independent*, 26 July 1996.

45 'Department of groundless optimism', *Fortune Magazine*, 9 September 1996, p. 17.

46 John Lichfield, 'Theft embarrasses slack Louvre', *The Independent*, 5 May 1998.

47 *Sunday Times*, 4 March 1990.

48 Hugh Muir, 'Buddhist's pique at RAF rescue', *Daily Telegraph*, 24 December 1996.

49 *Evening Standard*, 22 November 1988.

50 Adam Zagorin, 'Electronic debacle', *Time Magazine*, 12 November 1990.

51 *The Independent*, 19 July 1991.

52 *Financial Times*, 4 September 1991.

53 Fraser Nelson, 'Shoe specialists take backward step', *The Times*, 20 April 1998, Business News, p. 45.

Chapter 5

....

Case studies of total quality management

It must be considered that there is nothing more difficult to carry out, nor more doubtful of success, nor more dangerous to handle, than to initiate a new order of things.

Niccolo Machiavelli, *The Prince*

We are absolutely convinced that TQM is a fundamentally better way to conduct business and is necessary for the economic well-being of America. TQM results in higher-quality, lower-cost products and services that respond faster to the needs of the customer.

The CEOs of American Express Company, IBM Corporation, The Procter and Gamble Company, Ford Motor Company, Motorola Inc. and Xerox Corporation in an open letter sent to *Harvard Business Review* in 1991.

Changing company culture

Creating a total quality company culture is one of the biggest challenges of a total quality management programme. A firm's very survival may depend on how it adapts its culture to a rapidly changing business environment and to the new demands of its customers: 'Of corporations in the *Fortune* 500 rankings five years ago, 143 are missing today'.[1] In this chapter we first look at the elements of company culture and how it must change to accommodate TQM. We then look at six companies which have made the change and are still making it. These six brief case studies include two information technology service and manufacturing companies, IBM and Xerox, two service companies, British Airways and the Royal Mail, and Paul Revere Insurance Group.

But what is company culture? What are the different kinds of company culture? What is meant by a total quality management culture?

What is company culture?

Part of the fascination of foreign travel is observing the differences in national cultures. The British culture is very different from the French, Malaysian, Japanese or American cultures. And they are all different from the Eastern

European national cultures. Yet there are multinational companies that operate in strikingly similar ways across many national cultures. Oil companies such as Shell and Esso, car firms such as Ford and Nissan, computer giants such as IBM, Xerox and Hewlett Packard, and telecommunications consortiums such as British Telecom or Cable and Wireless or ITT, all have distinctive company cultures. In fact, these companies have ways of doing things which often override national culture. Their managers, in many different countries, often behave more like each other than like their fellow citizens. These companies have created cultures of their own.

In 1972 Roger Harrison described organizational culture as: 'The ideologies, beliefs and deep-set values which occur in all firms . . . and are the prescriptions for the way in which people should work in those organizations.'[2] In 1986, Charles Handy echoed Harrison's definition, but went further in clarifying culture as:

> Deep-set beliefs about the way work should be organised, the way authority should be exercised, people rewarded, people controlled. What are the degrees of formalisation required? How much planning and how far ahead? What combination of obedience and initiative is looked for in subordinates? Do work hours matter, or dress, or personal eccentricities? . . . Do committees control an individual? Are there rules and procedures or only results? These are all parts of the culture of an organisation.[3]

Recognizing culture

Culture is deeply rooted in organizations. It manifests itself in a number of obvious ways. Six expressions of a company's culture are the following:

1 *Regular ways of doing things.* Often there are observable patterns of behaviour among people of the same company. In one electronics company, the managing director called employees by surnames and expected everyone to be addressed formally. In a well known bank it was frowned upon if the male members of management did not come to work in a suit.
2 *Work group norms.* Standards of performance are formally/informally set by work groups: 'We make our decisions together and stand by them'; 'No rate busting allowed'; 'A fair day's work for a fair day's pay'.
3 *Main values espoused by a company.* A value is a deeply held assumption, which influences attitudes and behaviour. The US Marine Corps has its central value enshrined in the motto *Semper Fidelis* (always faithful). One of the key values of IBM is 'excellence in everything we do'.
4 *Philosophy that shapes a company's policies towards its employees or customers.* John Lewis expresses its philosophy in the phrase 'never knowingly undersold'. Tesco's was built on the barrow boy philosophy 'pile them high and sell them cheap'.

5 *Rules of the game for getting along well in a company.* Not attending a company's social events in many companies is seen as a lack of involvement and commitment to the company. Leaving the office before the boss in the evening can be viewed as having a lack of serious commitment to one's work in certain firms.
6 *Feeling or atmosphere created by the physical layout and decoration in a company.* The opulence of the Cartier watch company's retail outlet in London creates an aura of high sophistication associated with its expensive products. The VIP lounge of British Airways, with a special section filled with personal computers, fax machines and photocopiers, reflects its attention to detail in customer service for the business traveller.

All of these evidences of company culture Schein would argue are not, in themselves, the company culture, but they simply *reflect* the deeper level of basic assumptions and beliefs that are shared by people in a business. These assumptions and beliefs about how a company gets organized internally and deals with threats and opportunities in its business environment are deeply rooted and operate unconsciously and in a taken-for-granted fashion. Company culture then can be defined in Schein's words as:

> A pattern of basic assumptions – invented, discovered, or developed by a given group as it learns to cope with its problems of external adaptation and internal integration – that has worked well enough to be considered valid and, therefore to be taught to new members as the correct way to perceive, think and feel in relation to those problems.[4]

Peters and Waterman provided a list of seven basic values that are found in the best American companies.[5] These two management writers present corporate culture as a recipe for success in which quality is one of the seven essential beliefs. These basic values are defined as follows:

1 A belief in being the 'best'.
2 A belief in the importance of the details of execution, the nuts and bolts of doing the job well.
3 A belief in the importance of people as individuals.
4 A belief in superior quality and service.
5 A belief that most members of the organization should be innovators, and its corollary, the willingness to support failure.
6 A belief in the importance of informality to enhance communication.
7 Explicit belief in, and recognition of, the importance of economic growth and profits.

Peters and Waterman wrote *In Search of Excellence* nearly two decades ago while they were working as management consultants for McKinsey. It was there they learned the centrality of values in a company which is graphically

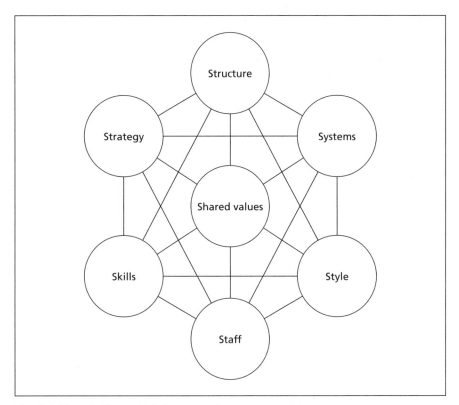

Fig. 5.1 The McKinsey 7-S framework

portrayed in Figure 5.1, developed by Tom Peters, Robert Waterman, Richard Pascale and others. When quality becomes the central shared value as in a TQM programme, everything else flows from it – systems, strategy, structure, style, skills and staff or choice of people. The framework is still valid today.

SAS, the airline (*see* pp. 26–28), underwent a radical cultural change by redefining its mission to meet its customers' 50 million moments of truth. Since most of the moments of truth were managed by front-line employees, they had to be empowered and educated to deal directly with them. They were backed by front-line management. The role of middle and top managers was changed simply to support the front-line people in dealing with the 50 million 'moments of truth'. SAS created a huge internal realignment to face up to the external adaptation of a new approach to customer service.

As a quality process which makes quality central to the business, total quality management recognizes a change in many of the basic assumptions and beliefs from former practices to future performance. Xerox made this cultural change explicit in its 'Leadership Through Quality' programmes. Examples

Table 5.1 Examples of cultural change required

From	To
Incomplete or ambiguous understanding of customer requirements.	Use of systematic approach to understand and satisfy both internal and external customer requirements.
An orientation to short-term objectives and actions with limited long-term perspective.	The deliberate balance of long-term goals with successive short-term objectives.
Acceptance of a certain margin of error and subsequent corrective action as the norm.	Striving for continuous improvement in error-free output in meeting customer requirements and doing things right the first time.
Unstructured, individualistic problem-solving and decision-making.	Predominantly participative and disciplined problem-solving and decision-making using a common approach.
A management style with uncertain objectives that instils fear of failure.	An open style with clear and consistent objectives which encourages problem-solving and group-derived solutions.

of cultural changes which could be required are shown in Table 5.1. The remainder of the chapter is taken up with the case studies which capture a variety of companies at a critical point in each of their histories when they made a radical choice for TQM for different reasons. These companies have all advanced their TQM experiences but remain loyal to the quality principle that motivated them in the first place.

The Body Shop – 24 years of customer focus

With over 1,600 retail outlets in 54 countries, The Body Shop pushes out the boundaries of meeting customer requirements to include a social dimension. No exploitation of animals, protection of the environment and a positive contribution to both the local community in which its retail shops operate and the global community from where The Body Shop derives its raw materials and trading base are part of the company's credo, not a marketing ploy. The business was also built on giving the customer value for money in the cosmetics industry notorious for the opposite.

Since opening her first Body Shop outlet in 1976, Anita Roddick has been customer focused. Today Anita Roddick still cannot leave the customer alone. She interrupted a tour guide's lecture about the start of her global business to a group of human resource managers from Cranfield School of Management to contribute to their knowledge of customer service and business ethics. Standing in a facsimile of her original store on the grounds of The Body Shop's international headquarters in Littlehampton, West Sussex, Anita Roddick said:

It's not difficult for us to know what the customers want from us; we ask them and then try to produce the product. We've always done that from the start.[6]

She has a particular grievance with the beauty business in which The Body Shop has carved out a niche by giving its customers value for money.

In my view the cosmetics industry should be promoting health and well-being; instead it hypes an outdated notion of glamour and sells false hopes and fantasy. With the muscle of multi-million dollar advertising budgets, the major cosmetic houses seek to persuade women that they can help them look younger and more 'beautiful'. Yet they know that such claims are nonsense.[7]

'Smile Dammit Smile!'

Anita Roddick attributes her success down to superb customer care. Her 20-second crash course in customer care asserts:

- Never treat customers as enemies, approach them as potential friends. Think of customers as guests, make them laugh.
- Acknowledge their presence within 30 seconds – smile, make eye contact, say hello.
- Talk to them within the first three minutes.
- Offer product advice where appropriate.
- Smile: always thank customers and invite them back . . .
- Treat customers as you'd like to be treated![8]

The Body Shop's policy is to communicate with the customer through use of leaflets, posters and information boards, books[9] and suggestion boxes in every shop. Six full-time members of staff catalogue customer suggestions and reply to them. The shops hold regular forums from 6 to 9 pm to invite customers to come and tell them what they want in terms of new products.

The Body Shop set up its own independent video production company called Jacaranda Productions in 1987 with a brief to produce staff training and educational weekly programmes – information, campaigning and documentary videos – especially for the company. One of Jacaranda's outputs is a monthly video *Talking Shop* which has global distribution through the outlets and is shown to all The Body Shop employees in their shops, factories, warehouses and offices.

A video production on customer care was entitled *Smile Dammit Smile*. Another was on loneliness in society and the need to do something about it. Videos on a general theme are being made available to a wider viewing public through schools, colleges and satellite or cable TV.

Reaching out to the public on wider social and environmental issues is part of The Body Shop's company culture. One cannot even obtain a franchise from The Body Shop to run a retail outlet unless the person has a track record of being involved in community issues, a plan for further community involvement and a genuine commitment to the company's core values.

Perhaps its most spectacular campaign to date was a drive to stop the burning of the rain forests. This major campaign had its roots in earlier action undertaken in 1989 when The Body Shop had displayed rain forest posters published by Friends of the Earth. This campaign had a four-year plan. In year one The Body Shop people from Anita Roddick and her husband partner Gordon to shop personnel and factory and warehouse workers educated themselves on the rain forest issues. In years two and three they launched a sustained campaign for the rights of indigenous tribes. Then in year four they offered the solution of reafforestation and the management of sustainable resources as the campaign's focus.

An immediate action was to campaign to stop the annual burning of the rain forest which took place during the dry season between July and September. In 1988 an area of rain forest larger than Great Britain was set ablaze to clear land primarily for cattle ranching. The burning wreaked havoc on the Indian population, destroyed wildlife and plants and contributed to the greenhouse effect by releasing tons of carbon dioxide into the atmosphere. Within a few weeks of the spectacular campaign, The Body Shop had collected over one million signed letters to the then President José Sarney demanding that Brazil stop the burning of the rain forests. These letters were hand delivered en masse to the Brazilian Embassy in London by 250 members of The Body Shops' staff, with massive media coverage.

There have been positive results from campaigns by The Body Shop and others like Friends of the Earth. Admitting that half the world's rain forest has been felled, Brazil has taken action to limit destruction. Dramatic new measures to save the Amazonian rain forest were decreed in 1996 by Brazil's President Fernando Henrique Cardoso. A two-year moratorium was imposed on the felling of mahogany and virola, two of Brazil's most important tropical hardwood trees.[10]

The Body Shop mixes business with politics unashamedly. A campaign in the summer of 1996 called on the Rt. Hon. The Baroness Chalker of Wallasey, Minister of State for Foreign and Commonwealth Affairs, Overseas Development Administration, to protect developments in Nigeria. The Body Shop was also one of the organizers of the United Nation's 4th World Conference on Women in Beijing.

Closer to home in Britain's capital, The Body Shop helped start and finance *The Big Issue*, a weekly newspaper written and sold in the streets by the homeless.

In such public ways The Body Shop puts into practice its deeply felt and championed values. It does, however, begin by putting its own house in order. A purpose-built child-care centre was opened in January 1990 at The Body

Shop headquarters at a cost to the company of nearly £1 million. It is for working mothers in the factories, offices and warehouses and The Body Shop pays a subsidy for all employees using the centre. To give its staff direct and personal experience of working in different cultures and countries, The Body Shop introduced an international job-swapping scheme, whereby staff change places with each other for periods of several months.

Whether it is looking after orphans in Romania or building a soap factory in a rough neighbourhood in Scotland with chronic high unemployment, The Body Shop aims at achieving social benefits. The corporate methodology is expressed in five huge silhouettes of its delivery lorries mounted like billboards on the landscape at its headquarters. The lorries form a convoy. The first lorry has the word 'THINK' in huge blue letters; beneath it in much smaller letters are the words 'how we can improve the quality of life'. It is followed by a lorry with the huge word 'ACT' 'because it we don't, who will?' The third lorry has the word 'CHANGE' emblazoned on it, followed by 'the way we work for the better'. The last lorry says simply 'THANK YOU' for resisting the ordinary, with the commemorative Body Shop logo. As Rosabeth Moss Kanter says in her new book *World Class, Thriving Locally in the Global Economy*, 'specific details are always subject to change as a company shifts strategy, a community gets its act together, or today's hero stumbles and becomes tomorrow's fallen star; it is a fact of life that no success endures for very long without both discipline and flexibility, both persistence and change.'[11] Indeed, The Body Shop is striving to change its structure.

In May 1998 Anita Roddick announced that she would relinquish day-to-day control of the company to become co-chairman with her husband Gordon. Patrick Gournay, a former director of Danone, the French food groups, took over the company as group chief executive officer in July 1998.

The American part of the business which was a loss-maker was restructured as a joint venture operation controlled by Adrian Bellamy; losses in the US operation were cut from £3m to £1.7m, but during the same time sales across the Pacific Rim fell 14 per cent, with Japan hard hit. Shares were trading at 120.5p in May 1998, down from their all-time high of 340p.

In addition to dealing with the Far East crisis in 1998 The Body Shop is struggling with fierce competition in America and in the UK where copycat products are sold by supermarket and chemist chains. The Body Shop's far-flung network of 1,600 shops spread across the continents is susceptible to rising rents in their high street and mall locations and this factor may lead the company to engage in direct selling to their wide customer base.

But management problems seem to lie at the heart of the company's current underperformance. The founders, Anita and Gordon Roddick, who still control a 26 per cent stake in the business, said that they were making the changes because they recognized that while they had certain skills they did not have the all-round management expertise to solve all the problems emerging in the far-flung parts of the sourcing, manufacturing and retailing business. Although new experienced management has been brought in, the charismatic founder is still very much involved in the business. All new ventures will have to remain true to the ideals of this extraordinary green company but the challenge for the future must be to maintain and increase the customer loyalty upon which the entire enterprise was begun over two decades ago.

British Airways – new routes to customer service

British Airways (BA) progressed in less than a decade from a shoddy airline known for its indifference to passengers to a world-beating, financially sound, trendsetting business. Total quality was the direct route it took to this transformation. The journey to excellence began when it was still a nationalized industry. It started by shedding jobs world-wide which was needed to stop the huge loss-making (£137 million in 1981) and to deal with the serious over-manning stemming from the 1970s merging of BOAC and BEA.

With Lord John King as Chairman and Sir Colin Marshall as Deputy Chairman and chief executive the airline then took a critical look at its route network. It withdrew from a substantial range of routes, a painful process for any airline, to focus on key economic sectors of the global market, namely Europe, the United States and the Pacific.

By October 1986, BA had regained its financial health. It signed the biggest deal ever made by an airline – an order for £2.5 billion worth of Boeing aircraft, thereby putting the final piece of its privatization strategy in place. With a £5 million advertising budget the airline sold itself. Four months later it was a private company. BA then began to sort out its poor reputation for customer service.

The leaner organization set out to become a fitter one by focusing on its customers. The 'Putting People First' programme was massive in scope. It aimed to reach every one of BA's 30,000 employees and did so. Colin Marshall made it his mission to support the initiative from the top. He personally introduced the courses and kept his weight behind them. Designed by Time Manager International, the Putting People First programme set the theme of service at the outset. 'This course and book are aimed at helping you to improve your skills as a giver of service to others. The basis of good service is that the person who gives it feels confident and at ease in a service situation' are the opening words of the handbook. The ambitious course and reading were designed to look at the nature of service, through the employee's own personal success, his or her aims in life and interpersonal relationships. One of the explicit messages was that behaviour breeds behaviour. Designed as a positive, uplifting experience the ten sessions covered the range of people skills from assertiveness to body language, from coping with stress to giving and receiving strokes.

It was the starting point for other quality initiatives including 'Customer First' teams. These teams needed training courses which were run by PA Management Consultants. The objectives of the course were:

1 To introduce the techniques and application of systematic problem-solving.
2 To give participants experience of group working and group leadership.
3 To discuss and solve practical problems concerned with business success.

Chris Swan, Deputy Head of Customer Service at the time, explained that research had shown that BA personnel were not very good at seeing things through their customers' eyes. They were not living up to their motto: 'We fly to serve'. The Putting People First programme and Customer First teams were aimed at changing that situation. To deal with the internal customer BA organized a programme called 'A Day in the Life', in which each department explained itself to the others in a cheerful convention-like atmosphere. Stands were erected with names such as 'The Golden Touch', 'Gold in the Hole' (cargo), 'The Magic of Flight', 'Money Matters', 'Tomorrow's World Today', 'Engineering Excellence', etc. More than 30,000 employees world-wide had the opportunity to understand what each of the departments really did. Seven years after the launch of their 'First Programmes', well known in the service sector, BA was running a fifth generation of the course.

In managing any large-scale organizational change there are four key processes companies go through:[12]

1 Pattern breaking in which old, dysfunctional, familiar ways of doing things have to be stopped or shattered so that new approaches can be tried. In that way the system is freed of structures, processes or functions that are no longer useful.
2 Experimenting processes in which new patterns better suited to the present environment are generated. The new ideas proposed will cause changes in a company's strategy, structure and culture. Here large-scale organizational change is often less disruptive than playing with piecemeal, incremental change.
3 Visioning is a process in which (of the many possible) a new perspective is selected around which the firm can rally its reorganization and reshape its system.
4 Bonding is a process of alignment in which people in the organization are led into the new ways of doing, thinking, learning, interacting and trusting.

BA went through each of these phases. The pattern-breaking phase began with the preparation for privatization with the massive 'de-manning' from 59,000 to 29,000 and the restructuring and the jettisoning of routes from Europe, the

United States and the Pacific. When the airline discovered that over seventy senior managers were actually blocking the cultural change to a total quality management approach and were incorrigible in their negative attitudes, BA gave them individual letters of dismissal all on one night known as 'the night of the long knives'.

The pattern breaking was brutal – even the old coat of arms and logo had to go as planes were repainted to reflect the new corporate identity and to look cleaner, sharper and more modern. The new corporate identity applied to the fleet, the terminals, retail outlets and uniforms for ground and cabin crew staff. Out went old central budgeting systems, unnecessary levels of management, old performance appraisal systems, poor information retrieval systems and old reward structures.

The experimenting and visionary stages were very difficult due to a rather hostile national environment for change in which BA operates. In a lecture, Sir Colin Marshall made the point that BA's cultural changes were made against rather unfavourable problems in the wider British society.[13] These were the following:

- an attitude fairly apathetic to business success;
- the absence of ways of developing good managers in the right type and numbers;
- an underachieving educational system with no effective, continuing education for present or future workforces;
- patchy or ineffective investment in new technology;
- the only effective motivation for good performance at work being the threat of loss rather than the hope of gain.

As Colin Marshall said:

> It is my opinion that when most people talk about the desirability of achieving cultural change in business, they are really talking about these five problem areas and the need to find a way to effect better approaches and hopefully better answers, than at present seems to be found almost anywhere on the business scene.[14]

Against the difficult, unique, national, cultural pull in the opposite direction of total quality, Colin Marshall cited a few of BA's accomplishments:

> ... the successes we have had in recent years derive primarily from our staff and their attitudes to what needed to be done. Whether in the cabin, behind the check-in desk, on the baggage ramps, in the cargo shed, at the service desk or on the ubiquitous telephone, our people have seen quickly and effectively what implications are to be drawn from an ever-increasingly competitive world, and often they have made major changes in working style and attitudes which our customers have noted favourably.[15]

Marshall argued for a critical change at the level of middle management culture, but then put his central view that cultural change is unswervingly linked to a change in underlying values. 'Thus for the phrase "culture change" to be meaningful', he said, 'it has to be time-qualified and it must be built on a firm base of truly altered value frameworks . . . In BA, this is something which has happened and hopefully will continue to be a prime focus of effort and attention for a long time to come.'[16]

Nicholas Georgiades as director of human resources (an appointment of Colin Marshall) established training programmes for senior and middle management which included 'Managing People First' and 'Leading the Service Business'. There were also off-site team-building meetings. These were experiential courses which included a good measure of individual feedback to individual managers about their on-the-job behaviour. To move the entire organization from a culture that was bureaucratic and militaristic to one that was service oriented and market driven required creating a new open, supportive and participative management style. Open learning programmes were offered to managers to help them develop themselves.

A 'Top Flight Academics' programme was started for various levels of management to encourage development. Through one of these courses a BA manager can earn an MBA degree. To show its ongoing commitment to employee education, BA purchased Chartridge as a permanent training centre.

Georgiades won acceptance from BA management of the concept of 'emotional labour', the high energy output individuals needed to meet customer demands in the uncertain environment of the airline business. Forms of emotional support were created to avoid excess stress and burn-out which included peer support groups.

There were many changes in the structures and systems at the airline. Task forces made up of people from different functions and from different levels of responsibility were formed to plan changes. The organizational hierarchy was flattened to remove unnecessary and dysfunctional levels of management. The budgeting process was radically altered making it less top-down and centralized. Profit-sharing bonus schemes were started. New performance appraisal systems were established to take into account one's behaviour as well as performance results. Personnel staff became internal consultants for the change process helping both line and staff managers with the new structures and procedures. A performance-based compensation system was put in place. A new data-driven feedback system on management practices was installed.

The bonding process at BA for the new change is still continuing to this day. One of the ways it is achieved is through advertising. According to Liam Strong, former Director of Marketing and Operations (before becoming CEO of Sears), BA's advertising is targeted just as much on BA's staff as on the public at large. Ideas such as 'World Traveller' class to replace the lacklustre economy class are first introduced to the staff before announcement to the public.[17] Imaginative ways are found to lure the internal BA customer into the change. For example, a pavilion in the shape of a huge sports or travel bag next to BA's main building was used to draw staff members into a briefing session on the new 'World Traveller' product. Employees were invited to visit the bag in a series of 'teaser posters'. This effort to build up an internal commitment to the new class of service before going public with it worked as over a thousand staff a week visited the building.

The rebranding of the various classes of service on a flight was part of BA's successful effort to meet customer requirements. 'Clearly British Airways already had the normal commercial functions – advertising, promotions, a market research function,' Liam Strong explained. 'What the company did not have was a brand function whose job it was to specify product standards throughout the business.'

The brand products within the cabin followed on the heels of each other – Club World for business class was introduced in 1987 (and imitated by other leading airlines within 18 months). Then came a revamping of First Class and Super Shuttle in 1989, Leisure in 1990 and economy – World Traveller – in 1991.

Part of the cultural change challenge was to establish marketing as central to a large, operationally driven business. BA had been dominated by the long planning lead times which required technically powerful functions of engineering and flight crew. 'We turn our back on the operational aspects of the business and make an intense effort to understand the aspirations and desires of our passengers . . . as people,' Liam Strong explained. 'For our economy [World Traveller] relaunch this entailed 5,000 interviews to establish not just physical requirements but emotional needs and preferences.' BA's research established 15 discrete groups travelling economy from grandma on her first long-range flight to a weary, thrifty export manager to a childless couple on their third annual holiday.

As Strong explained:

World Traveller was the brand name which, internationally, most effectively reflected the aspirations of the diverse group. It captured the excitement and sense of occasion for the many making a major infrequent trip; and it gave an appropriate status to the back end of the plane where most people are spending their own money on what is a significant expenditure. Our business definitions start with the traveller, not the journey.

The aspirations we stimulate must be met by the physical product we offer. Again taking economy, the logistics of this change are staggering. Product managers in BA would make good staff colonels in a medium sized war. On the catering side alone, 130 million items have been ordered to support World Traveller. 20,000 seats have been re-designed and 60,000 pillows delivered.

All our service staff go through brand camps so they understand the quality of service that travellers in each of our cabins can expect. The brand specification, therefore, creates a framework to guide and inform staff responses.

Obviously therefore, internal marketing is just as important as any activity we undertake to the final consumer. As we look at the major events we have undertaken in the past few years, the ones which have been most successful are those where we have succeeded in capturing the imagination of our staff, and marshalling their enthusiasm and commitment behind the product. Each major relaunch or new initiative has an internal marketing programme and campaign which is just as detailed as our consumer and trade programmes.

The splashy television and newspaper advertisements aim to capture the imagination of both the staff and the travelling public. This produces a deliberate crossover where BA uses the advertisements to tell the consumer what he or she can expect from the airline, while telling the staff members what is expected from them in service to the customers. It takes about a year to get a relaunch message across. For example, a spectacular television advertisement for BA's 1990 campaign which cost just under £1 million to produce, was made in Utah with more than 4,000 school children using picture boards overhead (like Chinese students in a stadium) that gradually made a massive smiling face on the landscape. The evocative music of 'The Flower Duet' from the opera *Lakmé* by Delibes was matched by emotional scenes of people meeting loved ones. The highly visual and dramatic scenes were pulled together with an authoritative voice-over that slowly said, 'Every year the world's favourite airline brings 24 million people together.'

BA's give-away of £10 million-worth of seats on all their flights on 23 April 1991 won the airline about £50 million worth of media publicity and global applause for such a magnanimous event. As a sign of their support for the celebration, cabin crew wore fancy dress on the day which was St George's Day. The airline's goals for the day were to take leadership of the business after the Gulf War airline crisis, to energize staff and to get people flying again. They also used the occasion to fly a thousand travel agents into Britain and to involve car hire firms. As a result of the extravaganza BA recovered from the Gulf War crisis faster in April, May and June than other airlines.

Results

BA is the fourth largest airline in the world carrying over 25 million passengers in 1990. It has a very large international network of routes, with over 160 destinations in 75 countries, including over 20 North American major city destinations. It controls 41 per cent of the lucrative North Atlantic market. Its fleet stood at 235 aircraft in March 1991, with the following long-range aircraft: 7 Concorde, 47 Boeing 747 (including 8 new 747–400), 17 Lockheed Tristars, 8 DC-10 and 4 Boeing 767. The 747–400s which were delivered during 1990 have a longer range and significantly reduced operating costs compared to the older 747–100s and 200s run by competitors.

BA's 29,000 employees continue to make strenuous efforts to improve customer service through customer care programmes and by the use of improved information technology systems (such as its investment in the Galileo reservations system). BA's 'Club World' Business Class is marketed aggressively. The airline makes extensive use of competitive benchmarking, measuring everything they do against the best of their competitors, from maintenance engineering turning around aircraft to in-flight menus for its various classes of service. 'Food has a powerful effect on the memory of a flight, far more than anything else,' says Kurt Hafner, British Airways chief of catering standards. 'The importance of the meal is that, if it is good, the passenger will feel cosseted, will feel loyalty towards the airline, and will want to try it again.'

The remarkable improvement in airline food that has taken place in the past few years started in 1983, when the BA management team hired Michel Roux as its consultant. Roux's advice and recipes have been augmented from time to time by other leading chefs, such as Anton Edelmann of the Savoy, Anton Mosimann (on Concorde) and by specialist help from restaurants such as the Bombay Brasserie for, in its case, advice on curries for Indian routes. This has helped give BA the competitive edge.[18]

Virtually all BA's performance indices show improvement – more on-time departures and arrivals, less time connecting for telephone reservations or information, fewer lost luggage complaints, fewer jets out of service, fewer angry passengers due to over-booking.

BA has suffered other set-backs. It has lost its monopoly at Heathrow. It has failed in its attempts to be allowed to carry onwards from the US 'gateway cities' and its principal routes are to countries in the English-speaking world, which are the ones that were severely gripped by recession in the early 1990s.

Change is expensive and sustaining change is very expensive. An organization must be extraordinarily single-minded. The most critical issue was not just defining the change and the initial implementation, it is consistency of execution over time. 'We have aircraft taking off and landing every two minutes around the world, 24 hours a day,' Strong explained. 'Our scope for getting it wrong with our passengers is enormous.'

However, prospects for BA getting it right are promising. In the 1990s international aviation – their market-place – will be one of the highest growth sectors. By the millennium the market for air travel will double.

Competition in an already fiercely competitive industry will continue. As Sir Colin Marshall indicated, BA intends to carry the fight to its competitors with bold initiatives:

We are looking at our involvement and investment in Sabena World Airlines in Belgium in the context of establishing a foothold on the Continent of Europe. We see this as a major niche in the market place in Europe, the creation of the first true hub and spoke airline operation, comparable to some of the major hub and spoke systems that have been developed in the United States. There isn't one in Europe today which provides convenient connections to a whole array of the secondary regional cities in Europe.[19]

And as Liam Strong put it to the Cranfield School of Management (31 July 1991):

Against the potential growth of the airline we are constantly checking to ensure that we are properly structured to meet market needs. In 1986 we restructured to a functional basis to give more central control; to help us maximize our network; to control service standards and get branding established.

In 1990 we re-organised again to give more power back to geographical operations; to help us manage deregulation; and to provide more focus against local competitors such as Singapore, American and Lufthansa.

Through the 1990s you will see us continuing to *adjust* the balance between function, geography and product as our market-place evolves . . . We must not get stuck with 1980s structures in the 1990s market-place. We must get our people comfortable with steady change . . .

For the 1990s all our people are focused on three simple messages. The importance of winning with key customers by building enduring relationships. The importance of delivery to specification in everything we do. And finally that only the highest quality planning will allow us to continue to manage double digit growth from a base of 25 million passengers a year. Above all, we remain committed to the highest product and service *quality*. If we falter for one moment in that commitment then we are back in the hands of the bean counters.

BA has already achieved its financial target of becoming the world's most profitable airline. Under the direction of its new Chief Executive, Robert Ayling, it is trying to achieve a greater competitive edge on the lucrative transatlantic routes by its planned alliance with American Airlines. But BA has yet to persuade Brussels and win approval of the alliance (at the time of writing) which opponents argue may violate EU policy by restricting competition.

A more immediate threat to BA's ability to maintain its total quality thrust lies with its employees' reaction to a new plan. BA announced in 1996 (Ayling's first year as Chief Executive) a radical proposal called its 'Business Efficiency Plan' to save BA £1 billion in three years up to the year 2000.

To achieve this target, BA announced that it will shed at least 5,000 jobs. The fear of the employees is that such massive downsizing will be accomplished by forced redundancies and outsourcing of operations to low labour cost suppliers. They fear a 'Day Zero' when new conditions will be imposed on them.

The massive cost-cutting in the wake of record profits strikes the workforce as unfair. They fear that entire parts of BA like engineering will be hived off into separate companies and sold.

Robert Ayling argues that change is needed to ensure competitiveness and that BA employees have been insulated from the painful changes inflicted on other employees:

> In a way what we're doing isn't fair. In the same way as it's not fair that nurses in the NHS are not paid more than they are, which we'd all like to see, just because we're human beings. We don't sit down and consider whether decisions may be fair or not. We try and find out how we can make people fly in our aeroplanes rather than other peoples'.

BA's route to change may be beset by industrial disputes that could send its quality programme spinning off course in the short term even before it achieves, in fact, the accolade its advertisers bestowed on it at the start of its journey – 'The world's favourite airline'.

IBM – creating a quality policy and plan

The unshakeable values that Thomas J. Watson Sr placed at the core of IBM from the beginning were good starting blocks for total quality management – respect for the individual, service to the customer, excellence in everything the company does. But the company's formal policy on quality dates back to nearly two decades ago.

Quality in IBM has had three distinct phases. It started with Quality Phase One which focused on product leadership and embraced quality circles, quality teams, and initiatives such as defect-free working and quality as an explicit management objective. 'The quality focus on the business process' was Phase Two and spelt out IBM's approach to quality with specific attention to getting processes right. Phase Three was launched in January 1990 and labelled 'market-driven quality'. Tracing the evolution of IBM's quality policy from the top is an illuminating exercise.

The full text of IBM's corporate policy statement on quality is as follows:

Subject: Quality

In IBM, quality has been a cornerstone since the early days of our company. Its importance in human relations, products, customer service, and the overall way in which we approach every business task is reflected in many of our policies including our basic beliefs. There can be no doubt that the emphasis on quality over the years has played a key role in our success.

Today, quality is of more significance than ever. We are operating in an environment that is highly competitive and rapidly growing more so. Many of our most able competitors are concentrating on quality and are using it as a means to attract and retain customers.

Product leadership is one of our goals for the 80s. An essential element of product leadership is quality: the delivery of offerings which are *defect free*. That is how our quality – and our competitors' – will be measured by customers.

We have to do things right first time. Each stage in the process must produce defect-free output. In other words, everyone in IBM has customers, either inside or outside the company, who use the output of his or her job; only if each person strives for and achieves defect-free work can we reach our objective of superior quality.

Quality is not the exclusive province of engineering, manufacturing, or for that matter service, marketing, or administration. Quality is truly everyone's job. Each function, each individual in IBM must assume the responsibility for a defect-free operation.[20]

But having a policy statement on TQM is not enough. IBM had to develop a workable strategy for implementing total quality. The essential ingredients of its strategy included the following elements:

1 A committed will to improve.
2 Senior management commitment.
3 Total organizational involvement.
4 Customer orientation.
5 Visible management – individual, departmental, functional and plant.
6 Defined (annual) goals and related targets.
7 Technical and educational support.
8 Visible recognition/reward.
9 'Relentless' communication.

In typical IBM fashion the company consulted various gurus and took from them whatever was congruent with the IBM culture. The success of IBM's quality programme focus on product quality was demonstrable. Such success led to Phase Two 'the quality focus on the business process'. Launched on 14 May 1985 with corporate quality document no. 101, this policy stated: 'The objective of Quality Focus on the Business Process is to improve the operational efficiency, effectiveness, and adaptability of IBM business processes.'

While recognizing the success of its traditional approach of managing through key business indicators and through functional productivity in the past, success in the future was to come from quality management. Specifically it would be accomplished through a critical and systematic analysis of the business process. In setting out the idea the policy document read as follows:

Concept
Quality management is a methodical approach to remove defects from a business process and to improve its efficiency. It includes an understanding of supplier and customer requirements, process definition, defect measurement, root cause removal, and adapting the process to assure relevancy to business needs.

It has been successfully applied in IBM to improve both product and non-product processes.

IBM's business operation can be characterized as a set of interrelated processes (e.g., Billing, Distribution, Accounting, etc.). Most business processes consist of sub-processes (e.g. Purchase Billing within Billing, Ship-to-Plan Distribution within Distribution, Inventory Accounting within Accounting, etc.).

Each IBM operating unit will apply quality management to its key functional and cross-functional processes. Line management will define and own these processes. They will have responsibility for and authority over the process results. An executive is named as the single process owner and must operate at a level high enough in the organization to:

- Identify the impact of new business direction on the process.
- Influence change in policy/procedures affecting the process.
- Commit a plan and implement change for process improvement.
- Monitor business process efficiency and effectiveness.[21]

Critical to IBM's approach to the quality focus on the business process was the allocation of responsibilities to line management as process owners at all organizational levels. The process owner specifically has responsibility for the following items:

- determining and documenting process requirements and securing customer concurrence;
- defining the sub-processes including information used by the process;
- designating line manager ownership over each sub-process;
- identifying implementers and assuring application of quality management principles;
- ensuring documentation of task level procedures;
- identifying critical success factors and key dependencies in order to meet the needs of the business during the tactical and strategic time frame;
- establishing measurements and setting targets to monitor and continuously improve process effectiveness and efficiency;
- rating the process/sub-process against defined quality standards and control criteria;
- reporting process status and progress;
- identifying and implementing changes to the process to meet the needs of the business;
- ensuring that information integrity exists throughout the process including integrity of measurements at all levels;
- resolving or escalating cross-functional issues.

The role and responsibility of corporate staff in IBM's approach to quality is to ensure that processes meet current and future needs and to focus on functional excellence which encompasses quality improvement, 'aggressiveness of objectives' and the wherewithal needed to achieve process effectiveness and efficiency. Other staff tasks include: providing direction in identifying and rationalizing processes and sub-processes and setting parameters at operational level; concurring with the designation of line ownership; and concurring with the owner's assessment of the effectiveness and efficiency of processes and sub-processes.

The roles and responsibilities of the quality, controller and communications functions within each group, division, IBM subsidiary and site are as follows:

- Assisting the process owner to prioritize process improvement activities.
- Consulting on the quality tools and techniques to be used.

Quality – support for:

- Coordinating education/training in the application of quality tools and techniques to the business processes.
- Providing an independent assessment of quality improvement activities to achieve appropriate efficiency levels.

Controller – support for:

- Assisting the process owner with implementation methods and process analysis tools.
- Conducting reviews and tests of process efficiency and effectiveness.

Communications – support for:

- Providing a comprehensive programme to communicate and reinforce the quality focus on business process.

Quality results – Phases One and Two

IBM quality programmes Phases One and Two have yielded great results. A few historic examples will illustrate the early successes that were multiplied across the company's global operations involving nearly a third of a million people.

Error-free installation of new products
Jim Harrington reports:

> For years we had believed that a defect-free installation of our large computers was impossible because of their complexity . . . But once we focused on error-free installation, the process immediately began to improve. Today the 308X series is seven times better than its predecessor product in terms of defect-free installation . . . [and] installation time has been cut by a factor of three.[22]

Enormous improvement opportunities in mature products
IBM uses about 2 million flat ribbon cables a year to connect electronic circuits. Harrington reported:

This is a well-known technology moved out to vendors years ago . . . Massive amounts of rework had been built into the product estimate and treated as normal expected yield. A young industrial engineer . . . mustered up enough interest from management so that a team was assigned to attack the high defect rates. Scrap per cable dropped from 94 cents to 28 cents, and rework dropped from 25 to 4 per cent. Problems in final tests fell from 12 to 1.2 per cent. Our annual savings are $5,000,000.[23]

Software coding yields to the improvement process

Process improvement technologies were applied to software, where quality is in part measured in terms of defects per 1,000 lines of code. An institute was even set up to aid the process. A threefold improvement ensued over a six-year period.

Stunning results from improving mundane accounting practices

Accounting data entry was 98 per cent accurate at the outset. But that means 20,000 to 30,000 miscodes per day! In two years, the number dropped to 0.4 per cent, a fivefold improvement.

Supplier partnerships hit paydirt

Harrington reports that:

In the 1970s we made the mistake of talking to our suppliers in terms of AQLs [acceptable quality levels] when we should have been talking parts per million. I am convinced that if in the 1970s we had been talking parts per million, today we would be talking parts per billion. Typical improvements, from 1980 to 1983, measured as defects per million: transistors, from 2,800 to 200, a 14-fold improvement; transformers, 4,200 to 100, a 42-fold rise in quality; and capacitors, from 9,300 to 80, a 116-fold rise.[24]

Quality results – Phase Three

Stephen B. Schwartz, an IBM executive with over 30 years' experience, was the senior vice-president for market-driven quality. He reported directly to IBM's then Chairman John Akers. Schwartz explained as follows:

Market-driven quality is not a program. It is a continuing journey. It is a way of life – part of the basic fabric of our business. It means changing the very core of the way we do things in order to meet customer needs and wants. In fact, it is a matter of survival for our company in the 1990s and beyond.[25]

Schwartz believed that line management – not staff – would roll out market-driven quality initiatives around the world. He said at the time:

I have a charter that allows me to go to line general management and to work with them to make things happen. But I plan – and I think it's essential – for the line to be the implementer. You can't put a very long life on things that are implemented by staffs.[26]

His mission was to create the structure for the five initiatives for leadership that supported IBM's market-driven effort. The five initiatives were spelled out at John Akers' senior management meeting in January 1990 and they were as follows:

1 Defining market needs better.
2 Eliminating defects.
3 Reducing product cycle time.
4 Increasing employee participation.
5 Implementing common measurements.

In addition IBM at the top designated executive owners of its key processes with the objective of reviewing and analysing each process to work to improve it.

In outline form the approach to quality contained nothing new. But Schwartz insisted that the 'level of intensity' brought to bear on quality issues was new and different. Because IBM's customers are more demanding everywhere and the industry has grown even more competitive it was imperative 'to raise the level of excellence of the whole corporation to a new plateau'.

Typical of IBM's quality efforts was that everything began with a massive commitment to quality education, starting with the top executives who then educate their management teams, who, in turn, bring the messages to their employees. While the education process was cascading through IBM, individuals were to assess their own roles and set their own objectives to achieve the improvement goals. The focus on key processes and cycle times was to concentrate the effort for maximum gain. The measurement or quality assessment used the US Department of Commerce Malcolm Baldrige assessment techniques.

Part of the measurement process aimed at zero defects included the use of statistical measurement tool 'six sigma', which is a statistical term for 3.4 defects per million opportunities (*see* the discussion in Chapter 6 on pp. 208–210). IBM applied sigma six to everything – products, billing, answering the telephone, etc.

The scope for defect reduction was very large. In 1989, for example, IBM paid $2.4 billion in warranty costs and most of these warranty claims were caused by defects. Another part of IBM's warranty claims or repair actions was unrelated to manufacturing and product design defects, but to do with customer error – not knowing how to use the system or how to load the initial program or supply power, or the communication line was a problem, and so forth. This part of the warranty costs were down to the company's whole distribution and support system. As Schwartz explained:

> If we hadn't had any warranty claims, all those funds would have dropped to
> the bottom line and would have significantly increased our earnings and our

Fig. 5.2 IBM's 'closed-loop' system for market-driven quality

earnings per share which would have had an impact on the price of IBM stock. And if you go across the whole business, think of reducing engineering changes, think of reducing the cost of service, think of not having a product where you've spent a lot on development and then you find out it doesn't meet the market need, think of the productivity impact of having solutions that hit the bull's eye every time . . . you can see very significant financial improvements in the IBM company.[27]

IBM policy letter no. 132 states: 'IBM should deliver defect-free total solutions to anything in the market place, and deliver them on time, every time.' To offer customers total solutions is to raise the game by an order of magnitude. The need in IBM is 'to attain a very tightly closed loop process between development, manufacturing, marketing, service, and the customer', as Schwartz put it. 'Much of the work we embarked upon was to try to close that loop' (*see* Figure 5.2). The design shown in the figure symbolized IBM's commitment to a closed-loop system of teamwork in which satisfying customer needs was the target of everything IBM did.

As part of IBM's benchmarking top IBM executives visited Motorola in the United States where they heard of the company's five top measurements of business health, described by Motorola senior managers as 'Five Ups'. IBM took away both the idea and the name. It was a way IBM decided on to track quality efforts. Despite the name, an organizational unit selects its own measures, generally three to eight 'Five Ups' – track activities which remove defects, reduce cycle times and ultimately lead to total customer satisfaction. 'Five Ups' were not end results in themselves but the means to the end. For example, IBM UK's marketing and service 'Five Ups' were the following:

- Warranty costs.
- On-time delivery.
- Billing accuracy.
- Customer Service first-time fix.
- Marketing and SE skill improvement.

Xerox 2000 – driving quality into the business plan

The preoccupation of 'The Document Company', Xerox, is the integration of quality into the business. Xerox saw its 'Leadership Through Quality' programme in the 1980s as '. . . a chance of survival' (David T. Kearns, the chairman and CEO of the Xerox Corporation). Due to the rigorous application of total quality management over a decade, in the 1990s the TQM programme is '. . . a chance of continued success' (Paul A. Allaire, the chairman and CEO of the Xerox Corporation until 1998). From 1987 to 1990 Xerox concentrated on quality assessment and refocus. In 1991 Xerox launched its Business Excellence programme.

'Leadership Through Quality' was inspired by attack from Japanese competitors who aimed at taking all of Xerox's market share. The impetus to change, accordingly, came from the external factors, namely intense competition, market share loss and changing customer requirements. The impetus to change was also stimulated by internal factors, that is bureaucracy, excessive costs and a blindness to the threats and changes occurring.

Xerox's indirect labour/direct labour ratio in the late 1970s was twice as great as its Japanese competitors. (Xerox had two non-productive people employed [indirect labour] for every employee who was producing the product [direct labour], whereas their competitors had a ratio of only half an employee in indirect labour to each direct labourer.) Production suppliers cost nine times more for Xerox than its Japanese competitors. In the manufacturing process assembly line, rejects were ten times greater than its Pacific Rim rivals, while product lead time was twice as long. Defects per 100 machines were seven times greater. All of these facts taken together meant that the Xerox unit manufacturing cost was equal to its Japanese competition's selling price.

Not surprisingly the Xerox quality policy was developed rapidly and enforced globally as a matter of survival. In launching Xerox's total quality management programme 'Leadership Through Quality', David T. Kearns cited the fierce global competition in the office machine business as the motivator for making the fundamental changes at Xerox to total quality in a $400 billion business. His company had enjoyed a near monopoly status for the sale and rental of photocopy machines until 1975. Five years later Xerox's market share of photocopy machines had fallen to below 50 per cent and the firm had over a hundred direct competitors for that core part of their business.

Japanese photocopy machine companies, led by Canon and Ricoh, began to match Xerox on copy quality, reliability and service, and to beat them on price. Xerox watched its position in the Fortune 500 (in terms of company revenue) fall from the upper 10 per cent to the bottom third of the ranking. Xerox responded to the serious threat to its business by taking the following steps:

1 Trimming its costs by about $600 million a year. World-wide, Xerox employees were reduced through redundancy from 120,000 in 1980 to 104,000 three years later.
2 Restructuring, led from corporate headquarters in Stamford, Connecticut, each part of Xerox reorganizing itself for greater efficiency.
3 Competitive benchmarking its new rivals in terms of products, service and practices.
4 Launching a total quality programme in February 1983 based on massive training in the teachings of Deming and Juran.

The policy statement was simple and direct: 'Xerox is a quality company. Quality is the basic business principle for Xerox. Quality means providing our external and internal customers with innovative products and services that fully satisfy their requirements. Quality is the job of every Xerox employee.'

The news from Japan was not all bad. Fuji Xerox had won the Deming prize for quality in 1980 and had provided the Corporation with a role model for managing total quality. A change in both company culture and management style was required. It all began with quality training, starting with the top 25 Xerox executives and cascading down through the Xerox world. David T. Kearns published the top-down commitment to total quality in a video which had him talking to the camera like an anchor man on television news. The message was equally straightforward:

> Customers have come to expect and demand quality from Xerox. They no longer merely use our products and services, they depend upon them. As the office becomes more and more sophisticated and automated, that dependency on Xerox products and services will grow. As a result, our customers will make ever increasing demands on us. Faulty design, billing errors and defects that might have been understood just a few years ago, will no longer be acceptable. Our customers won't tolerate it and our competition won't allow us to get away with it.
>
> We were faced with a challenge to bring ever increasing levels of quality to our products, services and practices and we responded. *We introduced competitive benchmarking and employee involvement to our management processes.* We reorganized our development activities so that we can bring out higher quality products faster and at less cost. We began to measure customer satisfaction and to take appropriate action to enhance our service to our customers.

Despite these, and other moves in the right direction, we have a long way to go. Xerox is clearly in a period of transition. *We are no longer the company that we once were and not yet the company that we must be.* If we are to successfully complete the transition and continue our record of success, every individual in this corporation will have to work toward our common goals. That is where you come in. Leadership Through Quality is neither a panacea nor a magic formula for success. It is a vehicle for change and an umbrella under which all Xerox people can work to improve quality. As I view it, there are three objectives for Leadership Through Quality:

1 To instil quality as the basic business principle in Xerox and to ensure that quality improvement becomes the job of every Xerox person.
2 To ensure that Xerox people provide customers with innovative products and services that fully satisfy *their* requirements. When we speak of customers we mean customers in the broadest sense of the word. Every Xerox person has customers internal or external for his or her work.
3 To firmly establish in the Xerox culture new management and work processes. We must unleash the creative talents and energies of all Xerox people so that they can continually pursue quality improvement.[28]

There were 8,000 UK Xerox employees who belong to the 30,000 strong subsidiary 'Rank Xerox', which has now dropped the "Rank" name. As part of the cost-cutting exercise Xerox moved its own international headquarters from central London to Marlow. A unique approach to shedding executive management took the form of 'networking' in which the company set up former employees in private business, giving them the computers they needed and contract assignments.[29]

The former 'Rank Xerox' was one of the Xerox Corporation's ten major sectors represented on an international 'quality implementation team' through its own vice-president of quality who reported to the managing director at 'Rank Xerox' and who, with the other vice-presidents of quality, had two tasks: to advise the board on quality issues; and to put the corporation's quality policy into effect in his or her own territory. The Xerox Corporation assisted the 'quality implementation team' in every way possible – from providing its own training material beautifully packaged under the 'Leadership Through Quality' label which would cascade from director level to the office and factory floor of Xerox world-wide, to the publication of the policy and plan and, most importantly, through the high level of senior management commitment to the cultural change the TQM process would set in motion.

In its early planning sessions at top level Xerox identified the cultural changes demanded by the new quality policy. The specially designed 'Leadership Through Quality' training material identified 'five change levels, interacting with each other, which are essential to achieving the desired change'. These were as follows:

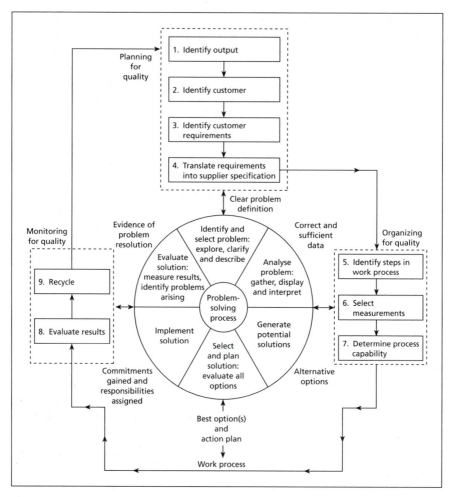

Fig. 5.3 Xerox Corporation's problem-solving process

1 Standards and measurements will provide all Xerox people with new ways of assessing and performing their work, solving problems and improving quality. Tools to do this include a six-step problem-solving process (*see* Figure 5.3), a nine-step quality improvement process, a figure of competitive benchmarking, an emphasis on error prevention and doing things right first time, and techniques for determining the cost of quality.

2 Recognition and reward will ensure that Xerox people are encouraged and motivated to practise the behaviours of leadership through quality. Both individuals and groups are recognized for their quality improvements – whether that takes the form of a simple thank you (recognition), or merit pay increase (reward).

3 Communications will ensure that all Xerox people are kept informed of the objectives and priorities of the corporation in general and their work group in particular and how they are doing in meeting these priorities. Communications includes both formal media such as magazines and films as well as informal media such as staff meetings.

4 Training will provide every Xerox person world-wide with an understanding of leadership through quality and a working 'knowledge' of the tools and techniques for quality improvement. This quality training is delivered in 'family groups' consisting of a manager and his or her direct reports. The manager, assisted by a professional trainer, conducts the week-long problem-solving and quality improvement training. During the course of the week, the group selects a problem or project for application of the quality processes and tools. After training, the manager guides the family group in the use of the quality process. Once the project is under way, members of the family group work with a professional trainer (consultant) to deliver the week-long training to their own subordinates, who then choose their own application project. This method of training top managers first and having them participate in the training of their subordinates is called a training 'cascade'. It is designed to ensure that managers are trained in and understand the quality process and to involve them actively in the training of their family groups.

5 Management behaviour and actions will ensure that the management team – at all levels of the corporation – provides the necessary leadership, sets the right tone and acts as examples for the successful implementation of leadership through quality. Managers must not only espouse the principles of leadership through quality, but also practise them day-in and day-out; in other words managers must walk like they talk.

Table 5.2 shows the time frame of the Xerox total quality programme. Cultural change takes years to effect.

There have been many pain barriers to such sweeping cultural changes in Xerox. These have included staff reductions on an unprecedented scale to such an extent that to many employees the 'new flexibility' simply meant job losses. 'Downsizing' operations mean redundancies which is difficult to square with employee involvement and personal commitment to change. Another major barrier had to do with Xerox's emphasis on reducing the cost of quality. It is difficult to control cost of quality when over 80 per cent of Xerox's production costs are attributed to buying in materials from their outside suppliers. To deal with the problem in 1986 Xerox set up a full-time consultancy group to carry its 'Leadership Through Quality' message to one hundred key suppliers. The plan was initially for three years and has been extended indefinitely.

Table 5.2 Timetable of 'Leadership Through Quality' programme at Rank Xerox

February 1984	First training group at top of Xerox Corporation.
April 1984	MD of Rank Xerox takes part in training group (along with MDs of nine other main Xerox companies).
May 1984	Rank Xerox senior executive group take part in first 'Leadership Through Quality' sessions to be held in UK.
late 1984	Top managers of Rank Xerox operating companies meet in training groups.
late 1984	Orientation video shown to all Rank Xerox employees.
during 1985	Training starts to cascade down management layers of all Rank Xerox operating companies.
late 1986	Final sessions completed within English-speaking companies.
late 1987	Final stages of training (at workgroup level) in European, African and Eastern areas.

Any change as bold and comprehensive as Xerox's attracts public attention and running commentary from critical academic observers.[30] Since total quality management at Xerox is a journey not a destination, there is no point at which its initiators will say they have arrived. Hence the verdict on how successful it has been will be an open one yet the benefits are as substantial as the challenges (*see* Figure 5.4). The financial indicators, however, are very positive and indeed measurable. Production costs are down in places by as much as 40 per cent. Customer satisfaction – the key principle – is increasing by 35–40 per cent in various parts of the business. Market share – once threatened – is increasing. And the Xerox Corporation won the Malcolm Baldrige Quality Award in 1989 for 'Leadership Through Quality'.[31]

Paul Revere Insurance Group – TQM in a paper and ideas business

Paul Revere[32] Insurance Group began its 'Quality Has Value' process in 1984 and called it a process because a programme implies an end point. Paul Revere was one of 12 finalists for the coveted Malcolm Baldrige National Quality Award in 1988 and had won similar quality awards in Australia and Canada. It was one of the first companies in the United States to use total quality management in a service industry and was singled out early in 1987 by Tom Peters as having the best quality process of any service industry in North America. The insurance company's main business is the provision of individual non-cancellable disability income insurance for professional corporate executives and small business owners. It carries a full line of group insurance products, and individual life insurance and financial products.

BENEFITS	CHALLENGES
• Engages all process owners in systematic continuous and breakthrough improvement	• Personal commitment and effort
	• Initial learning curve/workload
• Focuses and prioritises improvement actions	• Control the bureaucracy
	• Action must follow analysis
• Provides a comprehensive summary of a company's position and actions on enablers and results against its desired states	• Follow-up and inspection to ensure success and maintain momentum
	• Integration of Policy Deployment and the Management Process
• The model is more than a snapshot of our business, it is dynamic	• Align to changing Corporate Strategies
• Enables cross-functional learning and the sharing of best practices	• Consistency of examiners
	• Objectives without winners and losers – maintain motivation
• Enhances understanding and ability in process management	
• Examiners' understanding of and learning from other parts of the business	

Fig. 5.4 Xerox: sustaining the culture

Source: Xerox Training Material.

Within the first year of its total quality process, the company had recorded $8.5 million in savings. Its 1,200 employees at headquarters were so switched on to quality that they produced a phenomenal 568 ideas per 100 employees (while other US suggestion schemes only average 17 ideas per 100 employees). The ideas were carried out and the company began an upward spiral of quality improvement and cost-cutting while guaranteeing a no-redundancy policy.[33] In five years employees produced and implemented 26,000 ideas for total savings of over $17 million.

The insurance group was in a healthy financial state and began its quality programme, as many companies do, by a convergence of circumstances. Four separate events came together to kick-start the quality initiative. In ascending order of importance the first event was confined to one department where the manager invested heavily in the knowledge and ideas of his people, encouraged by public recognition, to turn around a negative situation. Although the activity was personal to the manager and unofficial to the company, it did broaden the spectrum of possibilities. The programme lasted only a year and died when the key manager was promoted to another department, but it had given a small section of the workforce a taste of what was to come and a chance to prove their capacity to contribute.

The second event was occasioned by the company, a consistent market leader, losing the number one position in disability insurance to its chief competitor. The operations vice-president suggested that total quality was the way to stimulate growth and regain market share. His idea was picked up by the Chairman of the Board of AVCO, then the parent company of Paul Revere Insurance Group[34] and turned into a directive for all AVCO companies to start quality initiatives.

The third event that propelled the company into quality was a simple directive from the company's president to the Vice-President of Human Resources to improve productivity which led him and his team to select 'value analysis' as a method. With the emphasis in 'value analysis' on defining products, services and information and the processes needed to deliver them, these efforts were a start in the analytical phase of a quality delivery process.

The fourth event was the simultaneous discovery, by the Chairman of the Board of AVCO and the Head of Paul Revere Operations, of Philip B. Crosby's book *Quality is Free*. Taken with his ideas – especially on cutting the cost of quality – they decided to apply Crosby's book on quality to their business. They gave ball park figures for the 'cost of quality' as $288 million for AVCO and $9.6 million for Paul Revere Insurance Group – $9.6 million at the time providing some financial motivation for the quality initiative.

The convergence of these four events led to the formation of a quality steering committee which then, armed with *Quality is Free*, set about planning the total quality programme for Paul Revere Insurance Group. The period of preparation lasted nearly a year, after which all the features of the 'Quality Has Value' process appear to have come to maturity all at once. These features, while revolutionary for the conservative, New England insurance company, are rather standard for total quality programmes. They started with commitment from the top to the total quality process, which cascaded through the management ranks down to the first level supervisors. A high-powered steering committee was a visible sign of top level commitment to the process. The committee developed the philosophy for the programme which was a blend of Crosby's book, Deming's ideas and Tom Peters' motivational lectures in a video cassette training package.

The steering committee provided a working definition of two distinct types of quality, namely:

1 'Quality in fact', which is the provider meeting his or her own specifications for the product or service.
2 'Quality in perception', which is the subjective element in quality as seen by the customer. It satisfies the customer's expectations.

In addition, the committee defined the procedures that framed the structure of the quality process. Members of the committee were sufficiently high powered to show both serious company intent and the priority given to the quality process and they represented different segments of the company.

The committee set the goal of the quality effort. At the outset of the effort the committee fused the 'value analysis' work from the human resources department with the overall quality process. Value analysis, they decided, essentially aimed at 'doing the right things', whereas a quality process was about 'doing things right'. The name they finally gave to the quality process reflected the marrying of the two ideas – 'Quality Has Value'.

The steering committee set in motion quality teams which were like quality circles in design and scope – they were composed of about ten people, drawn from the same work group and led by their own manager, who had a place on another quality team run by his or her own boss, thereby creating an interlocking connection between the teams at various levels. Like quality circles they met for a set period of time each week (30 minutes) to identify, analyse and solve problems. Unlike quality circles, however, membership was obligatory not voluntary and they were capable of implementing their solutions straight away, without presentations to management.

Once the ideas were certified by Quality Team Central, composed of four analysts and a secretary, the ideas or solutions to problems could be put into effect. As a control group, Quality Team Central had the advantage of a computer system with over 150 terminals already in place in the insurance company. 'The quality team tracking programme' was the vehicle created for filing all the quality ideas the teams were coming up with and working on. A piece of software merged the files of each team leader. Each quality idea was placed on a separate screen and coded '1' to tell everyone a team was working on the idea, '2' indicated a delay in the implementation of the idea, '3' signalled that the idea, upon reflection, was being abandoned, '4' meant the idea had been implemented, and the final code '5' indicated that the idea had been certified by Quality Team Central. Only these certified ideas were put forward for recognition.

Recognition

The year Paul Revere launched their total quality process, 1984, was an Olympic year. This gave the steering committee the idea of designing its recognition awards for Quality Teams along the lines of Olympic medals – bronze, silver and gold. Would they wear the medals? The question was answered by the Director of Quality Team Central, Patrick Townsend, who proposed the idea in the first place and who had the US Marine Corps on his curriculum vitae: 'I just came out of twenty years in an organization where people risk their lives for little pieces of ribbon. Believe me, people will wear decorations that have meaning and value attached to them.'[35]

As a team reached a defined level of achievement the members were awarded the corresponding lapel pin medals, based on the following criteria:

1 Bronze: ten certified quality ideas or $10,000 in annualized savings – each member received a bronze-coloured lapel pin. The awards were presented by one of the senior vice-presidents who was co-chairman of the steering committee.

2 Silver: twenty-five certified quality ideas or $35,000 in annualized savings – $20 gift selected from a prize catalogue was also given to each member in addition to the silver pin. The awards were presented by one of the senior vice-presidents who was a co-chairman of the steering committee.

3 Gold: fifty certified ideas or $50,000 in annualized savings – a $50 gift selected from a prize catalogue was given to each member along with the gold pin. The awards were presented by the company president.

Unwittingly the steering committee had set the lowest level of achievement target (bronze) at 167 per cent of the national average for suggestions implemented from quality circles in the United States. The gold target was 833 per cent higher but by giving the quality teams two different routes to the targets – through ideas certified or money saved – it gave equal status to improving working conditions and enhancing the customer's perception of the company's quality and cutting the cost of quality. The recognition also included lunches and dinners and photographs in the company newspapers. There were also the 'Most Valuable Player' and the 'Most Valuable Team' awards presented in a rented conference hall near the company's headquarters. There was a convention celebration spirit for these award ceremonies and up to a thousand dollars in cash and engraved bowls as awards.

In Townsend's words:

> The Great Hall of Mechanics [in Worcester, Massachusetts] where the celebration was held, has a large main floor and a horseshoe-shaped balcony. Winners of awards were from gold teams, and a request was made for silver and bronze teams to sit in the balcony so that winners could reach the stage more easily. When the company president asked everyone who was on a gold team to stand, virtually all those seated on the main floor, close to 750 people, rose. It sent a powerful message.[36]

Training at Paul Revere included 'groupAction' education from Zenger-Miller Inc., a California-based management development and training firm. All quality team leaders had training in working in groups and problem-solving. They also read *Quality is Free* and later *In Search of Excellence* by Peters and Waterman. The two books and an inspirational video tape, a packaged course by Peters called 'Towards Excellence', provided the academic grounding for the quality thrust.

As the programme matured the catalogue gifts gave way to Paul Revere gift certificates that could be spent in an array of local shops and restaurants. Teams went on to achieve gold and then double gold – 60 per cent of all certified ideas saved the company money. In 1984 Quality Teams put the company's cost of quality at $16.2 million. The following year using the same rigorous method of determining the cost of quality – converting time into wages and adding in material costs – the cost of quality was driven down to $14 million. For the 'Quality Has Value' process for 1985 the quality teams continued to focus on two questions, namely 'does this have an effect on your customer's perception of you or the company's quality?' and 'does this reduce your cost of non-conformance?'

'Quality Team Control' has been changed to 'Quality Management Department' but still serves a facilitation/control function with the quality teams. It contains analysts who still certify quality ideas. Their efforts, however, have been altered to meet the new needs and demands of the quality teams.

Penny La Fortune, an analyst from the Quality Management Department for four years, is a change agent in the new 'Quality Has Value' process. She sees her job as advising the teams on how their quality efforts link up with their departmental plans and the company's overall business strategy. Twenty years ago she worked at Paul Revere and then left the company to raise her family. When her three children were grown up she returned to find Paul Revere 'a thousand times better' due to the quality process and the new forms of employee involvement and participative management that have sprung from total quality. Her enthusiasm for the company has led her to encourage her two daughters, niece and sister-in-law to work there – the ultimate test of job satisfaction. They are part of the headquarters staff of 1,500. Adding in the field staff and the Canadian part of the company in Burlington, Ontario, brings the company's payroll to 3,200.

As Penny La Fortune explained:

> We have now taken responsibility for our own quality training and no longer use outside consultants for it. Our own Corporate Training Unit provides education for all. The training was good enough to carry the company into an onsite inspection for the Malcolm Baldrige National Quality Award as one of ten semifinalists in 1989 – we were one of the two companies from the service sector and we learned a lot from the committee's two-day, on-site inspection.[37]

She explained that the company still continued to encourage healthy competition between the quality teams with the Olympic award scheme. The prizes have increased in value and bronze now carries a $30 gift certificate, silver $50 and gold $60 plus a day-off with full pay. Diminishing some of the excessive American hoopla, they have discontinued 'double gold' awards. 'Gold is gold' she said and they still use the Great Hall for quality celebrations putting the hall's capacity of 1,500 persons under strain as the staff numbers have grown.

Joan A. Wackell, Director, Corporate and Government Relations for Paul Revere, has been with the firm for 12 years. She has played a part in Paul Revere's cultural change to a total quality management firm. As a quality team leader she has her team exploring community issues and the interface between their insurance company and government through seminars which they have arranged.

Cultural change

Seven years into the 'Quality Has Value' process there have been some structural changes. The steering committee was disbanded and replaced by the Quality Advisory Council which includes a mix of team leaders as well as senior managers. The 'Quality Team Tracking Programme' is still used but has become more sophisticated to reflect the changes in quality team activity. The teams themselves, having done a spectacular amount of problem-solving and sorting out of basic problems in the first few years of the process, now focus most of their efforts on goal-setting to achieve the department divisional operating plan which is part of the company's overall strategic plan.

In 1985 Paul Revere's 'Quality Has Value' process generated over 5,000 quality ideas certified and implemented in headquarters and another 1,000 from the field. In addition to the criteria of big ideas that saved $10,000 to $50,000 or an aggregate of small ideas that did the same, the teams came up with a third category – complicated ideas that needed a longer time frame, required some debate and had little immediate money savings. Most of these ideas fell into a category of changes that were the right thing to do for customers. As these types of improvement projects were more difficult to do, they were also more difficult to evaluate for recognition. The projects were labelled 'quality goals' by the quality steering committee and each team was encouraged to set them. A form of self-assessment was developed for these goals and teams to gauge their own progress towards the achievement of the goals and to decide what level of recognition they were due.

Being singled out as a role model for a total quality company by management guru Tom Peters[38] and others has created problems of its own. But Paul Revere copes well with the fish bowl factor: 'To process the many queries we get about our Quality Has Value process, we have produced a small pamphlet describing it and we send that out to anyone who asks for it,' Joan Wackell explained. 'It focuses their questions when they come back to us and is a more efficient use of our time.'

The president of Paul Revere Insurance Group shaped an advertisement around the accolades his staff/company were receiving under the banner heading 'We've always heard Paul Revere's "Quality Has Value" process was something special. Now they've made it into a federal case'.

G. Robert Lea, former Vice-President, Human Resources and Quality, summed up the goals of total quality in the following way:

At Paul Revere, we believe that quality is not a programme, or merely a process, but a way of life – the way we do business. We believe that our employees are our most important asset in providing service excellence to our customers.

Our customers are the reason we are in business today. Every Paul Revere associate pledges to provide superior customer service to his or her customers by meeting their requirements and treating them with courtesy, respect and a sense of urgency.[39]

The company has regained its position as the leading insurance company providing individual non-cancellable disability income insurance in North America. The cultural change has been sweeping, as Patrick Townsend sums it up: 'any person can walk into Paul Revere at any time and ask any employee, "which Quality Team are you on? What are you doing about quality this week?" – and get definite answers. That is revolutionary.'[40]

The accomplishments Paul Revere attributes to its Quality Has Value process programme include:

- market share – No. 1 disability income provider;
- finalist for the first Malcolm Baldrige National Quality Award (1988);
- low employee turnover throughout its quality initiatives;
- increased customer retention through improved customer service and the building of strong trusting relationships with its customers, both internal and external.

Successes that Paul Revere employees have initiated include:

1 Proactive phone calls – the company calls its customers to find out if there is anything they can do for them, or just to ask how their service has been. Paul Revere also calls them when they detect a potential problem or error about to occur. This way any negative impact the future problem may cause can be lessened or dispersed. They consistently ask their customers for input and feedback whenever they implement customer suggestions.
2 Paul Revere mails all of its claims checks before Christmas each year regardless of the due date, so that the claimants will be able to use them for the holidays.
3 The company offers rehabilitation services to its claimants. Claimants on disability are helped with their rehabilitation schedules and many have been helped to return to work within a suitable period time – whether it be to their own position or a comparable one.

Paul Revere acknowledges that its sustained strategic advantage in the market-place came from quality initiatives:

1 by having a focus on customer service and continuous improvement as a top priority;

Table 5.3 Paul Revere: savings

Dates	Ideas implemented	Documented savings ($)
1984–7	13,817	16,240,000
1988	3,257	1,952,921
1989	1,891	646,438
1990	2,542	1,854,429
1991	1,991	864,429
Totals	23,480	21,558,626

2 by making use of innovative new technologies to aid in product development and administrative procedures;

3 by making a commitment to building stronger relationships between the workforce, its customers and its producers to open up and enhance lines of communication and promote teamwork.

There has been many documented savings from Paul Revere's many quality initiatives over the past 13 years. Besides the actual dollars saved (*see* Table 5.3), there have also been a substantial amount of 'soft' savings, including computer run time and time saved for employees on any particular process or task.

Vision for the future

In 1995 Paul Revere celebrated its one hundredth anniversary. In its century of doing business Paul Revere had become so competitively successful – so attractive in the market-place – that its main competitor, Provident Companies Inc., bought it from AVCO in the spring of 1996 and merged the company with its own insurance operations Provident Life & Accident.

The attractive sale price of Paul Revere of $1.2 billion reflected not an incredible leap in real estate values in New England but over a decade of quality achievement that had built Paul Revere into a colossus in the insurance industry. The difficult task, however, of moving from fierce competitors to family friends is still underway three years after the merger. As spokesperson Jim Johnson pointed out in the re-engineering of the merged companies, 'the quality process has never been more important' as the united company moves to harmonize its rival cultures to better exploit its enhanced market position.

Royal Mail – projects for TQM

In May 1991 over a hundred total quality teams from Royal Mail across the country converged on the Post Office College at Milton Keynes to a convention scene under billowy white tents – this was Teamwork '91. On individual stands the teams displayed their quality improvement projects and explained to anyone who would listen how they were setting about implementing their ideas. One group from Manchester, for example, showed how they would recover many millions of pounds in their district alone strictly by adhering to procedures that required postal dockets from companies when picking up the post in bulk. Another explained how they were *preventively* dealing with forgery in the printing of stamps. The teams were all keen to hand out or show the printed materials of their data-driven projects to each other as well as to visitors. They were the representatives of 180,000 Royal Mail employees across the country who are now becoming caught up in a total quality management process that should reach out to offices, factories, businesses and 23 million households across the United Kingdom. Once TQM is flourishing in Royal Mail, it will spread to Parcel Force's 10,000 employees, to Post Office Counters' 15,000 employees and to the 5,000 people at central office who do the supplying, purchasing, training, etc., for such a vast organization.

One of the most lively stands at Teamwork '91 was the benchmarking group who had gone to America to learn from several superior companies. They communicated the following eight messages from the US benchmarking tour:

1 Total quality works – leading companies are applying the processes and getting success because of it.
2 Clear, simple and bold targets can be achieved – they strive for big improvements.
3 Personal leadership and passion from the top managers is everywhere – they are consistent, they walk the talk!
4 These companies have staying power and courage; they are not frightened to take risks or to make mistakes.
5 People in these companies have fun. They have opportunities to participate in their work environment, make decisions, talk to customers.
6 Key themes found in all benchmark companies include training, recognition, teamworking, measurement and display of performance.
7 All these companies really focus on the customer – they pay attention to the customer's requirements.
8 At Royal Mail we have a long way to go but we are on the right track.

In addition to the key messages the US study team developed a menu of good ideas taken from visits to US companies. The menu includes 'one-liners' such as: 'Promise what we can deliver and deliver what we promise!'; 'Quality – I take it personally'; 'Imagine what we can do together'; 'Steal shamelessly'; 'They watch your feet'; and 'Every organization is the lengthened shadow of its leaders'.

Flow charting work was an idea best illustrated at a US company visited – Corning Glass. The company used a simple technique for work process simplification. They took several people who performed the same task but at different places and asked them independently to draw a simple flow chart of the process for that task. They then brought them together and put all the diagrams on the wall. There were dramatic differences in the way that people did things – the number of steps charted varied between 67 and 150 and the people just got stuck into discussing the differences and were very keen to come up with the optimum process. Being done this way gave the Corning worker ownership of the new process. This can be built on given that the people are empowered to change things.

'Coffee clutches' were used to keep management in touch with the workers' ideas. Senior managers at Corning when visiting locations got together with randomly selected groups of employees to talk about climate and quality issues, or anything people wanted to raise. An informal atmosphere was created by the choice of room and the use of a coffee break approach. In addition to such informal spontaneous feedback, there were group discussions for more formal feedback.

Formal feedback from employees was essential. Corning, for example, brought groups of about 15 employees together with a facilitator and flipcharts and then went through the following steps with the group: what is right about quality here? what is wrong with quality here? form a dozen or so issue statements; prioritize by votes – usually two or three stand out; ask what should be done about the two or three; and finally, get the group to present their views back to the plant managers and union jointly.

Most companies benchmarked on the tour had more formal quality organizational structures than the Royal Mail. At location level Corning used 150 quality improvement teams (quality councils) whose function was to 'translate the corporation's quality principles into actions'. They supported union input at this forum.

The American companies were all using climate surveys. Corning saw its annual climate survey as an evaluative measure of the effectiveness of their quality process. An idea discussed at Corning, but not in place, was for an almost continuous update facility through having the system on computer with an open invitation for employees to input. Corning also developed 'key results indicators' as part of their annual plans at all levels. These KRIs then became the focus for their evaluative measurement of quality. KRIs did not appear to be top-down targets but were location management team initiated and discussed at the higher level. Corning's KRIs are indicators of the changes that are being sought and not bottom line number targets but they did have a very high profile in the corporation.

Royal Mail's study tour brought back more practical ideas, for example Corning's list of ten questions which those attending their management committee meeting answered on a form. The questions regard the attendees as customers and ask about things such as: 'have you received adequate direction?' and 'have you been provided with the opportunity to input?'

It was recommended that Royal Mail did something similar on an individual team basis. There was IBM's idea of incorporating quality measurements into performance appraisal through personal quality plans based on the requirements of the customers for the work. This formed part of the objectives of all managers and in their system nobody could get an overall better rating than was achieved in the quality area. IBM schemes of direct customer contact were of interest to Royal Mail. Front-line employees were given assignments of varying length with customers usually directed at some issue of common interest. The employee then spread the message and helped create an awareness of the reality of the external customers' requirements among his or her colleagues, creating a very strong message once they returned to their usual job.

The study group was taken with the way the US companies placed heavy emphasis on teamwork to resolve problems and improve quality. Teams were used to improve relationships with both internal and external customers. From corrective action teams to customer focus groups, the team efforts put people in direct contact with their internal and external customers as natural problem-solvers.

But individual effort was also important. The study group was impressed with how American Express (AMEX) used positive recognition at the individual level giving everyone real-time feedback on key aspects of their work. This was how the delegates from Royal Mail put it:

> The people at AMEX know exactly what their quality goals are in terms of their own job and their department. We tend to have rather high level goals whereas the AMEX ones are specific to the job. Through this they achieve a high degree of focus on quality and their quality effort provides a lot of feedback based on the quality goals set.

They were impressed by Westinghouse's process for relating stated priorities to actual time spent working on them. It enabled senior managers to think through their priorities and then measure how they actually spent their time. This time analysis which was fed back. It also put a process in place so that the manager could keep in view the way his or her time was spent. This helped establish what the real priorities were. The delegation recommend offering this process with a modest amount of training to Royal Mail senior managers.

One of the blunt American messages the delegation brought back to Royal Mail came from Westinghouse: 'People don't normally come to work thinking let's see what we can screw up today. Provided people understand goals and are given proper empowerment and training the evidence is that enormous improvements can be achieved.'

Entries for Teamwork '91 dealt with quality improvement projects from each district. The topics covered included those dealing with the internal customer, for example staff issues such as: the way of recognizing long-service employees; or crew conveyance in which employees themselves fitted out vans to carry in safety seven postal delivery staff, their pouches and bicycles; or dealing more effectively with 'Christmas casuals'; or recruiting permanent staff; or setting up miniature colour graphs for graphical presentation of performance data; or physical fitness centres.

Many quality improvement projects reached out to Royal Mail's 23 million households and to its business customers. The following are some examples taken from the Teamwork Exhibition:

Cleaners at Royal Mail Darlington wrote three cleaning up booklets which were produced on desktop publishers. As well as being used in the Darlington district they were sent out to every district head postmaster in the country.

Royal Mail Peterborough recognized a customer need through a mailshot for companies that used franking machines. Customers were not happy with Royal Mail coming to their sites to set the franking machine at a cost of £7 for each machine. They preferred to take the machines themselves to a newly established Meter Resetting Centre at Royal Mail in Peterborough. Before this centre was set up some customers were taking their franking meters to the Post Offices but Post Office Counters Limited charged Royal Mail about £5 for setting each franking machine. Royal Mail also lost the interest from the banked cheques for the franking service when they were collected by Post Office Counters. On average it took 17 days for the franking revenue to be credited to Royal Mail accounts. The new service centre pleased the customers and saved Royal Mail money.

Technical service field engineers at Guildford distributed questionnaires to their internal customers and were alarmed to learn that only two offices, out of the 23 returns, had any technical records or drawings on site. Sixteen offices did not know that main office copies of this information were held by the engineers at the District Office. Thirteen of the supervisors did not know of the location of the main water stop-cock. The team designed an impressive form providing easy reference for the location of the incoming main services such as water stop-cock, key location and number; mains gas valve, key location and number; electrical isolating switch, key location and number; and a space for further information.

The Sales Operations Department based in Oxford decided to enter a fiercely competitive market by introducing a quality branch pouch service from Royal Mail. The team described its project as a market opportunity in the financial market for a head office to branch and return daily pouch service. Although the finance market is already served by first class mail, the team identified the loss of business due to inroads made by small firms, namely

Insurance Couriers (ICS), Britdoc and Securicor. (ICS's turnover rose from £149,175 in 1985 to £13,500,000 in 1989.) The total market for the major banks, building societies and finance houses is put at £10,325,000 per year. (This figure comes from the formula 20,640 branches × 250 working days × 2 carriers = 10,325,000.)

The Royal Mail's proposed entry into this market would offer a collection at 5.30 pm and delivery before 9.00 am using Royal Mail supplied day-glo pink envopacks. Key features of the service include: optional late hand-in at mechanical letter offices (MLOs); guaranteed money back service; credit account facilities; packaging provided; optional compensation for loss through Registered Service Insurance; Monday through Friday service with Saturday delivery; a Saturday collection option; and minimal paperwork as the envopacks are all recorded by barcode marking.

Royal Mail's mechanized letter office at Cambridge set up in August 1989 a health and fitness centre with a qualified physiotherapist as part of its quality improvement thrust with the double objective of reducing exceptionally high labour turnover rates and absenteeism and promoting better employee relations. The location chosen primarily employed rank and file, blue-collar workers. Because both objectives were achieved another fitness centre was set up in 1990 at the Stevenage mechanical letter office. When a financial crisis in Royal Mail letters caused most of the initial funding for the new centre to be withdrawn, the quality team obtained alternative funds from the Civil Service Sports Council.

All of the Royal Mail quality improvement teams worked through their quality delivery process, going from output identification to meeting customer requirements to feedback loops. The process is expressed in Figure 5.5. The high level of analysis and data collection was reflected in printed handouts at the one hundred stands at Teamwork '91. From desktop printing to commercially printed booklets to computer graphics, the message emerged that people were serious about improving quality.

Ian Raisbeck, Quality Director at Royal Mail, together with his boss Sir Bryan Nicholson, Post Office chairman, are former Xerox Corporation senior managers who helped put Xerox's 'Leadership Through Quality' in place. Raisbeck worked with the process from its beginnings in America. Ian Raisbeck, who is an absolute believer in total quality management, studies the theory and practice relentlessly and has perfected the model of TQM that he worked with in Xerox in the implementation at Royal Mail. 'Feedback to the managers on how they are doing was always part of the Xerox model,' he explained. 'But it wasn't given enough importance in the early days. At Royal Mail we place a great deal of emphasis on it at the outset.'

He is a man with a mission that has an international dimension to it. US Mail with its 800,000 workers is relying on Ian Raisbeck to help it with a

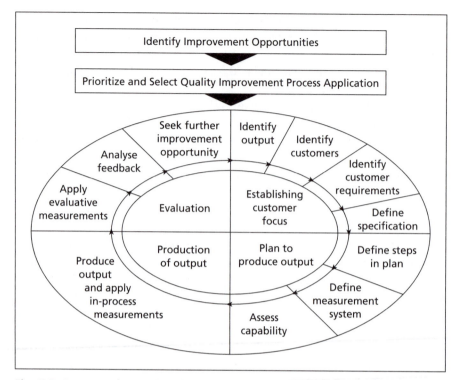

Fig. 5.5 Customer-focused performance improvement at Royal Mail

total quality programme, modelled on the British one, which is now into its tenth year. In turn a British delegation visited their American counterpart for an exercise in total quality benchmarking as part of a study tour in 1990 and 1991.

A key event in Royal Mail's recent history provided a spur to action on the quality front. The national postal strike in August 1988 raised an ugly spectre internally and for its customers. It shook up any complacency in the sprawling service organization. The strike also helped to focus people on the basics of their business. Ian Raisbeck came into the company to find it positively smug about the speed of its service and reluctant to hear from outsiders about it. When the Post Office Users National Council (POUNC) complained that only 70 per cent of first class post was reaching its destination in one day, Royal Mail countered with its own data that showed a 90 per cent success rate. The problem lay in the measuring. Royal Mail was not measuring the letter's journey from sender to receiver (a meaningful measure) but instead from when it was stamped to when it was ready to be delivered. Now Royal Mail measures its service end-to-end – pillarbox to doormat – and has watched its success rate rise to a European leading 86 per cent average score in getting

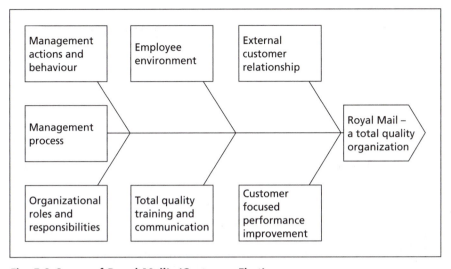

Fig. 5.6 Scope of Royal Mail's 'Customer First' programme
Source: 'Total Quality Benchmarking', USA Study Tour, 1–5 October 1990.

the letter to its destination the next day in August 1991. This average score rose to 88.5 per cent in September 1991.

The development of total quality started in Royal Mail in 1988 under the title 'Customer First'. The overall scope of 'Customer First' is shown in the fishbone diagram in Figure 5.6. 'That overall approach has now been adopted Post Office-wide, tailored appropriately to the specific needs of the other businesses and the corporate functions,' Royal Mail asserts. And:

> The implementation is now at a point that our understanding of the basics is such that we can learn from the actions of other companies who are already further down the total quality path without being overawed. There is then the probability of being able to take actions that will enable the Post Office to achieve its vision of total quality in a more effective and efficient manner. This could be through new specific ideas not previously considered by us or by avoiding blind alleys through understanding the mistakes made by others.[41]

Royal Mail's seven steps approach is shown in Figure 5.7.

To determine who to benchmark against Royal Mail turned to those companies that demonstrated clear achievements in total quality and who had been recognized through the Deming and the Baldrige Awards.

Royal Mail does not have a commitment, as some companies do, to a no redundancy policy attached to its TQM process. Like the leading-edge companies it does build in recognition events for quality progress and allows each postal district £10 per head to undertake its own preferred form of recognition. Given the civil service roots of Royal Mail, it came as no surprise to Ian

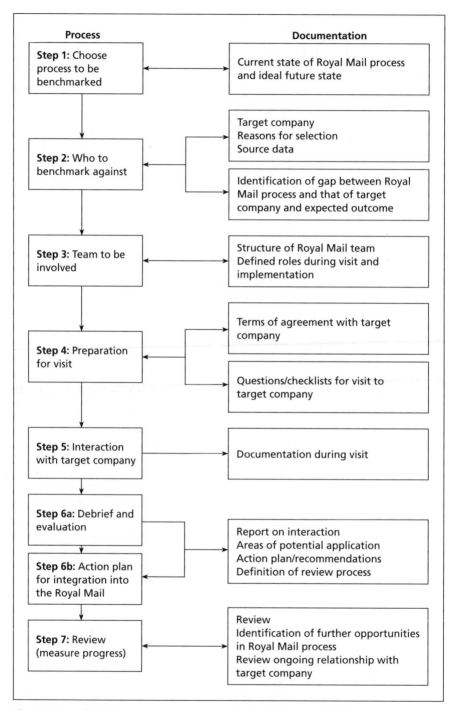

Fig. 5.7 Royal Mail's seven-step approach to 'Customer First'

Source: 'Total Quality Benchmarking', USA Study Tour, 1–5 October 1990.

Raisbeck to receive a response from senior managers to his open directive on recognition of 'when do we get the guidelines?'

Total quality begins with a clear, simple mission statement. Royal Mail's mission is to be recognized as the best organization in the world distributing text and packages. Royal Mail attempts to achieve its mission by achieving the following:

- Excelling in collection, processing, distribution and delivery arrangements.
- Establishing a partnership with its customers to understand, agree and meet their changing requirements.
- Operating profitably by efficient services which its customers consider to be value for money.

Caring for the customer in a total quality process is a massive effort for Royal Mail. In October 1989 every household in the country received a *Post Guide* booklet from Royal Mail. The new idea was aimed at helping people get the best from their postal service. An improved updated version of the guide was sent out in June 1991. The cover letter that accompanied the guide included two tear-off cards which listed postal prices. The letter was signed by the recipient's District Head Postmaster and pointed to some improvements and asked for suggestions. 'We have also been listening carefully to our customers' comments and ideas. Most of the improvements we have made are a direct result of customers telling us what they want,' it read. 'For example, we have re-introduced Sunday collections of mail from selected posting boxes. We have also invested in the latest electronic sorting machinery. More mail is now transported on direct links using our own vehicles. This is all part of our commitment to give you a more convenient postal service.'

Since 1986, when Royal Mail became a separate business within the Post Office, Royal Mail has achieved eight consecutive years of profit, free of any government subsidy. From 1990 to 1995 Royal Mail has had a steadily rising profit stream.

But far from relaxing in its success Royal Mail is gearing itself up for the fiercely competitive future. Its track record of success includes 12 successive years of volume growth of national mail which has been achieved despite an economic recession and the growth of alternative forms of communication such as telephone and television, and electronic communication such as fax, e-mail and electronic data interchange. In addition, Royal Mail is coming under increasing competition in the traditional hard copy transmission market from courier services, document exchange operations and other postal administrations.

However, Royal Mail is restless for improvement. An example of how it measures its performance against external best practice is Royal Mail's recent participation in the World Class Financial Benchmarks, a global study arranged by Price Waterhouse involving 46 participant companies world-wide.

Table 5.4 Financial process benchmarking

	Results		
	Royal Mail	Average	World class
Performance measurement and review			
• Cycle time to close the general ledger (days)	5	6	4
• Cycle time for monthly consolidation (days)	5	6	4
• Cycle time for annual budget preparation (days)	179	110	60
Revenue management			
• Average number of invoices per person per year	8,710	9,901	27,237
• Percentage of invoices paid on time	62%	78%	92%
• Bad debts as percentage of total revenue	0.05%	0.02%	0.00%
Procurement			
• Average cost to place a purchase order	$19	$24	$10
• Percentage of items received on time	71%	85%	95%
• Average payment period (days)	35	30	20

Source: Royal Mail Internal Publication. Used by permission.

The study involved 61 measurements against three areas of financial activity which correspond to Royal Mail's three principal financial processes (*see* Table 5.4).

The results of this study will be used to set stretching process targets with a view to attaining the world-class performance indicated in the table.

Royal Mail's Business Excellence Model

In 1992 Royal Mail adopted the European Foundation for Quality Management model of excellence as a new framework for working. The model is the basis for the internal self-assessment of total quality within Royal Mail. The model (*see* Figure 7.2 on p. 224) is based on the idea that:

> Processes are the means by which the organization utilizes and releases the talents of its people to produce continuously improving results.

Self-assessment in Royal Mail is at the core of its current thrust for total quality. It consists of four initiatives.

1 *European Quality Award* – an external business-wide assessment for European-based companies, e.g. Royal Mail in 1995;
2 *UK Quality Award* – an external business unit assessment for UK-based companies, e.g. Quadrant & Anglia Division in 1995;
3 *Business Excellence Reviews* – an internal Business Unit assessment by senior Royal Mail managers;
4 *Unit Excellence* – a self-assessment carried out at unit level.

Table 5.5 European Benchmarking of Excellence

Leadership
The behaviour of all managers and
employees in team leadership roles
in driving the organization towards
Total Quality.

Customer Satisfaction
The perceptions of Royal Mail's external
customers in meeting their needs and
expectations.

Policy and Strategy
Royal Mail's mission, values, vision and
strategic direction and the ways in
which it achieves them.

People Satisfaction
The perception of employees about
what it's like to work for Royal Mail.

People Management
The management of Royal Mail's
employees to release their full potential
to continuously improve the business.

Impact on Society
The community's perception of Royal
Mail's approach to quality of life, the
environment and the preservation of
global resources.

Resources
The management, use and preservation
of Royal Mail's resources in support of its
policy and strategy.

Business Results
The performance of Royal Mail against
its planned business performance.

Processes
Royal Mail's approach to the management
of all its value-adding activities.

Source: Royal Mail Internal Publication. Used by permission.

The Improvements to Business Excellence Reviews for 1995/96 involved a triple-pronged approach:

1 Good practice sharing – the identification and sharing of ways of working throughout Royal Mail that have proved to be effective and efficient to improve the company's performance. These are being shared throughout Royal Mail via the new Good Practice Database.
2 Business unit planning – the opportunities for improvement identified during the Business Excellence Reviews will be used to improve the business units' performance. These will be reviewed and actioned by the business units' Management Forums and where appropriate incorporated into business plans.
3 Increased senior management commitment – the most senior managers will have taken part in Business Excellence Reviews during the 1995 and 1996 cycle.

Meanwhile Royal Mail looks to its Business Excellence Review results.

Royal Mail compares the performance of its business units against the European Benchmark of Excellence (*see* Table 5.5).

Over 300 managers of the Royal Mail have been trained in the Business Excellence Review process, including 96 per cent of the most senior managers. Ten managers have been assessors for the European and UK Quality Awards.

Notes

1 Richard Pascale, *Managing on the Edge: How Successful Companies Use Conflict to Stay Ahead* (London: Viking, Penguin, 1990), p. 11.

2 Roger Harrison, 'How to describe your organization', *Harvard Business Review*, September/October 1972.

3 Charles Handy, *Understanding Organisations* (Harmondsworth: Penguin, 1976).

4 Edgar H. Schein, *Organizational Culture and Leadership* (San Francisco: Jossey-Bass, 1988), p. 9.

5 Tom Peters and Robert Waterman, *In Search of Excellence* (New York: Harper & Row, 1982).

6 Personal conversation with author on 6 August 1996, Body Shop Headquarters, Littlehampton, West Sussex.

7 Anita Roddick, *Body & Soul: Profits with Principles – The Amazing Success Story of Anita Roddick and The Body Shop* (New York: Crown Trade paperbacks, 1991), p. 9.

8 Ibid., p. 146.

9 For example, *The Body Shop Skin, Hair and Body Care Book* (London: Little, Brown, 1996).

10 Geoffrey Lean, 'Brazil moves to protect rainforest', *The Independent on Sunday*, 4 August 1996.

11 Elizabeth Moss Kanter, *World Class Thriving Locally in the Global Economy* (New York: Simon & Schuster, 1995), p. 13.

12 Gloria Barczak, Charles Smith and David Wileman, 'Managing large-scale organizational change', *Organizational Dynamics*, Autumn 1987, pp. 23–35. See also Leonard D. Goodstein and W. Warner Burke, 'Creating successful organizational change', *Organizational Dynamics*, Spring 1991, pp. 5–17.

13 Sir Colin Marshall, 'Culture change: no science but considerable art', Comino Lecture, 13 June 1990, *RSA Journal*, January 1991, p. 893.

14 Ibid., p. 893.

15 Ibid., p. 895.

16 Ibid., p. 896.

17 Liam Strong, unpublished talk at Cranfield School of Management, 31 July 1991.

18 *The Sunday Times*, 25 August 1991.

19 Sir Colin Marshall, Proceedings, Comino Lecture, *RSA Journal*, 1991, pp. 892–902.

20 John R. Opel, IBM's corporate policy statement on quality, no. 132, 30 November 1991.

21 IBM corporate quality document no. 101, 14 May 1985.

22 H. James Harrington, 'Excellence the IBM way', as quoted in Tom Peters, *Thriving on Chaos* (London: Macmillan, 1988), pp. 81 and 82.

23 Ibid.

24 Ibid.

25 Woody Klein, 'On market-driven quality', *Think*, no. 4, 1990, p. 26.

26 Ibid., p. 27.

27 Ibid., p. 27.

28 David T. Kearns, Xerox Company Video, *Leadership Through Quality*.

29 See David West and John Drew, *Networking in Organisations* (Philip Judkins, 1985).

30 See D.S. Mercer and P.E. Judkins, 'Rank Xerox: a total quality process', chapter in B.G. Dale and J.J. Plunkett (eds), *Managing Quality* (Hemel Hempstead: Philip Allan, 1990). *See also*: E.M. Giles, 'Is Xerox's human resource management worth copying?', 3rd Annual Conference, British Academy of Management, September 1989; Richard Upton,

'Xerox copies the message on quality', *Personnel Management*, April 1987; Irving J. De Toro, 'Strategic planning for quality at Xerox', in *Quality Progress*, April 1987.

31 The quality award is the US equivalent to Japan's Deming prize. It was named after the 26th Secretary of Commerce, Malcolm Baldrige, who served in the post from 1981 until his death in 1987. The award is meant to 'promote quality awareness, recognize quality achievement and publicize successful quality strategies'. The application form for the award is 75 pages long and those short-listed for the award have a two-day on-site inspection which scrutinizes all aspects of the claims companies make about themselves.

32 Paul Revere was an American patriot who on 18 April 1775 galloped through the night in a legendary ride celebrated in Longfellow's poem to warn the revolutionary forces of the British march on arsenals in Concord. He was a Boston artisan (goldsmith and silversmith) and an entrepreneur who built the first copper rolling mill in North America and set up a hardware store, bell foundry and metal casting plant.

33 The subject of this entire book is the total quality programme of Paul Revere Insurance Group, by Patrick L. Townsend with Joan E. Gebhardt, *Commit to Quality* (New York: John Wiley, 1987). The original edition covers the first two years of the total quality process start-up. Paperback editions (1989) have a 31-page, additional chapter dealing with the next three years. The authors have left Paul Revere and are now management consultants.

34 Paul Revere Insurance Group has its offices in Worcester, Massachusetts; both it and AVCO are now owned by Textron Inc., of Providence, Rhode Island, a conglomerate making products ranging from helicopters to motorized golf carts, from industrial fasteners to financial services. Its operating profits for 1990 were $789.4m.

35 Patrick Townsend and Joan Gebhardt, op. cit., p. 85.

36 Ibid., p. 134.

37 Conference telephone discussion with the author, 5 September 1991. When the women who participated in the discussion at first tried to refer the author's query to their senior managers, to their surprise and satisfaction they were told 'the query is about your programme, you deal with it'.

38 Tom Peters and Nancy Austin, *A Passion for Excellence* (London: Fortune, 1986), pp. 256, 257 and 259; and Tom Peters, *Thriving on Chaos*, op. cit., pp. 76–9 and 85.

39 G. Robert Lea, *Quality Has Value*, publication by Paul Revere Insurance Group.

40 Patrick Townsend with Joan E. Gebhardt, *Commit to Quality*, paperback edn (New York: John Wiley, 1989), p. 202.

41 *Total Quality Benchmarking*, USA Study Tour, 1–5 October 1990, Royal Mail Publication 1991.

Chapter 6

··

Tools and techniques of total quality management

When you can measure what you are speaking about and express it in numbers, you know something about it; but when you cannot measure it, when you cannot express it in numbers, your knowledge is of a meagre and unsatisfactory kind.

Lord Kelvin, 1881

'If only it weren't for the people, the goddamned people', said Finnerty, 'always getting tangled up in the machinery. If it weren't for them, earth would be an engineer's paradise.'

Kurt Vonnegut, *Piano Player*

Since the 1930s whole texts have been written on statistical quality control.[1] Many of the techniques presented in these texts are complicated and highly quantitative, written as they were for engineers and specialists. In addition to the rich literature on quality control going back over sixty years, individual companies have developed their own quality control books. For example, Ford has produced *Quality System Standard* as part of its QI programme for manufacturing operations and outside suppliers of parts and service products. Ford has its own eighty-page book on *Statistical Process Control* and its own manual on *Potential Failure Mode and Effects Analysis* (FMEA). Similarly, IBM produces its own quality literature, such as the 200-page book *Process Control, Capability and Improvement*.

This chapter will not attempt to sum up the extensive quality control literature, but rather will give a few examples of accessible techniques.

Techniques for analysing a quality process

There are four common and popular techniques for analysing a quality process and these are:

- flow charts;
- histograms;
- run charts;
- control charts.

190

Perhaps the simplest way of describing or mapping a process is to draw a flow chart. Figure 6.1 illustrates a flow chart of a customer using a bank's cash dispensing machine. The flow chart maps the stages of a process from start to finish, each action of the process shown in a rectangular box, each decision taken shown in the shape of a diamond, and arrows which point forward and at times point back to an earlier stage in the process.

The following steps should be followed to construct a process flow chart:

1 Identify the subject of the flow chart.
2 Determine the starting and end points.
3 Stratify the task(s) into the smallest possible sub-tasks and list them.
4 Identify each sub-task as one of five process flow chart symbols (*see* Figure 6.2).
5 Measure the time distance or quantity for each sub-task.
6 Calculate and record the frequency and time for each symbol.
7 Create the flow chart by utilizing the symbol for each task.
8 Include a legend which defines the symbols used.

In addition to the process flow chart which is used to illustrate tasks which normally follow a single path, there is a decision path flow chart which is used for tasks which follow multiple paths. These are drawn in a similar way to process flow charts, but sub-tasks are not illustrated. The actual drawing of a decision path flow chart begins with the allocation of responsibilities across the top of the chart. Column one in the chart lists the steps and the time frame for each step. These steps are entered under the appropriate column to match up with the responsibility holder (*see* Figure 6.3).

Histograms are visual representations of the spread or distribution of data. They are also called 'frequency distributions'. They are used to monitor a process to see if it consistently meets customer requirements. Measuring the process to see if it really does this usually requires the observation of several runs of the process, the recording of observations and then a comparison of these with the target, standard or specification for the process. Histograms can help those involved in preliminary data analysis find the distribution pattern of whatever variable is being studied. The information presented in histograms is represented by a series of rectangles or 'bars' which are proportional to groups of data (*see* Figure 6.4).

Histograms also illustrate the various measures of central tendency: the mean (average), mode and median. In that respect, a histogram can also show how the data are spread out or dispersed. This information can be particularly helpful in understanding the extent to which a process is operating normally (in control). The measures of central tendency are defined as follows:

● Mean – the sum of all the measured or counted data divided by the total number of data points, also called average or $\bar{X}$.

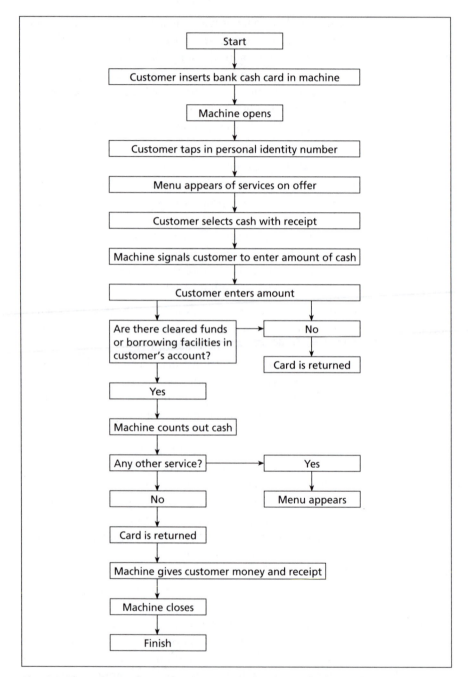

Fig. 6.1 Flow chart of a customer using a bank's cash dispensing machine

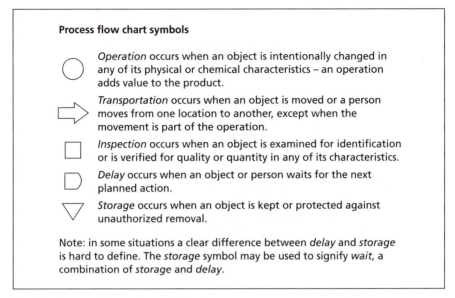

Process flow chart symbols

Operation occurs when an object is intentionally changed in any of its physical or chemical characteristics – an operation adds value to the product.

Transportation occurs when an object is moved or a person moves from one location to another, except when the movement is part of the operation.

Inspection occurs when an object is examined for identification or is verified for quality or quantity in any of its characteristics.

Delay occurs when an object or person waits for the next planned action.

Storage occurs when an object is kept or protected against unauthorized removal.

Note: in some situations a clear difference between *delay* and *storage* is hard to define. The *storage* symbol may be used to signify *wait*, a combination of *storage* and *delay*.

Fig. 6.2 Process flow chart symbols

Source: Eli Lilly and Company, published by Florida Power and Light Company, 1989, p. 35.

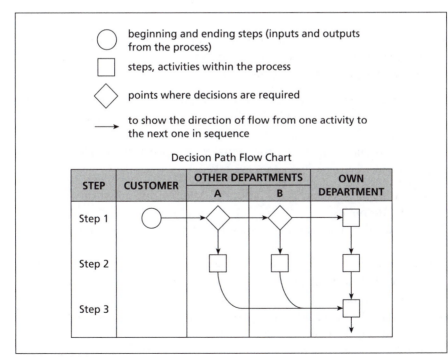

beginning and ending steps (inputs and outputs from the process)

steps, activities within the process

points where decisions are required

to show the direction of flow from one activity to the next one in sequence

Decision Path Flow Chart

STEP	CUSTOMER	OTHER DEPARTMENTS		OWN DEPARTMENT
		A	B	
Step 1				
Step 2				
Step 3				

Fig. 6.3 Decision flow path analysis

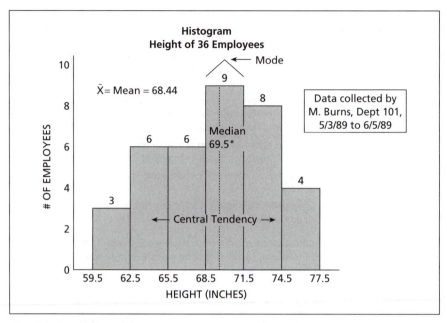

Fig. 6.4 A specimen histogram

Source: Florida Power and Light Company.

- Mode – the values repeated most often in the raw data or, in the case of a histogram, the most common class interval.
- Median – the middle value(s) of all the data points.

Histograms may even suggest ways of keeping a process in control. Deviations from normal or expected distribution can help teams locate root causes.

To make a histogram one draws a grid, defines a target for intended performance and then marks the actual performance level. The following steps for constructing a histogram are taken:

1 Collect the data to be charted (at least 30 points) and count the total number of data points.
2 Determine the range of the data by subtracting the smallest data point from the largest.
3 Determine the number of bars by taking the square root of the total number of data points; as a rule of thumb, it is a good idea to keep the number of data bars in a histogram to between 6 and 12.
4 Determine the width of each class interval (bar) by dividing the range (found in step 2) by the number of bars.
5 Determine the starting point by subtracting half of the unit of measure from the smallest data point.

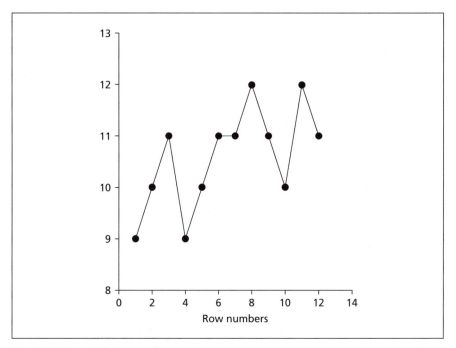

Fig. 6.5 A specimen run chart

6 Place the class intervals (groupings of data) on the horizontal or X axis.

7 Place the frequencies on the vertical or Y axis.

8 Draw the height of each bar to represent the number or frequency of its class interval using the scale on the vertical axis; each bar should be the same width with all data points included; bars should be touching.

A run chart is a line graph which illustrates how a process changes over a period of time. It is an effective tool for presenting data. Figure 6.5 shows tally chart data presented as a run chart.

Control charts are line graphs used to track a process's trend or performance. The operating data from an ongoing process are used to establish statistically normal operating limits or control limits on a control chart. These control limits provide a range for normal operations. The control chart, then, provides a picture of how the operations are staying or failing to stay within the control limits. Figure 6.6 shows an example of a control chart.

To construct a control chart take the following steps:

1 Decide on a unit measurement to use in monitoring performance; put this on the vertical axis.

2 Choose a time interval for taking measurements; put this on the horizontal axis.

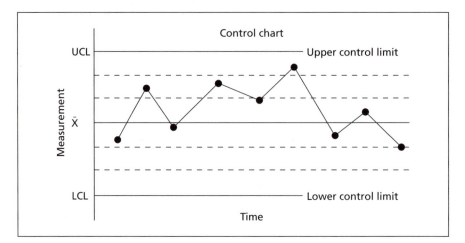

Fig. 6.6 A specimen control chart

3 Calculate control limits by determining the mean (average of X) and standard deviation; generally the UCL (upper control limit) is the mean plus 3 standard deviations; the LCL (lower control limit) is the mean minus 3 standard deviations.
4 Mark the mean and the control limits on the vertical axis and draw a horizontal line for each along the length of the chart.
5 Enter data points chronologically on the chart.
6 Draw a lien connecting the data points.

Statistical process control

Consistent performance of manufacturing and assembly processes, rather than extensive sorting and rework or scrap of defectives, can be achieved only by a process that is inherently capable of consistency in the long term. Any car manufacturer is aware of the fact that statistical techniques such as statistical process control (SPC) aim to achieve defect prevention and to pursue neverending improvement. SPC also reduces variability in delivery times, completion times, methods, attitudes, equipment and materials.

Process capability is a measure of the variation of a process and its ability to produce components consistently within specifications. Process capability can be defined only when a process is in statistical control, that is when it is being influenced only by common causes and special causes have been eliminated. Process capability is measured by the process capability index.

Special causes are sources of variation that are unpredictable or intermittent. Statistical control chart literature calls these types of cause assignable causes. They are signalled by a point beyond the control limits or a run or other non-random pattern of points within the control limits (*see* Figure 3.3 on p. 95). Usually special causes can be corrected at the process by the operator or supervisor. Examples are a broken tool, a change in the machine setting or a change in raw materials, or the errors of an inexperienced operator.

Common causes are sources of variation that are always present – part of the random variation inherent in the process itself. The origin of a common cause can usually be tracked to an aspect of the system which can be corrected only by management. Examples are poor lighting, bad workstation layout, old machines or badly maintained machines. It is management's job to improve process performance.

The process capability index (Cpk) is an index which measures the variability of the process relative to the specification and process setting. When Cpk is less than 1.00, a 100 per cent inspection must be implemented and action taken to increase Cpk value to a minimum of 1.00.

A process is said to be operating in statistical control when the only source of variation is common causes. 'But a state of statistical control is not a natural state for a manufacturing process,' wrote Deming. 'It is instead an achievement, arrived at by elimination, one by one, by determined effort, of special causes of excessive variation.'[2] The initial function of any process control system is to give a statistical signal when special causes of variation are present and to avoid giving false signals when they are not present. Such a signalling system enables appropriate action that can eliminate those special causes and prevent their reappearance.

As long as a process remains in statistical control, it will continue to be predictable with benefits in consistency of quality, productivity and cost. The process must first be brought into statistical control by detecting and eliminating special causes of variation. To help detect special causes control charts are employed. Once process performance is predictable, its capability to meet customer requirements can be determined. This is the basis for continuous improvement.

Machine capability studies (at times referred to as process potential studies) assess the short-term influences on component dimensions emanating from the machine/operation/process alone when the study is performed; for example, when special causes are not identified. Usually consecutive components are measured and the results are analysed using a suitable chart. It is therefore possible to calculate the machine's capability index. In these cases a minimum machine capability index of 1.33 is required for approval of initial samples.

Process capability is determined from control charts with the process operating under actual production conditions. When the process that will be used to produce a new component is essentially the same as that currently used for existing components, Cpk may be estimated from data from the current process. In this sense, a process is the combination of people, machine and equipment, raw materials, methods and environment that produces a given product or service.

The tools of SPC are of importance not in themselves but to further the efforts of continuous improvement by reducing variability. They help managers and workers alike to ask the basic question: can the job be done more consistently? Far from being limited to production or operations, SPC is applicable to administration and service. It can be used effectively in sales and purchasing, invoicing and finance, distribution and after-service, training and management development.

Organized problem-solving

For over sixty years psychologists have been using a simple ambiguous drawing to explain perception. The drawing by a cartoonist contains two images – that of an old woman and that of a young woman (*see* Figure 6.7). Once a person sees either figure it is difficult to see the other, one image tending to

Fig. 6.7 Old woman or young woman?

Source: Edwin G. Boring, 'A new ambiguous figure', *American Journal of Psychology*, July 1930, p. 444. Originally drawn by cartoonist W.E. Hill, published in *Puck*, 6 November 1915. As printed in *Games Trainers Play*, by John W. Newstrom and Edward E. Scanneil, McGraw-Hill Book Co., 1980.

block out the other. Similarly, in looking at problems people tend to lock onto one perspective, one aspect of the problem, to the exclusion of other viewpoints or perspectives. Organized problem-solving is used to pry loose a person from only one perspective on a problem. The techniques of organized problem-solving are used to get people to see problems from all angles.

The purposes of organized problem-solving in a TQM framework are the following:

1 To improve a company's performance by successfully solving problems that are causing dissatisfaction for internal or external customers.
2 To ensure that problem-solvers do not jump to solutions before they have analysed the cause(s) of the problems.
3 To provide a process that can be used by project teams to maximize the contribution from each individual.
4 To implement solutions to problems that really do eliminate the problems through prevention processes.
5 To reduce the cost of quality.

There are six steps in the problem-solving process. They should normally be taken in sequence. Step 1 is identifying and selecting the problem. Many people rush out and end up solving the wrong problem. It is important to define a problem as the difference between the target and the actual. A problem statement should be written based on measurements taken that will focus attention on the causes of the deviation (*see* Figure 6.8). Step 2 is analysing the problem causes. Spend time on the cause(s) and avoid jumping to solutions only to find they do not actually solve the problem.

Step 3 is generating potential solutions. It is essential to explore alternatives because the first solution is not always the best. Step 4 is selecting and planning the best solution. Planning the best solution results in cost effectiveness and makes sure the right people do the right things at the right time.

Step 5 is implementing the solution. Seeing the job through to conclusion is essential, with appropriate contingency planning in case some of the new ideas do not quite work out. Finally, step 6 is evaluating the solution. Reviewing the results is vital to be sure the problem really has been solved. For a review of these six steps *see* Figure 6.9.

Problem-solving tools

Brainstorming

Brainstorming is an effective technique to help a quality improvement team identify a problem, sort out its causes and come up with solutions. Invented by Alex Osborn, an advertising executive in the 1930s, brainstorming makes

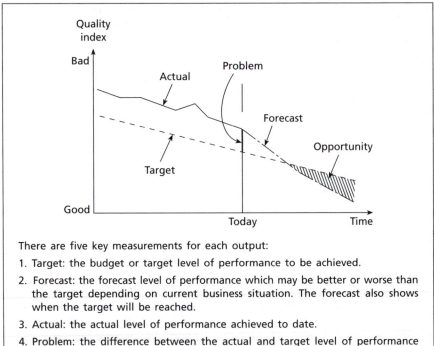

There are five key measurements for each output:

1. Target: the budget or target level of performance to be achieved.

2. Forecast: the forecast level of performance which may be better or worse than the target depending on current business situation. The forecast also shows when the target will be reached.

3. Actual: the actual level of performance achieved to date.

4. Problem: the difference between the actual and target level of performance where 'actual' is worse than 'target'.

5. Opportunity: the opportunity for improving quality better than target at no extra cost.

Fig. 6.8 Defining the problem

use of lateral or right-brain thinking. It is a way of getting a large number of ideas from a group of people in a short time. It can be used effectively for the first three steps of the problem-solving cycle – to identify problems, sort out causes from effects and come up with creative solutions.

There are certain rules for brainstorming which must be followed for the technique to be effective, which are as follows:

1 No criticism: participants should contribute ideas without fear of criticism from others. Likewise, they should suspend their judgement on the ideas of others.

2 Freewheel: the process of brainstorming should promote the free flow of ideas without analysis or evaluation. It allows apparently silly or far-fetched ideas which may develop into something useful.

3 Go for quality: the aim is to get as many different ideas as possible in the allotted time.

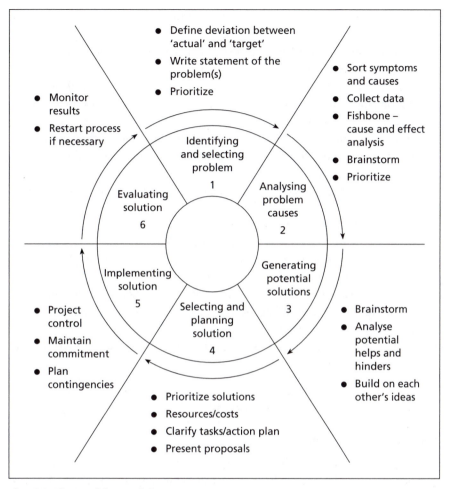

Fig. 6.9 The problem-solving process

4 Record: write down all ideas, even repetitions, on a flipchart for all to see. The written words themselves will trigger other ideas from the team.

5 Cross-fertilize: use other people's ideas as springboards for your own. Building on ideas is an effective way of creating the best ideas.

6 Incubate: after the allotted time for generating ideas, each person should identify those ideas he finds most useful. The team can then select the ideas which should be developed.

7 *Everyone* should contribute ideas, however unimportant they may appear to be.

To run a successful brainstorming session, the quality improvement team leader should use the following ten guidelines:

1 Write up on a flipchart the topic to be brainstormed and keep it in full view.
2 Write up the rules for brainstorming, review them with the team and post these also where everyone can see them.
3 Warm up for a few minutes with a practice brainstorming. It is helpful to use something simple, such as the uses of a paperclip, or a brick, or a wooden pencil, or 50 uses of Blu-Tack.
4 Choose a volunteer scribe to write up all the ideas on the flipchart as they are brainstormed. (Never pressurize anyone into being a scribe.)
5 Start the ideas coming.
6 Maintain a 'cheerleader' role with the team keeping up the momentum for ideas.
7 Make it fun. Laughter is often a sign of creativity.
8 When the team dries up, try to get more ideas of your own, urging the team on, or by selecting the wildest idea and building on it. Post-it notes can be used to get everyone to contribute.
9 Incubate ideas. Help each person identify those ideas he or she finds most useful. Team members might be asked to place a tick mark next to the ten ideas they find most valuable.
10 Reverse brainstorming. Think of all the things that could go wrong with the ideas the team has selected.

The case study given in Figure 6.10 can be used by quality improvement teams to demonstrate the power of brainstorming.

The fishbone diagram

The fishbone or Ishikawa diagram is a cause and effect diagram which when completed resembles the skeleton of a fish. This diagram helps the team to separate out causes from effects and to see a problem in its totality. There are several uses for cause and effect diagrams. For example, they can be used to:

- assist both individual and groups to see the full picture;
- serve as a recording device for ideas generated;
- reveal undetected relationships between causes;
- discover the origin of a problem;
- investigate the expected results of a course of action;
- call attention to important relationships;
- create a document or a map of a problem which can be posted in the work area or in someone's office.

Figure 6.11 shows a partially completed fishbone diagram.

Another aspect of diagramming causes and their effects is that one can tell at a glance whether the problem has been thoroughly investigated. A cause

An exercise for brainstorming. First brainstorm all the problems in this case in 10 minutes. Then brainstorm 50 solutions.

Fare play

A large European city uses double-decker buses as its principal means of public transportation. Each bus has a crew of two: a driver who occupies a cab separated from the rest of the bus and a conductor who has three functions. First, the conductor signals the driver whether or not to stop, one ring to continue, two rings if there are passengers that want to get off; second, the conductor signals the driver again when it is safe to start; and third, the conductor collects fares from those who have boarded. Fares are normally collected when the bus is in motion to make the stops as short as possible. During peak hours there are more buses in operation than there are stops. The number of passengers travelling during this time often requires the conductor to force through the crowd on both levels and on the stairs to be able to collect fares. The conductor frequently fails to return to the entrance on time to signal the driver whether or not to stop. In these cases the rules state that the driver must stop even though there has been no signal and so the bus stops even though often there are no passengers wanting to get off.

Such unnecessary stops bred hostility between driver and conductor, which was increased by the incentive system under which they operated. To encourage buses to run on time, an incentive system had been developed that paid drivers a bonus for being on time. There was also an incentive system for conductors to ensure they collected fares from everyone. Plain-clothed inspectors often rode on the buses and checked to see if the conductor got all the fares. If not, the conductor was penalized.

No wonder that in several cases a driver became so angry with the conductor that the driver stopped the bus between stops, got out of the cab, went to the rear, picked the conductor off the bus, and assaulted the conductor. After several such incidents, their separate unions became involved and declared war on each other. Violence flared.

The management was committed to the principle of participative problem-solving and arranged a set of meetings of small groups of drivers and conductors to discuss ways of resolving their differences, including changes in the incentive system. None of these sessions yielded constructive results, and neither union was prepared to consider the management's proposal to change to a 'pay bus' system, whereby the crew would consist solely of a driver who would collect fares from passengers as they entered the bus.

Fig. 6.10 A specimen brainstorming exercise

and effect diagram which contains much detail, if that detail is legitimate, indicates how deeply a group has gone into the process of investigation. On the other hand, a bare cause and effect diagram might indicate that the problem was not significant or that the solvers of the problem were not exhaustive in their search. Likewise, if the solution analysis diagram is complete, it will show the group's concern for the impact of a proposed solution.

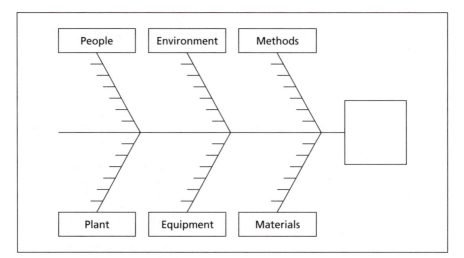

Fig. 6.11 Basic fishbone diagram

The following guidelines show how to construct a fishbone diagram:

1 Write up the problem statement, which is the 'effect', on the extreme right of a large piece of paper (flipchart, or several pieces of paper fastened together).
2 Draw in the main ribs of the fish and write a heading for each rib. There are general headings which cover most problems, such as: people, environment, methods, plant, equipment and materials; or there can be specific headings tailor-made to cover special problems (for a more sophisticated use of the technique *see* Figure 6.12).
3 Review with the team the rules for brainstorming and post them on a wall where they can be seen by everyone.
4 Brainstorm a list of causes on to the fishbone diagram. The brainstorming can be done in a free-style manner in which all ribs of the diagram can be brainstormed simultaneously, or the ribs can be taken one at a time and brainstormed in a more structured way.
5 Incubate the diagram to get a feeling from the team as to the key causes of the problem.
6 In a more formal way, apply the Pareto principle to determine the 20 per cent of the causes that contribute to 90 per cent of the effect.

The Pareto diagram

Vilfredo Pareto was an Italian economist who, between the world wars, conducted extensive research on income distribution. He found that in his native country 80 per cent of the wealth was held by only 20 per cent of the population. In international comparative research he established the same ratio. He

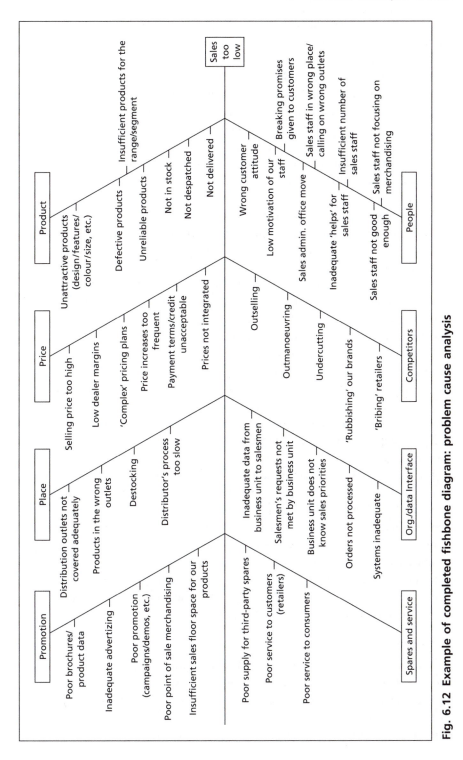

Fig. 6.12 Example of completed fishbone diagram: problem cause analysis

eventually realized that he had discovered a universal law – 80 per cent of any-thing is attributed to 20 per cent of its causes. For example, 80 per cent of road accidents occur on 20 per cent of the roads – or some roads are more dangerous than others. And 80 per cent of absenteeism in a company can be assigned to only 20 per cent of the workforce – or some people are off work and stay off work longer than others. Also 80 per cent of the shopping that takes place is done in 20 per cent of the time stores are open – or people try to shop at the same time. This 80–20 law has come to be called the Pareto principle after its founder. In problem-solving, it is helpful to determine the key causes – those 20 per cent – which lead to 80 per cent of the problem and cure them.

A separate diagram can be used to show the Pareto analysis. The frame-work of the Pareto diagram comprises the vertical and horizontal lines for a column graph. The left vertical scale will list the number of occurrences of problems. The right vertical scale is a percentage scale (100 per cent should be opposite the total number of problems). Space should be left on the hori-zontal axis to list the problems. Using the information from the data table, construct a column graph for each of the problems. Plot the data on the diagram, making one column for each of the problems. The data is plotted with the largest group or category on the left. The remaining categories are plotted in descending order and the 'other' category is on the right-hand side. The diagram should be labelled so that each axis is identified and so that each column is identified. A cumulative or 'cum' line can be drawn by plotting each point at the right-hand corner of each column and then connecting these points. A legend will provide useful information that will help others understand the Pareto diagram.

The completed Pareto diagram supplies much information. As a column graph, it tells about the relative sizes of the problems. With the exception of the 'other' column, the columns are in descending order and give some indication of which problem needs attention first. The cum line conveys an important message about the first few problems. This cum line indicates that if the biggest two problems are corrected, a large percentage of the total problems will have been determined. Such a visual display of the key causes helps a problem-solver to prioritize so that he or she spends the time attacking those causes that will eliminate most of the problem (see Figure 6.13).

Data collection

Collecting data is another aspect of analysing problems. Facts, not opinions, fuel good problem-solving. Team members must be insistent on bypassing opinion-based arguments to uncover the real facts of a problem. While it is difficult to collect reliable facts about some problems, this tends not to be the case with most problems that quality improvement teams tackle.

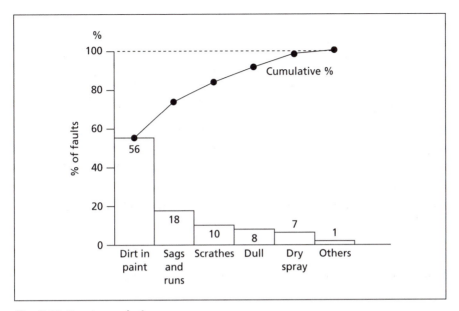

Fig. 6.13 Pareto analysis

The teams have the task of carefully collecting the facts that demonstrate the dimensions of the causes of a problem or point to potential solutions. The fact-based arguments these teams develop are not only more powerful and likely to be accepted, but they are also much easier to communicate. A very common tool for collecting data used by quality improvement teams is the 'check sheet', which is simply an organized way of recording information (*see* Figure 6.14).

The following guidelines will help you design check sheets:

1 Always state the full title of the data you intend to collect and the date or time period covered. For example: partial title – 'phone calls to Manchester branch'; full title – 'an analysis of incoming phone calls to the MDA Manchester branch of customer service each day over the next four weeks'.
2 Ensure that check sheets are uniform so that everyone uses the same form to collect comparable data.
3 Design the check sheets in such a way that writing is kept to a minimum, with ticking of boxes preferred using the '5 bar gate'.
4 Collect only the amount of information needed to solve the problem. Use statistical sampling rather than counting all items.
5 Look out for things that can distort the data giving a biased result, such as seasonal influences, unusual events in the normal pattern of working and happenings in the outside world that have an impact on the situation.

TYPE OF CALL		MON		TUE		WED		THU		TOTAL
		AM	PM	AM	PM	AM	PM	AM	PM	
NON-CUSTOMER	Crank Call	II	I		II	III		I		9
	Wrong Number		I	II		II	I			6
CUSTOMER	Service Out			II	III	III	I		III	II	14
	Questions on Service	I	I	II	III	II		I	I	11
	High Bill Complaint			I	II		I		I	5
TOTAL		3	5	8	10	8	2	5	4	45

Data collected by S. Smith, 3/4/88, oper. tally sheet

Fig. 6.14 Sample check sheet: an anlaysis of telephone calls from a particular telephone

6 Aim to get the full picture by covering all the variables that occur in the situation.

It may be necessary to collect data at step one of the problem-solving cycle. Certainly data are needed for step two, analysing problems. Probably some data collection is required to generate options for the solutions stage.

Six sigma

Six sigma is a statistical term which measures the extent to which a process varies from absolute perfection. At the six sigma level this is a 3.4 defects per million or 99.99971 per cent perfection. The technique was developed by engineers at Motorola as part of the company's TQM thrust in the 1980s. The technique was given a global boost in 1998 by Jack Welch, the controversial CEO of General Electric (GE), who has led this company to amazing levels of profitability. He adopted it world-wide for GE's renewed quality drive to stay the most valued company in the world. Jack Welch heard about six sigma from a former protégé, Lawrence Bossidy, CEO of AlliedSignal. During a golfing outing, Bossidy claimed to have used six sigma as a quality improvement technique to save AlliedSignal $14 billion in 1997.

By simply announcing his plan to introduce six sigma into GE world-wide before his retirement in 2000, Welch sent GE's share prices rocketing in the expectation that the quality initiative will generate even higher returns to the shareholders. GE predicts that the six sigma initiative will contribute an extra $10 billion to annual revenue and cost-savings. Projects that directly impact on customers are given top priority. The starting point is GE's definition of quality as:

Completely satisfying customer needs *profitably*.

GE has engaged in a global training programme to put the six sigma technique at the fingertips of all its employees. The company rigorously examines trainers – so-called 'Master Black Belts' – who work full-time throughout GE to drive out defects using six sigma. The rest of the workforce is offered 'Green Belt' training which is strongly supported by the CEO. In fact, employees can only be considered for promotion if they have completed 'Green Belt' training.

In summary, sigma is a statistical term measuring the extent to which a process varies from perfection. To calculate the sigma of a process, one multiplies the number of units processed by the number of potential defects per unit, divide that into the number of defects actually made and multiply the whole thing by one million. This produces the number of defects per million operations. A conversion table translates that number into sigma:

6 sigma =	3.4 defects per million
5 sigma =	230 defects per million
4 sigma =	6,210 defects per million
3 sigma =	66,800 defects per million
2 sigma =	308,000 defects per million
1 sigma =	690,000 defects per million

Other techniques used by GE employees in their quality efforts include the following:

1 *Chi testing* – an analytical table that tests the relationship between two possible causes of variation to see if the relationship is statistically important.
2 *Dashboard* – a scorecard on GE progress for the customer. It resembles a car's instrument panel and replaces the oil, mileage and temperature gauges with such gauges as order fill rate, billing accuracy and percentage of defective parts. One arrow on each dial indicates the level of quality that the customer is seeking. The other arrow measures how far the company is from meeting that requirement. Welch has said that he wanted a dashboard on every customer updated every week, but insiders say that the goal placed unrealistic demands on the existing workforce. Instead, businesses are aiming for monthly or quarterly dashboards on the most strategic customers.
3 *Design of experiments (DOE)* – a way of shifting or reducing variation in a process by carrying out a methodical sequence of experiments rather than attempting a scattershot trial-and-error approach. Each combination of adjustments becomes an equation that can either be solved as a matrix or entered into a computer for solution. DOE allows users to efficiently test a large number of variables. Black Belt trainees learn how to visualize this method by practising on an adjustable catapult that fires a table tennis ball

at a coffee can on the floor. They must become so familiar with the mechanism that no matter where the can is placed, they can adjust the catapult to hit it on the first shot.

Quality functional deployment (QFD)

QFD can be defined as a disciplined approach to solving problems *before* the design phase of a product. At the basis of this approach is the belief that all products and services should be designed to reflect customer desires. Therefore marketers, design engineers and manufacturing engineers or service providers must work closely from the beginning to ensure a successful product or service. This approach involves finding out early on what features are important to customers, ranking them, identifying conflicts and translating them into engineering specifications.

Quality functional deployment (QFD) is also called the 'house of quality' (HOQ). The technique is used in design management and was invented by Japanese workers in 1972 at Mitsubishi's Kobe shipyard. Toyota and its suppliers have developed the technique, as have many other users like Ford, General Motors, Jaguar, Hewlett-Packard, Xerox, AT&T, Digital Equipment, Procter & Gamble, ITT and Mercury over the last three decades.

QFD's starting point is to use customer demands and desires for designing a product or service. It is inclusive. All members of all functions of the supplier organization get involved in translating the customers' requirements into corresponding technical requirements for each stage of the system. They include market research, basic research, invention, concept design, prototype testing, final product or service testing and after-sales service or troubleshooting.

The strength of the approach lies in the fact that it is performed by a cross-functional QFD team whose members draw on their knowledge and experience in a systematic way. The team asks questions to identify *who* the customers are for the product or service, to determine *what* the customer needs and to decide *how* the needs will be met. These three terms are entered into the QFD matrix or grid of the 'house of quality' (*see* Figure 6.15). The 'whats' are entered in rows and the 'hows' are recorded in columns to create a quality table. When these matrices are fitted together they resemble the structure of a house, hence the name 'house of quality'. There are numerous examples of how this technique involved the customers at the design stage of a car to tease out their special requirements for an off-the-road vehicle, for example, and then fully satisfy these requirements at the design stage. It is the customers' requirements that should drive the construction of the house at the design and development stage rather than have everything driven by new technology.

The close co-operation of people from different parts of the business who traditionally may have had little to do with each other gives the process potency it would otherwise not have. HR people mix with engineers, designers and

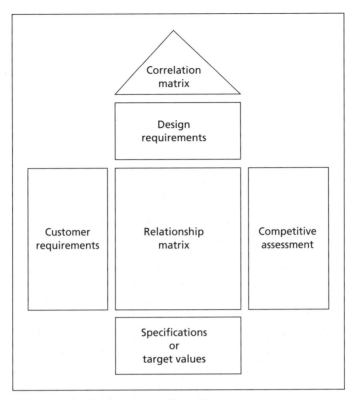

Fig. 6.15 The basic 'house of quality'

Source: V. Daniel Hurst, 'How to implement a competitive quality program',
Quality in America (Homewood, Ill.: Business One, Irwin, 1992), p. 270.

marketing people and work closely from the time the product or service is created until it is delivered to the customer. Inter-functional planning and communication takes place throughout, starting with the 'customer attributes', that is the descriptive words and phrases the customer uses to talk about the product or service provided. The goal is to gather all of the customer requirements in a series of 'house of quality' diagrams and translate them into individual, operational processes.

Figure 6.16 shows a fully worked model of the house of quality for Bharat Earth Movers. This simple house of quality was created to facilitate the continuing development of Bharat's earth-mover machines. It provides a good illustration of the main features of the HOQ which distinguishes this technique from other multi-attribute methods. The foundation or 'basement' of the house directs users of the technique to high-priority product design specifications (ECs) and thereby delineates target values. The body of the house builds up the crucial link between customer needs (CAs) and product design specifications (ECs).

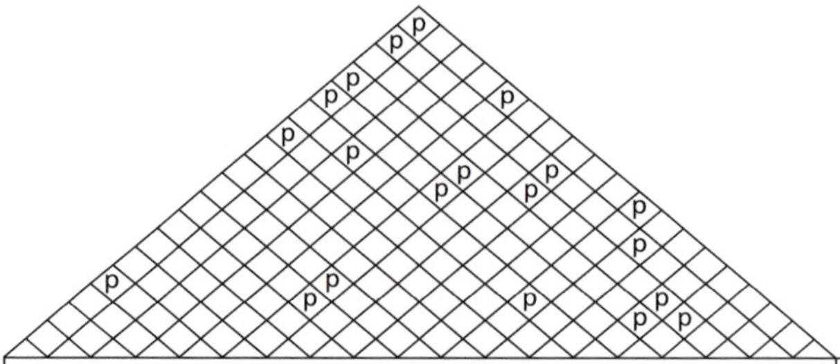

DESIGN FEATURES

Comparative Analysis

CUSTOMER NEEDS	RANKINGS	Center of gravity	Turning cycle	Suspensions	Operator cabin	Dashboard	Payload/GVW	Computer designed	Fatigue tested	Service brakes	Emergency brakes	Power steering	Telescopic hoist	Planetary axle	Spherical Brng. Migs.	Engine	Transmission	Refilling capacities	Tractive effort	Dumping efficiency
Stability	5	5	5	1	0	1	5	5	0	5	5	0	5	5	1	3	3	0	5	5
Riding comfort	3	1	1	1	3	1	1	1	0	3	3	3	1	5	3	1	1	0	5	5
Automation	3	1	0	1	3	5	1	5	0	3	3	1	5	5	0	3	3	3	5	5
Productivity	5	3	1	1	1	3	5	5	3	5	5	3	5	5	1	5	5	5	5	5
Long life	5	0	1	1	1	1	3	3	3	5	5	3	3	5	3	5	5	3	5	0
Safety	5	5	5	3	5	5	5	5	3	5	5	5	5	1	1	1	1	1	5	5
Steering	3	5	5	5	5	0	5	5	0	1	1	5	0	5	0	1	0	0	5	1
Compactness	3	3	1	3	3	5	5	3	3	3	3	5	5	5	1	5	5	5	0	0
Performance	5	3	3	3	3	5	5	5	5	5	5	5	5	5	3	5	5	5	5	5
Low operating cost	3	0	1	3	0	5	5	1	1	3	3	1	1	5	3	5	5	5	0	5
Serviceability	3	1	1	3	3	5	5	3	3	5	5	3	3	5	5	5	5	5	0	0
Maneuverability	3	5	5	3	1	0	5	3	0	1	1	5	1	5	0	0	0	0	5	3
RATINGS		128	117	102	104	138	196	178	178	182	182	149	163	200	81	155	152	124	185	157
(targets)	Possible low	~14.75	~5 CPS	Ergonomics	Electronics	~0.55	Maximum	2.5 M Cycles	12000 Kgs.	12000 Kgs.	No noise	Compact	No failures	~6°	~450 Hp.	~16.1	Optimum	~26 tons	~50°	

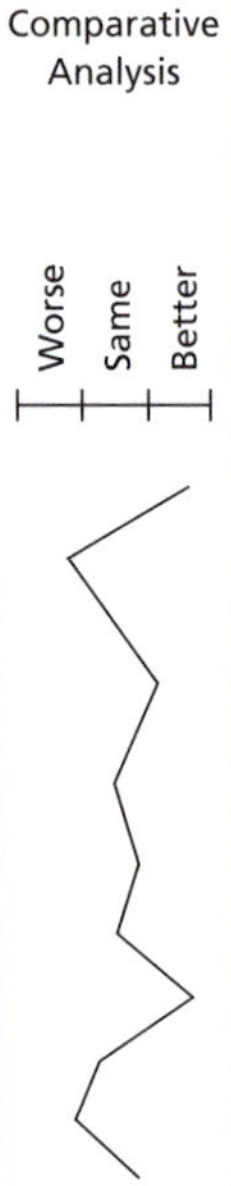

Comparative Analysis: Worse — Same — Better

Fig. 6.16 Completed house of quality for Bharat Earth Movers

Source: Rao, Carr, Daembolena, Kopp, Martin, Raffii and Schlesinger, *Total Quality Management: A Cross Cultural Perspective* (John Wiley & Sons, 1996), p. 408.

The roof of the house provides a matrix (p = positive correlation; n = negative) which signals potentially difficult trade-offs. Two examples are: (1) an increase in payload demands high brake capacities (2); a reduction of noise in the power steering puts demands on spherical bearing mountings. The HOQ overall, as straightforward as it is, provides a wonderful aid in product development and design.

Notes

1 One of the best texts on statistical quality control is A.V. Feigenbaum, 'Total quality control', *Engineering and Management* (New York: McGraw-Hill, 1951). Another good text, first published in 1982, is by R.H. Caplen, *A Practical Approach to Quality Control* (London: Business Books, 1982).
2 W. Edwards Deming, 'On some statistical aids towards economic production', *Interfaces*, 5(4), August 1975, p. 5.

Chapter 7

Evaluating total quality management

Science is usually an incremental enterprise, with most researchers toiling in the experimental thickets, trying to hack out a little clearing of enlightenment. Occasionally, however, a Darwin or Einstein comes along and with a flash of insight as blinding as a thermonuclear airburst, clears the entire landscape. Down below, ordinary scientists blink disbelievingly at their sudden ability to see from horizon to horizon. But their sense of wonder is tempered by regret. Tending your tiny patch seems like pulling weeds compared with such intellectual clear cutting.

Jeffrey Kluger[1]

Some writers have asserted that TQM provides a historically unique approach to improving organizational effectiveness, one that has a solid conceptual foundation and, at the same time, offers a strategy for improving performance that takes account of how people and organizations actually operate. A more sceptical view is that TQM is but one in a long line of programs – in the tradition of T-groups, job enrichment, management by objectives, and a host of others – that have burst upon the managerial scene rich with promise, only to give way in a few years to yet another new management fashion.

J. Richard Hackman and Ruth Wageman[2]

Testimonies from believers in TQM continue to celebrate it as a viable way of becoming customer-focused, cutting costs and delivering bottom-line results. Richard Buetow, Director of Quality at Motorola, puts the cellphone manufacturer's cost savings related to TQM at an amazing $6.5 billion over an eight-year period (1987–94). The company won the Malcolm Baldrige National Quality Award in 1988 and is regarded as world class.

But the evidence of TQM's success in the USA is mixed. Edwards Deming died in December 1993 at the age of 93, having lectured managers and quality forums to the end of his life. Joseph Juran gave his farewell tour in 1994, the same year that there was a sharp fall-off in applications for the Baldrige Award. But waning interest in the prestigious quality prize need not mean a sharp decline in TQM, rather a shift of emphasis that recognizes American advancement in the quality stakes. A joint study by Boston University, Tokyo's

Waseda University and the European Business School, INSEAD, concluded that US firms had already achieved quality on a par with their Japanese competitors or surpassed them.

The decline in Baldrige Award applications may also reveal a poor fit between TQM and the industrial imperatives of the 1990s. As *The Economist* observed:

> The most ardent adherents of quality are finding that TQM does not readily blend with wave after wave of restructuring, downsizing and re-engineering. And the challenge of developing products and bringing them to market even more swiftly – especially in industries where prices are tumbling, such as computers – adds to the strain on TQM.[3]

It is clear that downsizing creates job insecurity and demotivation among employees[4] and thereby undermines the employee involvement essential to any successful TQM programme. Rather than following Deming's dictate to 'drive out fear' as a prerequisite to quality, senior executives have instigated wave after wave of downsizing which instils fear in the survivors and makes TQM difficult to foster. Even in the photocopy company, Xerox, one of the US's greatest proponents of total quality since 1983, the TQM message has become harder to implement because of downsizing and delayering. Announcements that British Airways planned to shed 10,000 employees in 1996 in an attempt to save £1 billion costs[5] did little to inspire the levels of trust and commitment among BA personnel that are the prerequisites of continuing its total quality management programme.

A major survey published by the Institute of Management revealed that demoralized top managers were struggling to cope with record levels of stress due to the series of downsizings and delayerings. More than 80 per cent of the managers in the survey felt that their workload had increased[6] over the past year and nearly half of these said it had increased greatly. Ongoing research at Cranfield School of Management on survivors of corporate downsizing shows HR directors/managers expressing a range of perceived failures of the downsizing exercise. In some instances redundancy selection methods resulted in the departure of effective and experienced people and retention of poor performers. Against this backdrop, organizations also had a group of people who wished they could be 'released' but were not allowed to go. There is no doubt that survivors have been facing an increase in workload without the necessary resources or commensurate rewards; one HR manager described it as 'more work for higher risk'. Downsizing was carried out as a reactive measure with insufficient clarity of strategy and benefits to the organizations. After downsizing, survivors were expected to learn new skills in a relatively short space of time but people with years of experience were no longer there to coach them.

Some HR directors/managers reported that survivors do not see an end to the process, leading to demotivation, low morale, uncertainty and lack of trust in the organization. Loss of career opportunities appears to be another recurring theme in many companies. Survivors have been suffering from 'change fatigue' and 'initiative overload' without any tangible results as in many instances the envisaged improvements in business performance have not occurred. The expectations of initiators of change were overoptimistic and in some instances oversimplistic; they grossly underestimated the 'post-restructure workloads'. The process ended up, as one HR manager commented, as 'long and muddled' which was unsettling for all employees. Communication in terms of the reason for downsizing was not clear in many instances.[7]

'The process of restructuring that occurred during the recession has left many companies with just their "lifeboat staff",' Mark Hastings, a policy adviser of the Institute of Management, said. 'The result is fewer people are doing more and more work. Businesses are now asking themselves have they gone too far in taking the quick, easy route of reducing costs rather than addressing what it is about their company that creates value.'[8] The financial guru credited with starting the strategy of downsizing, Stephen Roach, Chief Economist at Morgan Stanley, feels it has gone too far.[9] Such a scene is very dysfunctional for total quality management where senior managers are supposed to create the fear-free, positive company culture needed for TQM to thrive while being role models of the new behaviours espoused.

While many companies experience a crisis of confidence and poor morale among their employees, they cannot escape from the unrelenting demands of their customers. They must become more customer focused even while they address the issues of the survivor syndrome (the state of shock and anger experienced by those who keep their jobs in downsizing), the new implicit psychological contract at work called 'the new deal' and the dictates of technological change. Empowering people at work is still a powerful option for companies trying to create a new *esprit de corps*. This effort in BT has given rise to a new programme called 'For a Better Life' which promoted more ownership of the customer's requirements and better interaction between employees at work and in the community. In the spring of 1998, the healthcare company BUPA put all 12,000 of its employees through a 'One Life' event which is part of an integrated customer orientation strategy.

BUPA's 'One Life' event objectives were:

To enable every person within BUPA to:
- Identify key customer relationships
- Understand the business rationale for customer orientation
- Recognise the behavioural impact and influence they can have on customer satisfaction/retention

- Feel valued, inspired, and motivated about the challenges facing BUPA
- Understand the brand new proposition and their role in fulfilling it
- Recognise the power, worth and value of the individual
- Feel committed to the change programme.

Since the private health-care market is flat, customer retention is critical for BUPA's survival. This is especially so in the face of massive competitive pressure from the Guardian Health merger with Private Patients Plan (PPP).

Empowerment at Xerox, which puts individual people and teams in direct contact with customer needs, is encouraged to increase motivation. Not surprisingly connecting people with the outputs of their work groups has positive benefits in Xerox, Hewlett-Packard and IBM. Studies show that where front-line people are put in charge of quality to meet customer requirements, TQM programmes have twice the success rate as those that rely on being driven by senior management.

Bill Hewlett, one of the founders of Hewlett Packard, is a believer in total quality the HP way. 'I feel that in general terms, it [the HP Way] is the policies and actions that flow from the belief that men and women want to do a good job, a creative job, and that if they are provided with the proper environment, they will do so.' Not surprisingly Hewlett Packard world-wide is famous for creating a company culture conducive for employee involvement and quality working.

For IBM, which has seen its employee numbers halved in a decade, the challenge is to develop its quality goals while continuing significant re-engineering. The two are not incompatible. Both TQM and re-engineering begin with meeting customer requirements. Both focus on *processes* that are set up to deliver work group outputs to internal or external customers. They diverge only in their strategies for change with TQM opting for continual improvement and re-engineering going for radical, mega-change.

Still it must be admitted that the increasingly mixed reviews TQM receives can create confusion. For example, a survey of 500 US manufacturing and service companies revealed that only 33 per cent say that their TQM programmes have had a significant effect on competitiveness. Another survey of 100 UK companies showed that 80 per cent of quality programmes failed to deliver due to poor management. A similar conclusion was reached by an Ashridge Management School report.

A Gallup survey sponsored by the American Society of Quality Control (ASQC), based on interviews with over six hundred executives, revealed that quality at board level is not seen to have strategic importance. Board members, lacking direct involvement in daily quality matters, find it difficult to establish a link between TQM implementation and an impact on profitability and market share.

Yet a world-wide survey of 3,000 managers revealed that more than 90 per cent of the sample believed that customer issues would be the most critical to success in the future. Managers in this study said that their organizations were far from achieving customer satisfaction. Commitment to TQM was revealed to be wavering – more talk than action – and that measurements of customer satisfaction – more often than not – were based on 'gut feelings' rather than data collection or organized intelligence systems. Other studies point to a wide chasm between the companies' perceptions of being world class and what their customers think of their products and services.

Both academics and consultants make a very valid distinction between TQM programmes that are properly implemented and maintained and those that are not. It is a fact that many managers try to do total quality management programmes 'on the cheap', failing to provide proper training at all levels in the organization or simply not giving a programme enough time to grow before raising the cost/benefit questions. Some managers choose only the easy or often rhetorical parts of a TQM programme and fail to develop the rigorous, scientific techniques required, and then blame others for failure rather than recognizing their own half-hearted approach to quality as the cause.

Quality consultants try to bring bottom-line accountability to TQM programmes with quality review processes. The new edition of *Quality on Trial*[10] claims to do just that – transforming the leap of faith in a quality programme into a planned, manageable, measurable business initiative.

As all these sorts of books do, *Quality on Trial* illustrates its review process with the ringing testimonials of its clients. For example:

> Our business in 3M has achieved significant improvements in sales productivity, as in effective management of customer relationships, thanks in substantial part to the Quality Review process described in *Quality on Trial*. In particular, the sensitivity that has been created by having our people involved in the process of finding out what customers *really* consider important has been invaluable.[11]

The Bradford Study[12] meets the mixed messages on TQM's success in Britain head-on by researching total quality management's impact on bottom-line results. The study was inspired by earlier research in American by the US General Accounts Office (GAO) which linked TQM with bottom-line results focusing on the top 20 scores in the Malcolm Baldrige National Quality Award in 1988–9. The GAO study used questionnaires and interviews to obtain information from the sample of 20 companies on performance measures which included: (1) employee related indicators; (2) operating indicators; (3) customer satisfaction indicators; and (4) business performance indicators. The companies consistently saw improvements in all the various performance indicators.

The Bradford study used 'harder' bottom-line business indicators than the GAO study, but had similar aims. The Bradford researchers focused on the following indicators:

- profit per employee;
- average remuneration;
- total assets per employee;
- return on total assets;
- turnover per employee;
- profit margin;
- fixed asset trend;
- trend in number employed.

The GAO study was undertaken at the beginning of a recession, whereas the Bradford research looked at a pattern of performance spanning five years in deepening recession. The 29 companies[13] were chosen from those that had had five to eight years' experience with total quality management.

Despite the inherent difficulties with the Bradford research the findings are impressive. The results indicated that a high proportion of the companies examined exhibited above industry average performance:

- for profit per employee 79 per cent of the companies showed positive quantums in comparison with industry median;
- average remuneration in 93 per cent of the companies studied is higher than their industry median;
- total assets per employee is positively exhibited in 79 per cent of the companies;
- 76 per cent of the companies are showing positive returns on total assets;
- turnover per employee in 79 per cent of the companies is higher than the corresponding industry median;
- 76 per cent of the companies studied showed healthier profit margins than industry median;
- 72 per cent of the companies examined showed an above industry median fixed asset trend;
- 76 per cent of the companies studied showed healthier profit margins than industry median;
- 72 per cent of the companies examined showed an above industry median fixed asset trend;
- the trends on number of employees were not clear, but 17 of the 29 companies have, over the five years studied, increased rather than shed employees.

The eight indicators chosen for carrying out the comparisons reflect business performance both in the short term and the long term. They include 'softer' or people-related measures, such as employee trends and remuneration. In combination, the eight performance indicators show a consistently positive pattern of performance between the selected companies and industry medians.

These patterns strongly suggest that there is a positive *association* between the introduction of TQM and tangible benefits. The companies studied were selected on the basis of existing knowledge of their TQM initiatives and not their standing in the market-place.

Although it is not possible to prove direct causality in the Bradford study since other factors may be present, the consistency of the results does point towards a strong association. This European-based study, together with the US GAO study and other studies in Japan, provide strong evidence that total quality management does have a direct impact on financial results, provided its implementation is well directed and planned and provided there is strong commitment to sustaining continuous improvements which focus on benefits for the end customer. TQM offers companies the opportunity to carry out improvements and focuses on getting closer to customers. Companies must still have the right strategies in place, the right products and services, the right commitment and the right investment strategies to be successful.

The only foreign winner of Japan's Deming prize (1989) – the Florida Power and Light Company (FLP) – used to have a quality department with 85 full-time staff and 1,900 quality teams. The programme achieved spectacular results and became a role model to other firms. It even spun off its own consultancy company. 'Throughout the postwar period FPL had pushed for productivity and cost control, but in the early 1980s we were not getting much of either,' said the ex-Chairman and CEO.

> Now we were trying a totally different approach: quality improvement. Because we did not want our employees to think that QIP was just another productivity improvement scheme in disguise, we did not talk about cost at all. Of course, we never lost sight of the fact that price is important to our customers, and earnings to our investors, but the way to satisfy both turned out to be the indirect way of quality improvement.

He added more evidence to link the power company's TQM to performance:

> FPL's quality indicators measure those things our customers say are important to them. We listen to the voice of the customer. Then we work to do a better and better job of meeting their needs and expectations. That is what policy management and the quality improvement process are all about. That is the scoreboard, and when you are winning it is exciting and fun – and it is reflected in the bottom line.

Somehow the quality bureaucracy eventually got in the way of this electrical utility company delivering better service to its customers. When a new CEO got rid of most of the quality bureaucracy, service improved. Doubts were raised everywhere about the value of quality prizes and what it took to win them.

Quality awards as assessment

The Malcolm Baldrige National Quality Award was launched in the USA in 1987 with two main objectives:

1 to raise the consciousness on quality matters of US business leaders;
2 to provide a comprehensive framework for measuring the quality programmes of the nation's businesses.

Named after Malcolm Baldrige, Secretary of Commerce (1981–7), the Award took its inspiration from Baldrige's direct approach to quality:

> We have to encourage American executives to get out of their boardrooms and onto the factory floor to learn how their products are made and how they can be made better.[14]

The first aim of consciousness raising was achieved as the press and other media used the Award as springboards for quality features and senior managers moved quality to the top of their agendas. The second aim of providing a framework to measure quality success was also attained. In the first five years of the Award over a half million copies of the Application Guidelines were requested by companies to use in their own quality programmes. This massive self-assessment has been, perhaps, the biggest achievement of the Award scheme. Federal Express, a 1990 Baldrige Award winner, is among a number of companies that originally went through a Baldrige self-assessment with only the goal of self-improvement in mind. But by the time the company completed the process, senior management reasoned that they might at least rate a site visit, so they opted to apply and won. For these Application Guidelines provide what Marion Mills Steeples called a 'non-denominational' framework of what it takes to be a quality organization, an objective measure department-by-department, goal-by-goal, area-by-area of the quality process. The Award's quality guidelines, then, have truly become for countless companies a means for learning how to integrate a total system of quality management. It also helps these companies benchmark themselves against those companies who have been shortlisted for the Award by on-site inspections or who have won the Award outright.

Marion Mills Steeples has had extensive involvement as a member of the Board of Examiners for the Malcolm Baldrige National Quality Award since its inception. She wrote:

> It would be difficult to overestimate the ultimate impact of the new Baldrige way of thinking. Properly applied, the science of quality management is a CEO's dream

come true. The systematic pursuit of quality has the ability to cut development and production costs, eliminate waste, streamline processes, enhance worker morale, improve customer relations, and increase market share and profits. What is more, there doesn't seem to be any sort of business – or any aspect of business – that can't benefit from an integrated system of quality management. From heavy manufacturing companies to high-tech electronics firms, from retail and service industries to hospitals and even city governments, organizations that have made the commitment to quality have reported stunning results.[15]

'No cash comes with the Baldrige Award – not directly anyway,' she added. 'Companies that have won the Award have made marketing hay of it, but those companies that have vied and lost have also come away big winners, with more muscular, streamlined organizations, higher profits, happier workers, and improved products and services.'[16]

There are three Malcolm Baldrige National Quality Award applicant categories: manufacturing companies, service companies and small businesses. Each year there can be a maximum of two Awards presented in each category. If the Award's challenging standards are not met, no Award is given. In the Award's first nine years (up till 1996) only 28 out of 54 possible Awards were bestowed.

The Baldrige Award encourages companies to successfully apply total quality principles to every aspect of their business. The principles of total quality that are encompassed in the Award criteria include the following:

- Customers define quality. Everything starts with their requirements.
- Senior managers need to create quality values and build them into company operations and company culture.
- Quality emerges from well-designed and well-executed systems and processes.
- Continuous improvement is an integral part of the management of all systems and processes.
- Companies must set goals and create strategic and operational plans to achieve quality leadership.
- Shorter response time for all operations and processes must be part of quality improvement efforts.
- Company operations and decision-making must be based on facts.
- Employees at all levels should be appropriately educated and developed to be involved in quality improvement activities.
- Quality systems include design quality and error prevention.
- Companies need to communicate quality requirements to their suppliers and help improve their performance.

Like any award, the Baldrige is subject to claims that its criteria are arbitrarily determined. 'Nevertheless, the Baldrige has succeeded in encouraging U.S. business leaders to address quality on a broad range of management issues,'

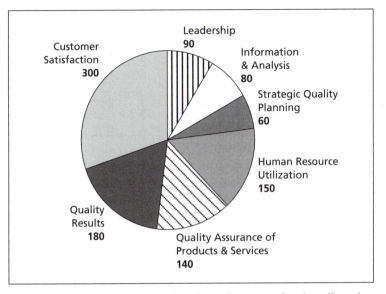

Fig. 7.1 Malcolm Baldrige National Quality Award point allocation

Source: Marion Mills Steeples, *The Corporate Guide to the Malcolm Baldrige National Quality Award*, 2nd edn (Milwaukee, Wis.: ASQC Quality Press, 1993), p. 22.

said Arden C. Sims, President and CEO, Globe Metallurgical Inc., one of the first small business winners of the Award. 'Companies that wish to compete for the award must produce evidence of leadership and long-term planning, initiate verifiable quality control procedures, address the happiness and well-being of the work force, and, above all, work toward the satisfaction of the customer.'[17]

The major components of a total quality management system are contained in the Award's seven examination categories:

1 Leadership
2 Information and Analysis
3 Strategic Quality Planning
4 Human Resource Development and Utilization
5 Management of Process Quality
6 Quality and Operational Results
7 Customer Focus and Satisfaction.

The total value of all examination categories is 1,000 points. The Award's category point allocations are shown in Figure 7.1.

The success of the Malcolm Baldrige National Quality Award served both as an inspiration and a model for the European Quality Award (EQA) begun in 1991. The European quality prize also includes the category of

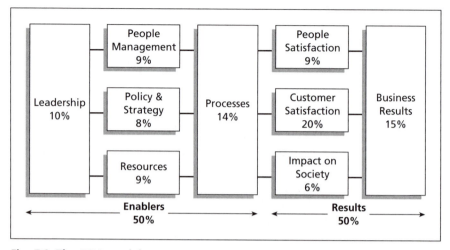

Fig. 7.2 The EQA model

public responsibility such as business ethics, environmental protection and waste management.

Unlike the Baldrige Award, the European Quality Award takes account of financial performance which is not an insignificant improvement. Author and publisher, Jerry Bowles, makes the point that 'Until the results of quality improvement are integrated into overall financial reporting and accounting systems, rather than being tracked and reported on their own, quality will not become a full partner in the strategic planning process.'[18]

In summary then, the European Quality Award model added to and enhanced the Malcolm Baldrige National Quality Award model by including 'impact on society' and 'business results' to Baldrige's existing categories for assessment (*see* Figure 7.2).

TQM – just another fad?

The Florida Power and Light Company experience of total quality management going from the dizzy heights of winners of the Deming prize in 1989 to partial demise within a few years strengthens the opinion of some writers that TQM is simply a management fad in the long series of fads that have dominated management thinking over the last few decades.

'Over two dozen managerial techniques have waxed and waned since the 1950s. More interestingly, half were spawned in the past five years. The list reads like a Who's Who of business hype: Theory Z, Matrix, Managerial Grid, T Groups, Entrepreneurship, Demassing, and One Minute Managing.'[19] Others are: corporate culture, kaizen, MBWA (Management by Walking (or Wandering) Around), portfolio management, restructuring, excellence, quality

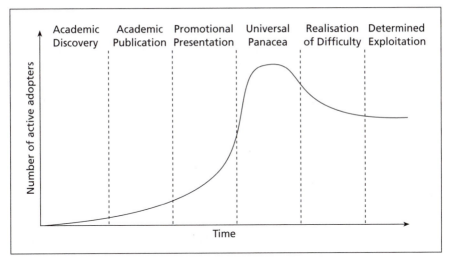

Fig. 7.3 Lifecycle of a management fad

Source: Gerard Burke, 'Business process redesign – hype or hope?', *Management Focus*, Cranfield School of Management, no. 2, Autumn 1993, pp. 11 and 12.

circles, wellness, decentralization, value chains, zero based budgeting, strategic business units, experience curves, diversification, management by objectives, conglomeration, brainstorming, theory X and theory Y, satisfaction/dissatisfaction, decision trees.

The fads are often contradictory. John Byrne, writing in *Business Week*, captured the frustration of managers:

> In the past eighteen months, we have heard that profit is more important than revenue, quality is more important than profit, that people are more important than profit, that customers more important than our people, that big customers are more important than our small customers and that growth is the key to our success. No wonder our performance is inconsistent.[20]

These fads, usually of American origin, continue unabated. Among the latest are the balanced scorecard, 360° feedback, the virtual value chain, empowerment (as practised by some companies), the learning organization and managing diversity. They follow a 'product lifecycle' as illustrated in Figure 7.3 from academic discovery to academic publication, from promotional presentation to universal panacea, from a realization of the difficulties to determined exploitation. At each phase of the fad's lifecycle the numbers of participants increase over time until it peaks at the universal panacea stage. Thereafter the numbers fall away fast.

In addition to fads there are well founded psychological theories which are picked up by management consultants and packaged for popular consumption among the managerial population. Serious psychoanalytical techniques such as transactional analysis (TA) and neuro-linguistic programming (NLP) appear in pop management manuals, training packages and the kit bags of consultants quick to make applications in the management world even though (often unwittingly) these applications amount to abuse of the scientific theories.

The balanced scorecard perhaps provides a clear illustration of a management fad's lifecycle. The balanced scorecard was first developed by Robert S. Kaplan, a professor of accounting at the Harvard Business School and David P. Norton, the president and co-founder of a Massachusetts-based consultancy firm, Renaissance Solutions. In 1990 they were both working on a one-year multi-company research study 'Measuring Performance in the Organization of the Future'. The study, sponsored by the Nolan Norton Institute, the research body of KPMG, was prompted by the hypothesis that existing performance measures, relying primarily as they do on financial accounting systems, were becoming irrelevant and obsolete. The core ideas appeared in an article in the *Harvard Business Review* January–February issue 1992, which illustrated how the scorecard tracks the key elements of a company's strategy – from continuous improvement and partnership to teamwork and global scale (*see* Figure 7.4). The idea is to have a swift, accurate measurement of a company's performance, which like the dials in a jet cockpit gives managers complex information at a glance.

The balanced scorecard permits managers to look at their business from four important perspectives instantaneously. The balanced scorecard provides answers to four main questions thereby giving vital information on key performance indicators. First, it tells managers how customers see the company – the customer perspective. (The technique of course owes a great debt of gratitude to the quality movement for this starting point.) Secondly, it answers the question: 'what must we excel at?' (the internal business perspective). Thirdly, it queries: 'How can we continue to improve and create value?' (the innovation and learning perspective). And fourthly: 'How do we look to shareholders?' (the financial perspective). The aim is to limit the information load to these four key measures – the most critical ones.

After the publication of the idea came the promotion which included consultancy by the founders and thousands of other consultants world-wide who helped sell the scorecard techniques to companies. This was followed by more documentation in the forms of 'Putting the balanced scorecard to Work'[21] in the *Harvard Business Review* and, four years after the initial publication of the idea, a further Harvard Business School article by the same founders of the fad showing managers how to use the balanced scorecard as a strategic management system:

> Recently, we have seen some companies move beyond our early vision for the scorecard to discover its value as the cornerstone of a new strategic management

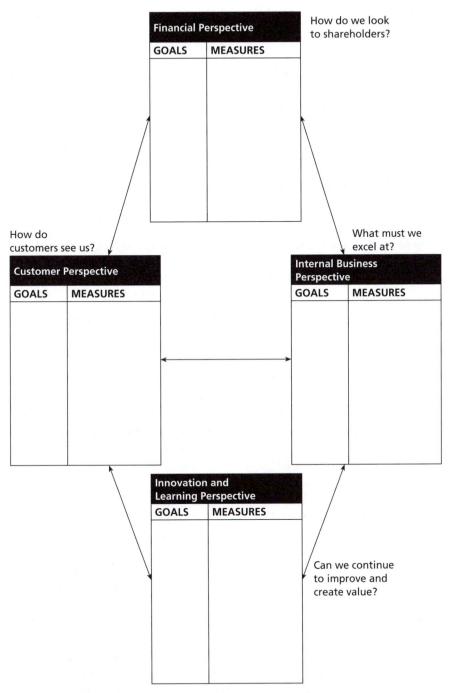

Fig. 7.4 The balanced scorecard links performance measures

Source: Robert S. Kaplan and David P. Norton, 'The balanced scorecard links performance measures', *Harvard Business Review*, Jan.–Feb. 1992, p. 72.

system. Used this way, the scorecard addresses a serious deficiency in traditional management systems: their inability to link a company's long-term strategy with its short term actions.[22]

By then the technique had been adopted by thousands of companies across the world which included household names in Britain such as BT and Cellnet, the Swedish financial services company SKANDIA and the global engineering company Kellogg based in Houston with an international office in London. The usefulness of the balanced scorecard was already proclaimed as a panacea.

> At Sears, we have successfully used the principles of the Balanced Scorecard to help shape our transformation.
>> Richard T. Quinn, Vice President, Quality, Sears & Roebuck & Co.

> At Mobil, the Balanced Scorecard has served as an irreplaceable agenda for discussion of business strategies, strengths, weaknesses and performance.
>> R.J. McCool, Executive Vice President, Americas Marketing &
>> Refining Division, Mobil Oil Co.

> CIGNA Property & Casualty Insurance Company has used the Balanced Scorecard to manage its transformation to a top-quartile specialist.
>> President, Gerald A. Isom

Even as the founders of the scorecard technique's first book on the topic came on stream in September 1996 from the Harvard Business School Press, many companies among the first users of the technique in 1992 were already moving out of the 'universal panacea' stage of a management fad into the 'realisation of its difficulty' stage, which will be closely followed by 'determined exploitation or abandonment'.

Is TQM anything more than a management technique like the balanced scorecard? J. Richard Hackman and Ruth Wageman, in their 25-page article in the prestigious *Administrative Science Quarterly*, argued that the jury is still out on whether TQM is a fad or rather a unique approach to improving managerial effectiveness with a solid conceptual foundation and staying power as a strategy for improving organizational performance. More empirical studies are required, but there are other real problems with TQM raised in the powerful article which proponents of total quality would do well to ponder.

These academic authors chart the many beneficial outcomes of TQM and the fit of many TQM practices today with the principles of the founders – specifically W. Edwards Deming, Joseph M. Juran and Kaoru Ishikawa. Much of what is prescribed by current TQM practices, when implemented fully and well, they judged, is in alignment with research evidence about the factors that promote performance effectiveness. However, they stated that TQM, itself, by philosophy and design avoids head-on, large-scale, intervention in four areas of work which are critical to organizational behaviour and performance. These four features of work systems include:

1 how front-line work is structured;
2 how gains are allocated;
3 how opportunities for learning are apportioned;
4 how authority is distributed.

In terms of the design of work, apart from some employees joining quality teams or supporting initiatives normally undertaken by other staff members, 'the motivational structure of front-line jobs is unaltered in many, perhaps most TQM implementations'. This leads to the problem: how does a manager motivate front-line people to deliver continuous improvement and the highest quality outputs without radically redesigning their motivation package or the structure of their jobs?

Extrinsic rewards such as pay are outside the scope of TQM programmes since neither individual performance nor team performance should be measured. Management by objectives (MBO) is seen by Deming as an enemy of total quality. The problem that arises is a dilemma. How does a manager win commitment to organizational goals through collective gains and intrinsic rewards without disturbing the normal distribution of extrinsic rewards.

A TQM company is inescapably a learning organization. The learning takes place at the start of a company-wide quality programme at the top level and is cascaded down to all levels of the organization. The statistical techniques are continued through training and behavioural learning because the aspiration of continuous improvement in meeting customer requirements is ongoing. Moreover, quality efforts include benchmarking other organizations, learning best practices from them and meeting standards in the wider quality world promoted by quality associations and accrediting organizations. But there is a problem with quality learning, as Hackman and Wageman illustrated:

> Learning is indeed a core value in TQM organizations, but there are non-trivial constraints on what is to be learned about, who is to do the learning, and when learning should be set aside in favour of performing . . . [This leads to a dilemma of] achieving continuous learning by front-line organization members – while also requiring them to adhere closely to standardized best practices that have been developed by quality teams or imported from other organizations.[23]

A final set of problems flagged by the authors has to do with the distribution of authority. Traditional approaches to TQM as espoused by Deming and others predicate that it is the manager's job to design the systems within which workers do their jobs. By definition this reinforces the top-down chain of command and legitimizes the managerial power that creates cross-functional quality teams and taskforces. Front-line people are involved and empowered to actively analyse and solve problems and implement the solutions. Yet very often there is a great gap between their problem-solving processes and their power to make decisions. In fact, as the authors pointed out, this leads to a final dilemma – that of 'empowering organization members to be full participants in achieving collective purposes – but doing so without threatening top-down managerial control of the enterprise'.[24]

The authors admitted that expecting a TQM programme to radically change the design of work, reallocate rewards, restructure the learning options and redistribute functional authority in a company would be expecting a mission impossible for TQM. Moreover, such quality initiatives would be opposed by vested-interest groups of managers afraid of losing their authority and by employees threatened by radical changes in their own beliefs and prospects.

Were it possible to achieve all those goals, they surmised, the long-term success of those radical programmes that survived the opposition and took hold might be higher. One of the strengths, however, of TQM programmes world-wide is that, while having a demanding and rigorous agenda, they are not too radical to be embraced by most organizations. Once implanted the quality programmes work to achieve significant changes that ultimately alter the company culture irrevocably for the better.

The authors ended their long discussion of TQM today with a pessimistic forecast about the future of total quality management. They predicted problems for TQM due to three trends. The first is that 'rhetoric is winning out over substance',[25] the authors warned. Despite the significant outcomes of total quality management programmes which adhere to the principles of the TQM founders, Deming, Juran and Ishikawa, many so-called TQM programmes are a pale reflection of the real thing. The difficult-to-do scientific parts of a genuine TQM programme are passed over and only the slogans kept.

The second worrisome trend is that TQM is becoming a catch-all for every intervention dreamed up by managers, academics or consultants. TQM becomes an umbrella for virtually anything, blurring its focus with add-on interventions and putting it at risk.[26]

The third and final worrying trend touched on the role of the authors themselves and is simply stated:

Research is not providing the corrective function for TQM that it could and should . . . We researchers have not been carrying our share of the load: too much of the TQM literature consists of anecdotal case reports or simplistic before-and-after evaluation studies that may be of more use politically in promoting TQM (or, for sceptics, in debunking it) than they are in building knowledge about TQM processes and practices.[27]

Their appeal for more proactive research is especially attractive and an appropriate ending to a chapter on total quality management evaluation.

Total quality management as articulated by Deming, Ishikawa and Juran is a set of powerful interventions wrapped in a highly attractive package. When implemented well, TQM can help an organization improve itself and, in the process, better serve its community and its own members. If TQM is to prosper, however, rhetorical excesses will have to be kept in better check than they are at present, and researchers will have to do a better job of illuminating the mechanisms through which TQM practices realize their effects. For only if the continuous improvement idea comes to apply to TQM itself will this provocative philosophy have a chance of sustaining itself over time.[28]

Notes

1 Jeffrey Kluger, *Time*, 23 September 1996.

2 J. Richard Hackman and Ruth Wageman, 'Total quality management: empirical, conceptual, and practical issues', *Administrative Science Quarterly*, June 1995, p. 309.

3 'The strains of quality', *The Economist*, 14 January 1995, p. 65.

4 Noeleen Doherty, John Bank and Susan Vinnicombe, 'Managing survivors: the experience of survivors in British Telecom and the British financial services sector', *Journal of Managerial Psychology*, vol. 11, no. 7, 1996, pp. 51–9.

5 Barrie Clement, 'BA to jettison 10,000 workers', *The Independent*, 9 September 1996, p. 1.

6 Patrick Tooker, 'The boss is demoralised, downsized and delayered too', *The Independent*, 16 September 1996.

7 Kusum Sahdev and Susan Vinnicombe, 'Downsizing and survivor syndrome: a study of HR's perception of survivor's response and the changing role of HR', unpublished working paper, pp. 16 and 17.

8 Ibid.

9 Stephen Roach, interview on the BBC's *Money Programme*, 20 October 1996.

10 R.J. Howe, D. Gaeddert and M.A. Howe, *Quality on Trial* (New York: McGraw-Hill, 1995).

11 Pat Chelf, Marketing Development Manager, 3M Company Medical Division, as quoted in ibid.

12 M. Zairi, S.R. Letza and J.R. Oakland, *Does TQM Impact on the Bottom Line Results?* (The Bradford Study), University of Bradford Management Centre, March 1993.

13 The companies used for the Bradford Study were: Thorntons Plc, BRS Ltd, Bass Plc, NCR Ltd, Motorola Ltd, British Telecom Ltd, Avis Europe Ltd, Johnson & Johnson Ltd, Rover Group Ltd, ICI Plc, Elida Gibbs Ltd, Mercury Communications Ltd, Milliken Industrial Ltd, CMB Fodcan Plc, Rockware Glass Ltd, Kodak Ltd, BP Chemicals Ltd, Tetra Pak Ltd, Digital Equipment Co. Ltd, British Airways Plc, IBM UK Ltd, Exxon Chemicals, BICC Plc, Procter & Gamble Ltd, 3M (UK) Plc, Northern Telecom Europe Ltd, Rank Xerox Ltd and H.J. Heinz.

14 Marion Mills Steeples, *The Corporate Guide to the Malcolm Baldrige National Quality Award*, 2nd edn (Milwaukee, Wis.: ASQC Quality Press, 1993), p. 22.

15 Ibid., pp. x and xi.

16 Ibid., p. xi.

17 Arden C. Sims, 'Does the Baldrige Award really work?', *Harvard Business Review*, Jan.–Feb. 1992, p. 126. *See also* David A. Garvin, 'How the Baldrige Award really works', *Harvard Business Review*, Nov.–Dec. 1991.

18 Arden C. Sims, op. cit., p. 127.

19 Richard Pascale, *Managing on the edge: How Successful Companies Use Conflict to Stay Ahead* (London: Viking, Penguin, 1990), pp. 18 and 20.

20 John Byrne, 'Business fads – what's in and out', *Business Week*, 20 January 1996, p. 53.

21 Robert S. Kaplan and David P. Norton, 'Putting the balanced scorecard to work', *Harvard Business Review*, Sep.–Oct. 1993.

22 Robert S. Kaplan and David P. Norton, 'Using the balanced scorecard as a strategic management system', *Harvard Business Review*, Jan.–Feb. 1996.

23 J. Richard Hackman and Ruth Wageman, op. cit., p. 29.

24 Ibid.

25 Ibid.

26 Ibid., p. 31.

27 Ibid.

28 Ibid.

Chapter 8

···

Avoiding the hype

There is too much evidence to suggest that behind the brilliance of our world-class performers is a comet's tail of under-performing companies, too many of which are not as good as they think they are. While 70 per cent of UK companies think they perform at world-class level, only 2.3 per cent actually do so, according to an IBM London Business School study.

Sir Denys Henderson, President of the British Quality Foundation,
Chairman of the Rank Organization[1]

I believe there is a bright future ahead for mankind, and that future holds exciting technological advances that will enrich the lives of everybody on the planet . . .

We proved it in Japan by changing the image of the words 'Made in Japan' from something shoddy to something fine. But for a single nation or a few nations to have accomplished this is not enough. My vision of the future is of an exciting world of superior goods and services, where every nations' stamp of origin is a symbol of quality.

Akio Morita, Chairman of the Board and CEO,
Sony Corporation[2]

This chapter consists of a selection of a dozen books which are among the very best on total quality management in print today. A short critique of each book should help the reader with making choices for further reading.

Further reading

W. Edwards Deming: *Out of the Crisis*[3]

This book is Deming's last and a modern classic in total quality. As it represents further developments in his thinking, it presupposes a working understanding of his basic teachings. Serious students of Deming will find the book illuminating.

Unlike Juran in his most recent books, Deming does not give a detailed, prescriptive plan of action for installing total quality processes. For example, in a chapter entitled 'Organization for Improvement of Quality and Productivity', Deming advocates 'leadership in statistical methodology', which networks with the managing director and other senior managers, as well as all sections of the company. But he does not get more specific.

Sample extract

Malpractice in medicine. This can only be understood with the help of statistical theory. The result of a medical intervention is interaction between physician, treatment, and patient. Two thousand million (2×10^9) medical interventions take place every year in the United States. A hundred thousand cases of unfavourable results seem like a large number, yet this number represents reliability of 1 part in 20,000. It would be difficult to find a mechanical or electrical system with greater reliability. Most of the 100,000 unfavourable results (if that be the number) belong to the system. Some small fraction of the 100,000 unfavourable results could possibly be caused by carelessness, including incompetence.

One per cent of 100,000 is 1,000, still a large number. Any number is too big. The problem is to discover whether the cause of an unfavourable outcome (a) lies in the system of medical care, including the patient; or (b) may be ascribed to some special cause such as carelessness on the part of the physician, or carelessness on the part of the patient, who may fail to follow instructions or to get in touch with his physician as directed. An important step would be for medical people to construct operational definitions of special causes of unfortunate results from medical interventions of various kinds. This is a huge task, and a never-ending one, but until it is brought to a usable stage, physicians in the United States, and their insurance companies, will continue to fight off unjustified accusations of carelessness and will live a life liable to legal tangles.

(pages 484–5)

V.A. Zeithaml, A. Parasuraman and L.L. Berry: Delivering Quality Service[4]

Delivering Quality Service grew out of seven years of serious, academic research on quality service in America. The research had four phases. Phase one was extensive qualitative research of service customers and service-company executives from which the authors developed their model of service quality. Phase two was a massive empirical study which tested the customer half of the authors' service-quality model. Phase three was another empirical study but based on the service-provider part of their model. It focused on the eighty-nine field offices of five national service companies. Phase four focuses on customer service expectations.

The research consisted of a rich assortment of methods used to explore three central questions, namely: what is service quality?; what causes service quality problems?; and what can organizations do to solve these problems and improve their service? The book breaks down the little-understood notion of service quality into well-defined, manageable increments that are closely linked to customer perceptions. It uses sharp illustrations drawn from the authors' consultancy experience with major US companies.

Sample extract

Our extensive research focusing on the provider's side of our gaps model indicates that seven key conceptual factors contribute to Gap 3, the service performance gap. These factors . . . include: 1) role ambiguity; 2) role conflict; 3) poor employee–job fit; 4) poor technology–job fit; 5) inappropriate supervisory control systems leading to 6) an inappropriate evaluation/compensation system; and 7) lack of teamwork. (page 90)

David Halberstam: *The Reckoning*[5]

This massive book tells the story of the Japanese and American cultures through the case studies of two car companies – Nissan and Ford. The in-depth study – five years in the writing – is by one of the United States' best documentary journalists, a Pulitzer Prize winner. It is written with the force of a great novel.

In the book the Japanese are credited with heeding the advice of the American experts on quality and efficiency who were ignored in the United States. It is Ford's preoccupation with profit at the expense of quality and innovation under the leadership of J. Edward Lundy and his team of MBAs that is responsible for the widening gap between the two car makers. In microcosm, Ford's miscalculations and consequent decline reveal the reasons America lost its industrial supremacy to Japan, a defeated country only recently scorned for the low quality of its goods.

Sample extract

But when Japanese productivity teams visiting America mentioned Deming to their hosts, the Americans rarely knew his name. The few who did seemed to regard him as some kind of crank. To the Japanese that was particularly puzzling, for when a Japanese team came to America and made the rounds, city after city, factory after factory, the one American all its members wanted to see was Edwards Deming. It was like a pilgrimage. When they did come to see him at his home in Washington, Deming knew many of them by name, because he had visited them in Japan, and he was always able to ask about their colleagues back home . . . Deming's passion was for making better products, or more accurately for creating a system that could make better products. It was not for making money . . . There was another way in which he differed from the other Americans they were visiting. The others would lecture them and the lectures were, however unconsciously, an exercise in power. Deming listened as much as he talked.

(pages 311–12)

J.M. Juran: *Leadership for Quality*[6] and *Juran's New Quality Road Map*[7]

Both of these books are comprehensive guides to setting up total quality management programmes. Juran bases both books on his own method for planning, setting and reaching quality goals – his 'quality trilogy' (*see* Figure 3.3, p. 95 above) – a paradigm built on his own approach to quality planning, control and project-based improvement.

Leadership for Quality is a companion volume to his earlier work *Planning for Quality*. He provides senior managers with the proven, field-tested methods they need to be successful in leading their companies in the search for quality. He demonstrates how leadership for quality must come from the top. In his approach to strategic quality management he draws on the experiences of thousands of chief executives around the world to create a clear plan of action which is just as applicable to the service sector as to manufacturing.

Sample extract

A further significant post-war phenomenon was the rise of product quality to a position of prominence in the public mind. This growth in prominence was the result of the convergence of multiple trends:

Growing concern about damage to the environment.
Action by the courts to impose strict liability.
Fear of major disasters and near disasters.
Pressure from consumer organizations for better quality and more responsive redress.
Growing public awareness of the role of quality in international competition (e.g. in trade and weapons)

Collectively these trends are a consequence of mankind's adoption of technology and industrialization. Industrialization confers many benefits on society, but it also makes society dependent on the continuing performance and good behaviour of a huge array of technological goods and services. This is the phenomenon of 'life beyond the quality dikes' – a form of securing benefits but living dangerously. Like the Dutch who have reclaimed so much land from the sea, we secure the benefits of technology. However, we need protective dikes in the form of good quality to shield society against service interruptions and to guard against disasters.   (*Leadership for Quality*, pages 9–10)

Sandra Vandermerwe: *From Tin Soldiers to Russian Dolls*[8]

This is a stunning book that does more than call for better customer service. It creates a mindshift about one's thinking about customers, markets and organizations. In it the distinction between industrial and service sectors of the economy become blurred as all really successful companies must today create value for customers through services.

The book is both theoretically sound, grounded as it is in empirical as well as qualitative research, and very practical in giving the reader valuable ideas of how to pursue a service-focused strategy.

Sample extract

But, as the new sciences have so amply taught us, we do not live in a deterministic system. And, as we now know, we cannot extrapolate from our present state what the future will bring. Yet, when we look around, it's obvious that high-value corporations already have an image of the future. They have begun to articulate an agenda for the new millennium, thereby already setting it into motion. So, the stage has been set for the next century – one in which the immaterial will, more than ever, affect what firms will do and how they make their money. Opportunities for wealth will come consistently from making and moving intangibles rather than 'things', regardless of time, space or distance. Value is being found where it never was sought before – in the natural world, and from a communal and global sense of individual responsibility.

The inroads made by services will continue into the next millennium. In fact, they are likely to be even more predominant, bringing success to those corporations which have made the transition from tin solders to Russian dolls – from an industrial to a service ethos. Ironically, services have become the contemporary manager's way of making the intangibles more tangible for customers. As the industrial age fades still further into history, so the criteria for success and failure become more apparent.

But, whereas the service ethos is now the competitive differentiator, it will become a condition for corporate survival in the future. As the year 2000 draws nearer, rather than having to make dramatic changes – from high volume to high value – managers will be looking for new and better ways to keep adapting to ever changing conditions and customer requirements. Having established the groundwork for the design, delivery and support of service-intensive solutions, they will be intent on avoiding the industrial trap of simply delivering more of the same uniform offerings more cheaply.

Will the added-value services continue to give business the astonishing opportunities for satisfying customers that we are witnessing now? There can be no doubt. Can firms develop these services in the next century at the same pace that they did for 'things' in the last? Well, they must. For how else will they compete?

Never again can the material matter as much as the immaterial, or matter be as important as no matter.

The only question is: who can be best at it?   (page 224)

Patrick L. Townsend: *Commit to Quality*[9]

This is a quality manager's hero story of how his company, the Paul Revere Insurance Group, went through the first two years of a total quality process which has made it a role model for TQM in the service sector. Filled with day-to-day detail of the effort and written conversationally, the book is a unique document. It provides a blueprint for improving quality from the philosophy to the implementation of TQM. The emphasis on recognition and rewards is noteworthy. The paperback edition of the book, also from John Wiley, contains an extra chapter which describes the next three years of the programme.

Sample extract

The installation of a quality process such as that described in this book is not cheap. The return on investment, once the process is rolling, will satisfy even the greediest stockholder, but it will take some faith up front – faith in the employees to both know how to improve things and to be willing to share that knowledge once the forum is provided.

It will cost in people to run the process; it will cost in time devoted first by the steering committee and then, on an ongoing basis, by the teams in their meetings; it will cost to do the training; and it will cost to run a recognition program. Correctly established, costs will be returned quickly. At The Paul Revere, the costs for recognition alone in the first year were $80,000, but the annualized savings were over $3.25 million.

(page 67)

Philip B. Crosby: *Quality is Free*[10]

This is the best of Crosby's seven books. It is an account of Crosby's thinking and practice on total quality management. Everything is rooted in his own experience and punctuated with success stories. For example, ITT saved $720 million while he was corporate vice-president quality director at the company, using his 14-step quality improvement programme, which is the core of *Quality is Free*.

He has a readable, folksy style. He also uses many examples and some case studies to illustrate his basic teaching on quality.

Sample extract

Speaking about giving the quality business some thought, I feel it is time to discard a lot of the useless appendages that have made quality management difficult to understand. The word 'quality' is good enough to stand by itself. We should eliminate 'control', 'assurance', and other modifiers that too often accompany it. These identify relatively insignificant and minute differences in approach.

The term 'quality assurance' came into being during the first frantic missile years so a few astute individuals could move into higher salary brackets and at the same time be involved in more dignified work. They were soon peering over shoulders, rather than making quality happen. Certainly I have no objection to a little nest feathering, but it is possible to make an excellent living actually doing the job of quality rather than just auditing to find out why it wasn't done.

There is absolutely no reason for having errors or defects in any product or service. The concepts of quality management listed throughout this book, plus some hard, dedicated work, plus continuous exercise of personal integrity, make preventing error a realistic possibility. That in turn makes it realistically possible for the error preventer to become one of the most valuable executives in any company. You can get rich by preventing defects. You can never make much by simply 'assuring' or 'controlling'. Police officers try to keep things under control. Lawyers often work at prevention. You have never seen a rich policeman. There are a lot of rich lawyers.

Think about it.

(pages 58–9)

Brett Whitford and Rebecca Bird: *The Pursuit of Quality*[11]

Fifty case studies chosen from across British industry are used to demonstrate in a practical way virtually all aspects of a quality programme.

Topics are illustrated by anecdotes and examples, stories, facts and evidence. Nearly 600 pages in length, the book encompasses the following aspects of TQM:

- managing change;
- building supplier partnerships;
- quality audits;
- ISO 9000 and BS 5750 certification;
- UK/European Quality Awards;
- self-assessment;
- investing in people;
- continuous improvement;
- creating a quality culture.

Sample extract

Bentley Chemicals is an example of a smaller size company competing to supply what could be described as a galaxy of multi-million pound industries and to succeed it has had to advance as quickly as the industries it supplies. So, it should come as no surprise that this distributor of silicone, resin and adhesive products was the first in its field to achieve ISO 9002: 1994 and did so within 11 months of commencing the programme.

It provides the lesson that a small company can achieve quality registration and achieve it quickly without sacrificing day-to-day efficiency and the high level of personalised customer service on which small companies often pride themselves. Initially the company was working towards BS 5750: Part 2. However, a month prior to the official assessment date, the company decided that it would be of benefit to aim for ISO 9002: 1994. Subsequently, all the documentation was revised and updated to incorporate the changes within the standard.

The motivation to go for quality registration initially came from a couple of customers and the potential of winning accounts in the aerospace industry which insisted that suppliers be ISO certified. However, the original motives were further reaching than just obliging customer requirements. 'From a personal point of view, the company had grown so much in such a short space of time, it was becoming impossible for me to control and required systems to be put in place. Once we had introduced ISO 9000, it was satisfying from everybody's point of view that a total system was in place and there were actually good reasons for it. If everybody adhered to the system then they know, and I know, that the job is being done and that the customer is getting what they want. This ultimately gives me peace of mind in knowing that the business is being run ensuring total customer satisfaction,' explains Mr Watson, Managing Director.

James Dyson: *Against the Odds: An Autobiography*[12]

Against the Odds is the passionate, personal story of James Dyson, a maverick English inventor who designed, marketed and even made money from his own invention – a new kind of vacuum cleaner called the Dual Cyclone. He outwitted the market leaders for vacuum cleaners in the process whose attitude was 'if a better vacuum cleaner was possible, we would have made it.' Electrolux sued Dyson for his advertising claims that his bagless vacuum cleaner is better, but both parties in the case were issued with warnings from the court for publicly criticising each other's products.

His book captures the years of personal struggle he had to pass through as an inventor and entrepreneur before achieving success. It is as engaging to the modern reader as a story of an ancient hero proving himself through rights of purification and trial. His first successful invention – the Ballbarrow – was a wheelbarrow-shaped container with a pneumatic balloon in place of a wheel.

His iconoclastic remarks occur throughout the book which he describes provocatively:

> This is not a glib guide to instant wealth or effective management by California-style happy-talk and company outings to assault courses. This is not even a business book. It is, if anything, a book against business, against the principles that have filled the world with ugly, useless objects, unhappy people, and brought the country to its economic knees.
>
> We all want to make our mark. We all want to make beautiful things and a little money. We all have our own ideas about how to do it. What follows [his 300 page book] just happens to be my way.[13]

James Dyson's commitment to quality shines through all aspects of the remarkable case study. 'My experience shows that creativity alone is not enough to succeed. You have to be as dogged in solving the commercial problems that you meet, as you were in solving "the creative" challenge that turned your idea into reality in the first place.'[14]

Dyson is a great believer in continuous improvement and the concept surfaces continually throughout his autobiography. He refers to the West's mocking appraisal of Japan's first industrial products. 'But they were learning all the time. Improving little by little until they've reached supremacy.' He warns that now that the Japanese designers are understanding 'individualism', they are beginning 'to design beautiful things'.[15]

He knows Japan well and is ambivalent about the country, where he first marketed his new vacuum cleaner, in terms of doing business in their culture. But he greatly admires their perfectionism.

The Japanese got to their hard-won supremacy the same way he did – through gradually making things better. 'And all their success is born out of a theory of gradual development that is the very antithesis of the British obsession with the quantum leap,' Dyson argued. He made 5,127 prototypes of his vacuum cleaner to bring the product to market.

> In Britain we have laboured for years under the tyranny of expectation of a certain kind of excellence. For years, all that mattered was that you went to Oxford or Cambridge and got a first, that you were a genius. We placed our hopes in quantum leaping, and as our industrial decline continued, so the leap required grew bigger. It was going to take a lot to catch up. We put our faith in dreams of one brilliant idea that might put us back on top of the pile.
>
> The Japanese always took the opposite view. They put no faith in individualists, and lived anti-brilliance culture. And that was healthy. They know full well that quantum leaps are very rare, but that consistent development will result, in the end, in a better product. And that is a mindset I share with them. I am not a quantum leaper.[16]

Dyson cites figures to diminish the arrogance of his fellow countrymen about British inventiveness. He says that, according to recent research by the Design Council (of which he is a celebrated member) Britain is placed 11th in a league table of numbers who have filed patents with only 7.93 registrations for every 100,000 people in the country, putting Britain behind Japan, Germany, Taiwan and even Switzerland.

In the same research Britain is ranked 27th in a table of countries in terms of spending on research and development with a net 'growth' of 0.9 per cent (behind even Chile). South Korea came top of the league table with a growth of 45 per cent. Ireland showed an R&D growth spend of 9.1 per cent while even Spain had a 7.6 per cent growth.

Dyson was clearly fighting for his company's honour. There were separate and collective law suits from his competitors. Electrolux, the Swedish multinational, sued him for 'defamation' over his criticism of the efficiency of their new Powersystem vacuum cleaner which he incorrigibly says 'features a cyclone backed by a huge nappy filter, which might as well be a bag for all the clogging it causes'.[17] In addition, six multinational competitors were attacking his advertising in Belgium. The cases were about truth in advertising and centred on Dyson's claim that a bagless vacuum cleaner is better. In a tit-for-tat hearing in February 1999, Justice J. Parker dismissed the companies' actions against each other for "malicious falsehood".

But Dyson continues to collect glittering prizes – a CBE in the New Year's Honours List of 1998, design awards in Japan and the Czech Republic, the Prince Philip Designer's Prize and an Oscar from the French book *Inventions of the World*. The Dyson Dual Cyclone is the only domestic appliance in the Twentieth Century Gallery at the Victoria & Albert Museum and is uniquely on permanent view at the Science Museum and the Design Museum.

Dyson has founded another subsidiary in Germany and has made distribution agreements in New Zealand, Turkey, Belgium and Sweden. He has invested £15 million in a new 65,000 sq. ft R&D facility adjacent to his existing factory in Malmesbury that will employ 200 young people generating ideas and developing new product designs. It was opened in July 1998 by Prime Minister Tony Blair.

His present total workforce has expanded to 950 and the small company has enjoyed a compound growth rate of 300 per cent. Everyone who starts working at Dyson's factory, from the lowliest employee to a non-executive director, makes a vacuum cleaner on their first day of work. It is done in part for the fun of it. But also it reinforces Dyson's own view that 'anyone can do anything' and it also shows the new employee how the vacuum cleaner is built, how it works and why it is a better design. The employee then takes it home to use it and can keep it if he or she pays £20 for it.

At the workplace the new employees enjoy architectural design features developed by Chris Wilkinson that include a tubular and sheet tension structure to shade the factory. They enjoy a lilac, lavender and purple interior colour scheme and high-tech office tables. The colourful factory reflects the product. After all, the striking mix of colours in the vacuum cleaner – pink and lavender and yellow – were inspired by the light and colour of Provence where the Impressionists first found inspiration.

Each employee has a Vitara chair, designed by Antonio Citerio, to sit on which costs £400 a piece. All offices are open plan. The graphics and engineering people are located in the geographic centre of the office to underscore the centrality of their roles to the entire business and to encourage design consciousness and creative contributions from everyone.

Sample extract

That is what development is all about. Empirical testing demands that you only ever make one change at a time. It is the Edisonian principle, and it is bloody slow. It is a thing that takes me ages to explain to my graduate employees at Dyson Appliances, but it is so important. They tend to leap into tests, making dozens of radical changes and then stepping back to test their new masterpiece. How do they know which change has improved it, and which hasn't?

Let us say that we are looking at the brush bars. They are inefficient, and we don't know why. 'Why we need', says some bright spark, 'is softer, longer bristles.' So they order a brush bar with softer, longer bristles. And the new brush bar is better. But they still don't know why.

What the bright spark should do is order three new brush bars, one long and stiff, one long and soft, and one short and soft. And test each one against the other, to see wherein the improvement lies.

This is why development is such a slow process. But the British obsession with the quantum leap holds us back. We always want to create something new out of nothing, and without research, and without long hard hours of effort. But there is no such thing as a quantum leap. There is only dogged persistence – and in the end you make it look like a quantum leap. Ask the Japanese.

(pages 124–5)

John S. Oakland: *Total Quality Management*[18]

Professor Oakland holds a chair in total quality management at the University of Bradford Management Centre. His book, in its second edition, reflects his current career as a teacher and quality consultant and his past career in research and production management. He has roots in quality control.

The book covers the entire field from the basic concepts and definitions to policy development to organizing a quality programme and measuring costs of quality. He presents a detailed plan for TQM in two chapters and looks at quality system design and contents, documentation and implementation. He discusses special quality techniques such as SPC and other modern methods of quality control. Teamwork is important, as is training for total quality, and both are discussed fully.

The book is well written and thorough, enhancing Oakland's reputation for being a British expert in the field so dominated by Americans.

Sample extract

Quality has to be managed – it will not just happen. Clearly it must involve everyone in the process and be applied throughout the organization. Many people in the support functions of organizations never see, experience, or touch the products or services that their organizations buy or provide, but they do handle or produce things like purchase orders or invoices. If every fourth invoice carries at least one error, what image of quality is transmitted!

Failure to meet the requirements in any part of a quality chain has a way of multiplying, and failure in one part of the system creates problems elsewhere, leading to yet more failure, more problems and so on. The price of quality is the continual examination of the requirements and our ability to meet them. This alone will lead to a 'continuing improvement' philosophy. The benefits of making sure the requirements are met at every stage, every time, are truly enormous in terms of increased competitiveness and market share, reduced costs, improved productivity and delivery performance, and the elimination of waste. The Japanese have called this 'company-wide quality improvement' or CWQI.

(page 9)

Masaaki Imai: *Kaizen, The Key to Japan's Competitive Success*[19]

Of all the books on Japanese management this one is superior. *Kaizen*, the Japanese word used in the title, means gradual, unending improvement, doing 'little things' better, setting – and achieving – even higher standards.

The Japanese author is now the head of his own consultancy business based in Tokyo. He helps companies – usually non-Japanese or joint venture companies – use Japanese management methods.

The book is a practical 'how to do it' handbook, focused on 16 *Kaizen* management practices. They are illustrated by over a hundred examples and over a dozen case studies.

Kaizen applies to the following: profit planning; customer satisfaction; total quality control programmes; suggestion systems; small-group activities; just-in-time production; just-in-time information processing; systems improvement; cross-functional management; policy implementation or 'deployments'; quality deployment; total productive maintenance; supplier relations; top management commitment; corporate culture; and problem-solving in such areas as labour–management relations.

Sample extract

The implications of TQC or CWQC (Company-Wide Quality Control) in Japan have been that these concepts have helped Japanese companies generate a process-oriented way of thinking and develop strategies that assure continuous improvement involving people at all levels of the organizational hierarchy. The message of the KAIZEN strategy is that not a day should go by without some kind of improvement being made somewhere in the company. . . .

The belief that there should be unending improvement is deeply ingrained in the Japanese mentality. . . .

After World War II, most Japanese companies had to start literally from the ground up. Every day brought new challenges to managers and workers alike, and every day meant progress. Simply staying in business required unending progress, and KAIZEN has become a way of life. It was also fortunate that the various tools that helped elevate this KAIZEN concept to new heights were introduced to Japan in the late 1950s and early 1960s by such experts as W.E. Deming and J.M. Juran. However, most new concepts, systems, and tools that are widely used in Japan today, have subsequently been developed in Japan and represent qualitative improvements upon the statistical quality control and total quality control of the 1960s.

(pages 4–5)

Malcolm McConnell: *Challenger, A Major Malfunction*[20]

This powerful case study of poor quality management emerges from the writer's sifting through thousands of pages of documents and interviewing major actors in the *Challenger* disaster. He offers a sad tale of politicking within NASA, duplicity and dissembling from outside contractors, and dysfunctional interference by Congress, the military and a series of US Presidents.

One of his sources is the *Report to the President by the Presidential Commission on the Space Shuttle Challenger Accident*. He was also an eyewitness to the tragedy at Cape Canaveral as he was there to report on *Challenger*'s teacher-in-space flight on the day of the disaster.

Sample extract

In January 1986 Morton Thiokol was involved in an ostensibly urgent field joint redesign effort to find a solution to the problem. The urgent effort had been underway almost a year. But before each mission, both NASA and Thiokol officials continued to certify that the solid rocket boosters were ready for safe flight.

Marshall Center managers tried to minimize the problem to protect their reputation within NASA's jealously competitive bureaucratic hierarchy, for fear of exposing past incompetence and losing scarce funding.

The motives of Morton Thiokol appear equally venal. Thiokol had gained the lucrative sole source contract for solid rocket boosters thirteen years earlier, during a bitterly disputed award process that veteran observers have characterized as a low point in squalid political intrigue. At the time of the award to the then relatively small Thiokol Chemical Company in Brigham City, Utah, both the newly appointed chairman of the Senate Aeronautics and Space Science Committee, Democratic Senator Frank Moss, and the new NASA administrator, Dr James Fletcher, were insiders in the tightly knit Utah political hierarchy. This apparent Thiokol-Utah leverage has persisted over the years; James Fletcher was reappointed NASA Administrator following the Challenger accident, and the chairman of the Senate committee currently overseeing NASA's budget is Utah Republican Jake Garn, who rode aboard the shuttle in April 1985. By summer 1985, however – the year the catastrophic potential of the flawed field joints became obvious – Thiokol's monopoly position was under attack, and the corporation's executives were afraid to risk their billion-dollar contract by halting shuttle flight operations long enough to correct the faulty booster joint design.

In reality, as Challenger's crew smiled down from the launch pad catwalk at the massive white columns of the solid rocket boosters, they were looking at the final product of flawed policy and political corruption.   (page 7)

A.V. Feigenbaum: *Total Quality Control*[21]

Total Quality Control, by the man who coined the term, is a collector's item. The original book was published in 1951 under the title *Quality Control* and revised ten years later. The book reviews the entire field of quality control in depth. Its author helped take the idea of quality control from its more limited and fragmented work to the new systematic body of principles, practices and technologies called total quality control.

Feigenbaum was Manager, Manufacturing Operations and Quality Control at the General Electric Company in New York City and the President of the American Society for Quality Control at the time of the writing. He defined the total quality control of his day as: 'An effective system for integrating the quality-development, quality-maintenance, and quality-improvement efforts of the various groups in an organization so as to enable production and service at the most economical levels which allow for full customer satisfaction.'

In the phrase 'quality control' the word control for him represented a management tool with four steps: setting quality standards; appraising conformance to these standards; acting when the standards are exceeded; and planning for improvements in the standards. It is not wide of the mark as it is used today.

Sample extract

PRODUCT QUALITY AS A SALES MOVER

It is an established fact that customers will buy where they receive the greatest value. Some of the values customers look for in products are durability, convenience, reliability, attractiveness, adequate performance – all these are qualities of the product. The manufacturer who can provide these desired qualities without exceeding the price for competitive offerings gains product leadership.

If a manufacturer has provided the customer with good value and met his quality expectation, he has established his reputation with the customer and can expect the customer's continued patronage. Even beyond that.

The customer may become an active booster for the company's products and recommend them to his associates. Any salesman knows the advantages of being able to sell quality as compared with selling price.

When a manufacturer has established his reputation as a producer of quality products, there is a great deal of advantage in his advertising the fact. This is a case where acts must back up words. If they do not, the words can prove to be very embarrassing and very damaging to the manufacturer. Examples can be identified where firms are no longer in business because they could not back up their claims for quality products. On the other hand, those companies which have been able truthfully to advertise themselves as producers of quality products have established themselves in a very sound position.

The best product-quality assurance a manufacturer can provide his customers is the operation of a total-quality-control program.

The company with a well-established, effective total-quality-control program in place can emphasize it as an added-value for the customer.

(pages 617–18)

That was written nearly fifty years ago.

Conclusion

There are those who know and those who don't want to know. If the latter remain in the majority, and we prove so unimaginative, cowardly and self-interested that we fail to tend the early growth of this small seedling, we will soon ourselves wither and die with it. But taken together, this knowledge constitutes the basis for the millennial society that is gradually beginning to unfold, not only in the worlds of business and work, but also in those of physics, biology, medicine, physiology, economics, and doubtless eventually in education, law, religion and politics as well. Its pioneers will have to be insistent, consistent and persistent, but if they are they will predominate.[22]

These words from Kinsman's *Millennium: Towards Tomorrow's Society* remind managers and workers alike of their responsibility for the new knowledge.

The 75 million phone numbers registered in 1995 equal the total number distributed from 1876 to 1956. And Internet access is growing even faster . . . the Internet as we know it today will be over 100 times more powerful an information tool by the century's end; and that each newly connected PC boosts the power of the network not geometrically but exponentially.[23]

If *Time*'s Joshua Cooper Ramo's predictions for the future are to be believed the networked society is well underway and unstoppable. At the start of the 1990s, about one million people were connected to a rudimentary copper cable network. An estimated 47 million use the network today. But that figure is predicted to rocket to 700 million by the end of the century and explode to half a planet's worth of newly connected people by 2010. Such a knowledge explosion will reshape the Earth as we know it today.

Total quality management is part of a holistic approach to progress. It is in ascendancy as the year 2000 approaches. In every company that genuinely commits itself to total quality, there is a tremendous unlocking of energy in management and the workforce. The image that comes to mind is the Chinese tangram – millions of these ancient puzzles with individuals locked into tight boxes. Total quality has the potential power to transform the tangrams into running figures, liberating people at work to become more truly themselves and more creative.

Notes

1 Sir Denys Henderson, 'Foreword' to Brett Whitford and Rebecca Bird, *The Pursuit of Quality* (London: Prentice Hall, 1996), p. viii.
2 Akio Morito with Edwin M. Reingold and Mitsuko Shimomura, *Akio Morita and Sony, Made in Japan* (Glasgow: Fontana Paperbacks, 1989), p. 309.
3 W. Edwards Deming, *Out of the Crisis* (Cambridge: Cambridge University Press, 1986), 507 pages.
4 V.A. Zeithaml, A. Parasuraman and L.L. Berry, *Delivering Quality Service: Balancing Customer Perceptions and Expectations* (New York: Free Press, 1990), 226 pages.
5 David Halberstam, *The Reckoning* (London: Bloomsbury, 1986), 752 pages.
6 J.M. Juran, *Leadership for Quality: An Executive Handbook* (New York: Free Press, 1989), 376 pages.
7 J.M. Juran, *Juran's New Quality Road Map – Planning, Setting and Reaching Quality Goals* (New York: Free Press, 1991), 384 pages.
8 Sandra Vandermerwe, *From Tin Soldiers to Russian Dolls: Creating Added Value Through Service* (Oxford: Butterworth-Heinemann, 1993), p. 280.
9 Patrick L. Townsend (with Joan E., Gebhardt), *Commit to Quality* (New York: John Wiley, 1989), 189 pages. *See also* by the same authors: *Five-Star Leadership* (New York: John Wiley, 1997), 254 pages.
10 Philip B. Crosby, *Quality is Free: The Art of Making Quality Certain* (New York: New American Library, Mentor, 1980), 264 pages.
11 Brett Whitford and Rebecca Bird, *The Pursuit of Quality* (London: Prentice Hall, 1996), p. 582.
12 James Dyson, *Against the Odds: An Autobiography* (London: Orion Business Books, 1998), p. 287.
13 Ibid., p. 9.
14 Ibid., p. 286.

15 Ibid., p. 168.

16 Ibid., pp. 167–9.

17 Ibid., p. 285.

18 John S. Oakland, *Total Quality Management* (Oxford: Butterworth-Heinemann, 1993), 463 pages.

19 Masaaki Imai, *Kaizen, The Key to Japan's Competitive Success* (New York: Random House, 1986), 259 pages.

20 Malcolm McConnell, *Challenger, A Major Malfunction* (London: Unwin Paperbacks, 1987), 290 pages.

21 A.V. Feigenbaum, *Total Quality Control: Engineering and Management* (New York: McGraw-Hill, 1961), 667 pages.

22 Frances Kinsman, *Millennium: Towards Tomorrow's Society* (London: Penguin, 1990), pp. 269–70.

23 Joshua Cooper Ramo, 'Welcome to the wired world', *Time*, 3 February 1997, p. 32.

Appendix

....

Global benchmarking organizations

Australia Quality Council
69 Christie Street, PO Box 298, St Leonards, New South Wales 2065, Australia
Tel: + 61 2 901 9999

Australian Centre for Best Practice
7 Parkes Street, Parramatta, New South Wales, Australia
Tel: + 61 2 891 3677

The Benchmarking Centre
Truscom House, 11 Station Road, Gerrards Cross, Buckinghamshire, SL9 8ES, UK
Tel: + 44 1753 890 070
http://www.benchmarking.co.uk

The Benchmarking Club
Business Italy, Via Isonzo 42/C, 00198 Roma, Italy
Tel: + 39 6 841 3608

The Best Practices Club
IFS International Ltd, Wolseley Business Park, Wolseley Road, Kempston, Bedford MK42 7PW, UK
Tel: + 44 1234 853605
http://www.bpclub.com.

European Foundation for Quality Management
Avenue des Pleiades 19, B-1200 Brussels, Belgium
Tel: + 32 2 755 3511

German Benchmarking Club
Frauhofer Institute, Pascalstrasse 8-9, D-10587 Berlin, Germany
Tel: + 49 30 31424127

International Benchmarking Clearinghouse
123 North Post Oak Lane, 3rd floor, Houston, TX 77024-7797, USA
Tel: + 1 7133 685 4654

Korean Benchmarking Centre
2F FK1 Building, 28-1 Yoido-Dong, Yeongde Ungto-Ku, Seoul 150-7576, Korea
Tel: + 82 2 820911

Northern Ireland Quality Centre
Midland Building, Whitla Street, Belfast BT1S 1NH, Northern Ireland
Tel: + 44 1232 352999

The Norwegian Institute of Technology (NTH)
University of Trondheim, Department of Organization and Work Science, NTH/ORAL, 7034 Trondheim, Norway
Tel: + 47 7 359 3800

Strategic Planning Institute
1030 Massachusetts Avenue, Council on Benchmarking, Cambridge, MA 02138, USA
Tel: 1 617 491 9200

Swedish Institute for Quality
Fabriksgatan 10, Benchmarking, S-41250 Goteborg, Sweden
Tel: + 46 31 35 1700

Source: BBC, *Benchmarking for Competitive Advantage*, BBC for Business, Woodlands, 80 Wood Lane, London W12 OTT, 1995.

Index